DEADLY ENCOUNTER

We seemed to be on the enemy's beam, and so the German minesweeper M 3821 was the first to open fire.

Never had I forseen that the enemy's fire would be so like a curtain; a safety curtain to him, since for us to fire torpedoes with any hope of success we had to see the target. . . . Now the only points of aim were gunflashes, memory was the only guide. . . . I saw little future either for our torpedoes or ourselves and felt extremely frightened, and worse, totally lost and incompetent.

"Crash start," I told Guy. "Steer towards, full speed."

The main engine exhausts coughed, then roared, and with speed came fierce, primitive courage. Cannons to the right of us, cannons to the left of us, cannons in front of us volleyed and thundered as we sped towards our target. I knew then how the Light Brigade felt as it charged into the valley of death. . .

NIGHT ACTION
by Captain Peter Dickens

THE BANTAM WAR BOOK SERIES

This series of books is about a world on fire.

The carefully chosen volumes in the Bantam War Book Series cover the full dramatic sweep of World War II. Many are eyewitness accounts by the men who fought in a global conflict as the world's future hung in the balance. Fighter pilots, tank commanders, and infantry captains, among many others, recount exploits of individual courage. They present vivid portraits of brave men, true stories of gallantry, moving sagas of survival and stark tragedies of untimely death.

In 1933 Nazi Germany marched to become an empire that was to last a thousand years. In only twelve years that empire was destroyed, and ever since, the country has been bisected by her conquerors. Italy relinquished her colonial lands, as did Japan. These were the losers. The winners also lost the empires they had so painfully seized over the centuries. And one, Russia, lost over twenty million lives.

Those wartime 1940s were a simple, even a hopeful time. Hats came in only two colors, white and black, and after an initial battering the Allied nations started on a long and laborious march toward victory. It was a time when sane men believed the world would evolve into a decent place, but, as with all futures, there was no one then who could really forecast the world that we know now.

There are many ways to think about that war. It has always been hard to understand the motivations and braveries of Axis soldiers fighting to enslave and dominate their neighbors. Yet it is impossible to know the hammer without the anvil, and to comprehend ourselves we must know the people we once fought against.

Through these books we can discover what it was like to take part in the war that was a final experience for nearly fifty million human beings. In so doing we may discover the strength to make a world as good as the one contained in those dreams and aspirations once believed by heroic men. We must understand our past as an honor to those dead who can no longer choose. They exchanged their lives in a hope for this future that we now inhabit. Though the fight took place many years ago, each of us remains as a living part of it.

NIGHT ACTION

MTB Flotilla at War

Captain Peter Dickens,
D.S.O., M.B.E., D.S.C., Royal Navy

Vessels large must keep near shore,
but little boats may venture more.

BANTAM BOOKS
TORONTO • NEW YORK • LONDON • SYDNEY • AUCKLAND

*This low-priced Bantam Book
has been completely reset in a type face
designed for easy reading, and was printed
from new plates. It contains the complete
text of the original hard-cover edition.*
NOT ONE WORD HAS BEEN OMITTED.

NIGHT ACTION

*A Bantam Book / published by arrangement with
Naval Institute Press*

PRINTING HISTORY
*Naval Institute edition published 1974
Bantam edition / July 1981
2nd printing . . . March 1987*

*Illustrations by Greg Beecham, Tom Beecham and
M. Stephen Bach.
Maps by Alan McKnight.*

ISBN 0-553-26625-X

PRINTED IN THE UNITED STATES OF AMERICA

KR   11 10 9 8 7 6 5 4 3 2

*To all who fought with the 21st MTB Flotilla,
and to the dead and wounded of both sides*

ACKNOWLEDGMENTS

I am most grateful to copyright holders not mentioned in the Preface for permission to reproduce the following: the verse from Cautionary Tales by H. Belloc published by Duckworth & Co.; the verse by Michael John Pugh, published in 1936 by Sampson, Low Marston in 'More Last Words' edited by Cecil Hunt, with the permission of Mrs. Hunt; and for the photographs to Associated Press, Central Press Photos, Fayer, Ford Jenkins, Her Majesty's Stationery Office and the Imperial War Museum.

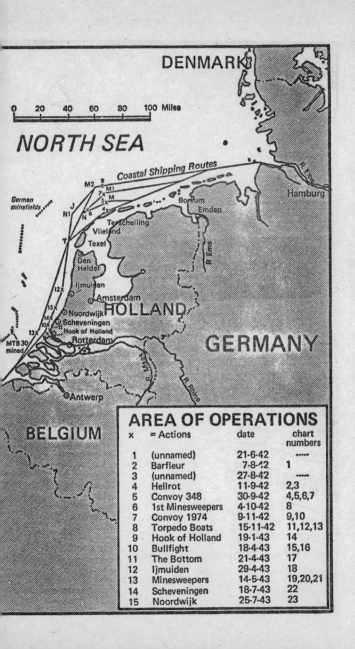

DENMARK

0   20   40   60   80   100 Miles

NORTH SEA

Coastal Shipping Routes

German
minefields

M2 ×—M1
7× ×M
5×
N× ×4×
J
N1

Hamburg

R. Elbe

Borkum

Emden

R. Ems

Terschelling
Vlieland
Texel

T

Den
Helder

Ijmuiden
12×

Amsterdam

HOLLAND

15×
14×
10×
13×

Noordwijk
Scheveningen
Hook of Holland
Rotterdam

MTB 30
mined

GERMANY

R. Maas
R. Rhine

Antwerp

BELGIUM

AREA OF OPERATIONS

x	= Actions	date	chart numbers
1	(unnamed)	21-6-42	----
2	Barfleur	7-8-42	1
3	(unnamed)	27-8-42	----
4	Hellrot	11-9-42	2,3
5	Convoy 348	30-9-42	4,5,6,7
6	1st Minesweepers	4-10-42	8
7	Convoy 1974	9-11-42	9,10
8	Torpedo Boats	15-11-42	11,12,13
9	Hook of Holland	19-1-43	14
10	Bullfight	18-4-43	15,16
11	The Bottom	21-4-43	17
12	Ijmuiden	29-4-43	18
13	Minesweepers	14-5-43	19,20,21
14	Scheveningen	18-7-43	22
15	Noordwijk	25-7-43	23

CONTENTS

Captain Peter Dickens
DSO, MBE, DSC

Preface

It is presumptuous for someone as unimportant as I am to write about his own doings, and some attempt at an excuse is called for. To most people small, fast fighting craft were exciting and glamorous, but to the Royal Naval Establishment they were anathema and now we have none. There seems a case therefore for trying to pass on some of the thrill, the delights and disappointments, failures and successes, problems and their solutions, experienced by a very young man in the enviable and uncommon job of Senior Officer of a Motor Torpedo-Boat Flotilla.

Being quite unprepared and untrained for the task I was avid to learn from anyone's experiences in World War I, but none had been recorded that I could find. It is just conceivable today that the Establishment will be proved mistaken, such miscalculations being not unknown, and that we shall again find ourselves having to resuscitate small craft to help dispute some narrow sea where nothing larger can be risked. Perhaps our off-shore oilfields may be a trigger, for we are told that they will soon become the foundation of our economy but not so far how we propose to protect them.

Should such a change of policy come about I must admit that to be 30 years behind the times in the 1970s means that our efforts will have little technical relevance to what might happen in the future. So primitive were our boats that we had neither radar nor voice radio which worked, if that can be imagined, and so it is no part of my present job to point tactical lessons. What I must do is tell the story as accurately as possible so that our successors may pick out any lessons there may be for themselves, and history can usually provide such lessons to those with the wit to distinguish the principle from the transient. I have therefore checked my memory against all relevant documents and the recollections of many of my brothers-in-arms; I have sincerely tried to write the ungilded truth, except for two very minor deliberate mistakes perpetrated for the sake of brevity and neatness. I hope the old and bold will concede that I have done so; but they must be ready for some shocks when they read the enemy's story for the first time and learn that many cherished beliefs were so much wishful thinking. They can however be reassured that we did not fall into the trap of claiming more enemy ships than we actually hit over the whole period, it was just that we did not always select the right ones in the dark.

I am enormously indebted to many people who have gone out of their way to help me, and often entertained me generously as well. Of the old salts: David Felce, Henry Franklin, Basil Gerrard, Douglas Gill, Ken Hartley, Ken Harris, Alan Jensen, Tommy Kerr, Arthur Lee, Jim Macdonald, Peter Magnus, Tom Neill, Percy Odell, Val Ohlenschlager, John Perkins, Alun Phillips, Walter Salmon, Jim Saunders, Ted Smyth, Peter Standley, Ian Trelawny and Edwin White. Almost though not quite in the same category is Friedrich Paul who gave me his personal account of a hectic few minutes, which neither of us wish to repeat, when he commanded the German torpedo-boat T23. On the research side I owe much to the invariable kindness, patience and erudition of Mr. J. D. Lawson and the staff of the Naval Historical Branch and Naval Library of the Ministry of Defence; also to that eminent German naval historian Vice-Admiral Friedrich Ruge, to Christopher Dreyer, Mr. W. G. P. Fraser, and the staff of the Rolls Room at the Public Record Office.

Many of the above have lent me photographs, and I am also extremely fortunate to have had access to the magnificent collections of Geoffrey Hudson and Grahame Nicholls, and to those of the Bibliothek für Zeitgeschichte through Dr. Jurgen Rohwer, Vosper Thorneycroft through John Brooks, and the Director General Ships (M.O.D.) through Miss M. E. Joll. In other ways I have been greatly helped by Kapitän zur See Hans Dehnert, Douglas Hunt, Kapitän zur See Herbert Friedrichs, Michael Benson, Bremer Horne, Guy Sells (who translated many German documents, mostly in difficult nautical jargon), ex-Chief Wren Mrs. Maud Parrett, ex-Wren Mrs. Joan Davey, my wife, and my family who have helped me write the story of what Dad did and did not do in the Great War in a way that may have some chance of appealing to their generation. The arduous task of reading the typescript critically has been undertaken by Alan Jensen, John Perkins, Jim Saunders and Ian Trelawny; while the book has been immeasurably improved by the masterly editing and insight of Derek Priestley (of Peter Davies). My gratitude to everyone is very deep and sincere.

Vosper Seventy-Footer

I

THE SECOND BATTLE
OF BARFLEUR

August 7, 1942 my friends and I stood forth for mortal combat against the foe, with an ardent desire to get at him but with woolly thoughts on how to do so.

I led my three operational motor torpedo-boats straight south from the Isle of Wight into the gathering darkness, the only friendly element in our natural environment off the enemy-held coast. By day the Vosper seventy-footers had delighted the eye with flowing grace as their bows surged over the wavelets, and their sterns pulled plumes of white water which sluiced and heaved in constant motion, while yet seeming to be rigid extensions of the boats' structures, and glittered gaily in the summer sunshine. But as darkness closed in, the wakes became gray and sullen; black, uncompromising guns obtruded from the shadowed silhouettes, powerful torpedoes in their tubes made the hulls seem as though they crouched to spring, and unsilenced engines growled. (For more prosaic details of the Vosper MTB, see Appendix I.)

Menace was our hallmark, appropriately since we were predators to the Germans' coastal traffic; but whether we should prove to be real or paper tigers was as yet undetermined. That would depend largely on me, the Senior Officer of the 21st Motor Torpedo-Boat Flotilla, who felt woefully unfitted for the task despite the grand-sounding title; with no experience, no guidance because there was none to be had, few tactical ideas except an intellectually unsatisfying hope that if I did not know what I was doing the enemy could not possibly guess and would consequently be confounded, all I could bring to the task was a determination to go hard because I had at least learned that that was the key to success at anything.

It was quite dark when, twelve miles off Cape Barfleur at the eastern tip of the Cherbourg peninsula, we cut our main engines and engaged our little Ford V8 auxiliaries which drove us at a pitiful six knots, though quietly, because I felt we must soon be heard by our enemies ashore or afloat. After a very long hour and a quarter of growing tension I judged we had reached the enemy's convoy route and turned down it into the Baie de la Seine as our orders required.

We were in historic waters, and students of naval history will recall the first battle of Barfleur which was fought between Admirals Russell and Tourville in the War of the English Succession. It was noteworthy for Sir Cloudesley Shovell tacking through a gap in the enemy line, and resulted in ex-King James II being permanently thwarted from invading England. Its date, May 19, 1962, is therefore memorable, as the second battle's, 250 years later, is not. No marks will be awarded for quoting it in any examination, and the only excuse for retrieving it from the oblivion in which it rightly belongs is to illustrate with hideous clarity how such affairs should not be conducted.

The German force which had left Cherbourg to escort the seagoing tug *Oceanie* to Le Havre comprised six armed auxiliary vessels, mostly requisitioned fishing trawlers, such as we were often to encounter on our forays during the months to come. (For details of German ships and craft, see Appendix III.) There were four Minensuchboote (minesweepers) of the 38th Flotilla and an ex-French motor minesweeper, the *RA 2*, all under Oberleutnant zur See Wunderlich; this was an experienced team but at the last moment another trawler, Vorpostenboot (patrol craft) *1520*, joined for the passage and her captain assumed overall command, being senior to Wunderlich. This the German operational authority afterwards thought to have been a pity, but my considered view was that the force was handled quite efficiently enough as it was. Having rounded Barfleur the Germans struck out directly for their objective on a course of 108 degrees, and that converged with ours.

All my boats were new but *MTB 237* was the newest, a beautiful craft built by Camper Nicholsons with the finish of a rich man's yacht. So recently joined was she that I had hardly come to know Guy Fison, her captain, except to realize I liked him; and it was for that reason that I had decided to use her as my flagship, though no flags were allowed to lieutenants aged twenty-five and quite right too. Keeping station on our starboard quarter was 232 commanded by Lieutenant Ian Trelawny, RNVR, an extremely competent and enterprising Cornishman six months older than me, which meant he was old. Ian used his upturned mouth and deep-set, humorous eyes to mislead one into thinking that nothing mattered very much to him; but I soon learned that he was uncommonly perceptive, determined, and sensitive for the welfare of others. I had warmed to him for he accepted me graciously when I joined Coastal Forces as a tyro, and taught me my job with loyalty and without presumption.

The port barb of the arrowhead was 241, commanded by Sub-Lieutenant Jim Macdonald from New Zealand, who was young even by Coastal Force standards. Indeed he was believed to be, at twenty, the youngest captain in the King's navies but there could be no doubt that he had earned his boat, even if one did not notice his DSC which had been awarded some months earlier for an act of outstanding gallantry before his promotion. Mac's smile was charming and generous, but he had no wish to appear other than he was, earnest, singleminded and disconcertingly direct; especially when he sized me up on first acquaintance and concluded, transparently, that I was unlikely to measure up to his standards. In return I stood in awe of him while determining to put the young blighter in his place as soon as possible; though I realized that this was not to be done by any means short of earning his loyalty by deeds.

Deeds for us meant attacking the enemy. There must be no shirking the issue since our flotilla existed for no other purpose, and I had said so unambiguously to everybody in it, not excluding myself. That was important for it was I who would take the decisions, and my own words declaimed publicly in the security of the base must allow me no loopholes for revisionism should stark enemy silhouettes suggest a more flexible approach. To attack the enemy we must first see him, for we had no other means of detection, and to that end I rammed my elbows into the bridge-top to hold the big night binoculars steady, and peered ahead with all my might.

I had already learned that much could be done to augment the natural keenness of healthy young eyes. First one

had to *want* to see, to bore into the darkness and extract
what it strove to hide; and that was different enough from
ordinary life in which one waits for objects to swim into
one's ken, and makes little attempt to see in the dark at
all without a light. With us lights were anathema; adaptation of our eyes to the dark, to a condition of really being
able to see, took at least twenty minutes. Then, the pupils
wide, an errant gleam could destroy night vision for a
possibly vital minute and evoke cries of, "Switch off that
bloody light!"

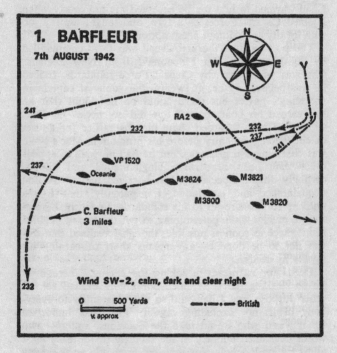

1. BARFLEUR

7th AUGUST 1942

Wind SW-2, calm, dark and clear night

0   500 Yards   ——·—·—— British
      ⊾ approx

Thirdly the lenses must be polished until they gleamed,
continually so if there was but a hint of rain or spray,
and adjusted with meticulous exactitude to one's own foci
and interocular distance. Fourthly one had to be aware of
the blind spot at the eye's center, whereby an object was
detected slightly to one side and to look straight at it
caused it to disappear. Fifthly one had to know from

experience what to expect, nothing more than the faintest break in the horizon's often indeterminate continuity; if it showed up more clearly than that one had not seen it at the earliest moment and had consequently failed. Sixthly one had to hold oneself and one's glasses rock-steady in a rolling, pounding, vibrating boat.

Having studied the art and practiced it assiduously I thought I was pretty good, and so it was with a mixture of shame and confusion that I heard Mac's cry, "Enemy in sight!"

"For God's sake!" I croaked. "Where?"

"Starboard beam."

There they were like pikestaffs, sore thumbs or what you will, and should have been seen at least ten minutes earlier; but I had been searching in the obvious though wrong direction, ahead. Clearly the technique of looking out demanded yet another discipline, ignore no section of the horizon; Mac made no mistake, and ignominiously for the rest of us reported the enemy to *starboard* from his position on the *port* wing. In the darkness I thought the enemy was a fat convoy; of course I did, one usually sees what one expects and rarely what one does not. That the unexpected is to be expected in war should be obvious, even if it were not emphasized in every treatise on the subject; so why does it, like all worthwhile lessons, have to be learned the hard way? Only one thing redeemed the night's work, the resolution to attack. The final profit and loss account would not have confirmed that view but then no business should be controlled by the Finance Manager; had we not gone in I have no doubt that a defensive pattern would have been stamped on our enterprises, and the investment would not have been made for future profits. As it was my mind was already made up and I shouted, which I could easily do for the eerie silence was the more bated for its shattering to come, "Separate and attack!"

Separation seemed indicated so that we should keep clear of each other and in this way offer the greatest number of targets to the enemy's guns, and perhaps give at least one boat the chance of closing the range unscathed. Ian and Mac needed no other order and we all turned towards, still on our quiet auxiliary engines in the faint hope that the enemy had been as blind as us. That quickly proved forlorn, the 38th Flotilla indeed knew its business and several ships flashed the challenge, "L for London," or perhaps for Leipzig.

We seemed to be on the enemy's beam, but as the map shows we were on their port bow and so the German minesweeper *M 3821* was the first to open fire. She estimated the range as 500 yards, but that would have been point-blank and I cannot believe we were quite so close at the start. I guessed two miles, thinking I saw big merchant ships beyond the escorts, but that was much more in error and reveals lack of experience in judging distance at night when the size of the object is not known. At two miles we should not have had to worry about the enemy's gunnery but that we most certainly did; *M 3820* and *RA 2* joined in almost at once, and then I realized I had had my last complete view of the enemy. His tracer was startlingly bright and completely blinding; emanating from a dozen points it stabbed the darkness with cones of brilliant light of which we were the apexes, though at first it was high and I still had time to think before we started to be hit.

Never had I foreseen that the enemy's fire would be so literally like a curtain; a safety curtain to him, since for us to fire torpedoes with any hope of success we had to see the target, assess her movement, and steer the boat so that the fore and back sights pointed squarely at her vitals. Now the only points of aim were gunflashes, memory was the only guide to course and speed which an alerted enemy would certainly alter drastically. I saw little future either for our torpedoes or ourselves and felt extremely frightened, and worse, totally lost and incompetent; but to run away would be worse still and it was at least possible that we should get a clearer view if we pressed closer. Did I think of my friends' possibly wasted lives? Perhaps, but when a commander is in the same danger as his men he must mistrust such a sentiment lest he is really applying it to himself.

"Crash start," I told Guy. "Steer towards, full speed."

The main engine exhausts coughed, then roared, and with speed came exhilaration and fierce, primitive courage. Cannons to right of us, cannons to left of us, cannons in front of us volleyed and thundered as we sped between *RA 2* and *M 3821* towards *M 3824*. I knew then how the Light Brigade felt as it charged into the valley of death, even though its troopers' lives were being squandered by the most appalling blunder; it felt good. A 40-knot slip-stream seared the cheeks, engines trumpeted, shells whined and some cracked with sonic booms as they whipped close overhead; the boat was clear of the water for a third of her length, and astern the foam rushed away into black-ness like a mountain cataract. Adrenalin flowed as fast, turning the senses to the highest pitch and the brain to react, analyze and decide on the instant.

M 3821 reported that we passed her closely, though I had no means of judging the range, and the firing became even more intense as *M 3824* joined in. Then suddenly, "There!" I shouted in Guy's ear, "there's your target."

It may have been the 585-ton ex-pilot vessel *M 3800* which, while not large, was certainly worthy of our torpedoes; we should have to turn to port to aim the boat and bring the sight to bear. I might have saved my breath, for Guy was already trying to turn but something was wrong; the boat kept straight on and—O Lord!—slowed down. Then I realized that my adrenalin had failed in not alerting me to the simple and entirely to be expected fact that we were being hit.

No large shells came inboard or the shocks would have been noticeable, but the results were none the less dis-turbing. One 20mm in the radio set prevented my enemy report from being sent and worse, started a fire. Another severed the after petrol supply which was connected to the center engine, so that stopped; there was no immediate blaze but it must be presumed that free petrol was flooding the bilge. A third entered the wheelhouse and nicked the hydraulic pipes of the steering gear, so that little capability remained to Leading Seaman Stiff, the coxswain, of obeying his captain's order.

Guy throttled back on the port engine to help the boat turn that way; she did so gradually, but then only the star-board engine was developing full power and the speed fell to little more than 20 knots. The enemy's fire was intense and our target was lost in the tracer's network, but when we thought the boat must be pointing somewhere near the right direction we fired both torpedoes. That at least was the right thing to do according to both common sense and the doctrine which exhorted one never to miss such an opportunity which will probably never recur. A boat com-ing home after contact with the enemy with her torpedoes still on board was viewed with raised eyebrows; though placed as we were I began to wonder whether we were likely to take anything, or anybody, home. We never saw the torpedoes again, and neither did the Germans.

Quick work in the engine room had connected the center engine to the midship tanks, and Guy had pushed his port throttle hard forward so we were up to our full speed again, but still heading for the enemy. All fluid had leaked from the steering, the rudders trailed, and if there had been a ship in our path we should have hit her and that would have been that; but we had no alternative but to go on. There was a certain relief in knowing we were doing the only possible thing but I cannot pretend there was any longer a pleasurable thrill. I knew now what a hit felt like and there were many; nothing larger than 20mm, but each could kill and I wondered how many had done so.

The fire slackened; it had to or the Germans would have hit each other, and ahead and just, but just, to port was a ship. I thought it was the tall stern of a merchantman for it looked huge and adamantine, but it must have been the whole of *M 3824* so close that her guns would not bear down on us. Terror followed hard, but our speed was such that we flicked past before it could overtake. Now, surely, every yard would take us further from danger? Not so, for whereas I thought we had penetrated at right angles we had in fact done so slantwise and *VP 1520* was ready for us; as soon as her line of fire was clear she gave us all she had.

We were a high-deflection target to be sure, and our twin machine guns fired back manfully, but we were also very close and vividly obvious. With our lifted, planing hull, streaming wake and following plume we must have seemed magnificent to any German with an eye for beauty and the leisure to appreciate it; but for our part we could only pray that our hitherto splendid engines would not falter for just a minute longer. More hits arrived, including this time a brute of a 37mm, *VP 1520*'s largest weapon, in the wheelhouse just before and below the bridge.

That Bob Gaunt, the lithe and alert First Lieutenant, and "Fish" Salmon, the Spare Officer, who were trying to navigate in the wheelhouse were not killed instantly was one of those miracles of war that one comes to accept as normal; and that would be fine if they did not work the other way just as readily. The quickest way out was through the shell hole, and after a shout from the captain, Bob was aft with the coxswain in a flash to rig hand steering. They did it most commendably in a moment, and we started to disengage to starboard. That this was a mistake is obvious from the map, but that was pieced together 30 years later and at the time we could see nothing but gun-flashes and tracer.

The turn took us close down the *Oceanie*'s starboard side and she gave us 45 rounds from her single 15mm, but the weapon cannot have been well directed or we should have suffered dreadfully. Then quite suddenly the gun, which was forward, would no longer bear, *VP 1520*'s range was fouled by the tug, and we were through. I waited in trembling anguish for the blood-count, but not one soul was apparently hurt. Poor *237* was no longer a rich man's yacht though, but quite a problem.

Ian Trelawny had turned *232* hard round on to a westerly course at the start so as to separate from me and aim for the enemy's rear; she passed inside the outlying escort *RA 2* and was instantly engaged. The Canadian First Lieutenant, Charley Chaffey, was navigating in the wheelhouse (an anachronism for there was no wheel there and the boats were always steered from their bridges), and with him was a charming young Sub-Lieutenant called Douglas "Gertie" Gill whose helpful enthusiasm led to his being present at nearly every battle, in one boat or another. He was a Spare Officer, another misleading title which denoted in fact an essential functionary, and came up to see what was going on. He was little the wiser: "Couldn't see a damned thing except all this stuff flying around." Ian however had caught a fleeting glimpse as I had done of what seemed a suitable torpedo target, and ordered, "Port wheel."

After that the sequence of events is indeterminate as every recollection differs from the next, but the essentials are only too clear. As Douglas peered into the brilliant void an explosive shell came over the bridge top from the port bow, ripped through his clothing, and burst against the inside of the bulletproof plating against which his captain was leaning. Ian fell, punctured and seared by fragments from his right shoulder to his ankle. The agony should have been unbearable but he says he felt no pain at all, and that can be believed because although he proved his bravery many times his honesty is no less evident. He struggled up but instantly fell back again because his right Achilles tendon was severed, though at first he thought the whole leg had gone. He then lay on the deck observing events and continuing to give orders, becoming much aggrieved when nobody paid the least attention; but whether there was anyone to hear him is doubtful because the wheel would not answer, and Douglas and the coxswain had dashed aft to rig hand steering.

When Chaffey came up he found himself alone on the bridge, except for his crumpled captain, and took charge with the wholly admirable aim of continuing the attack. He noted that 232 was now to the south of the enemy; he tried to take the safety latches off the torpedo triggers but the mechanism was damaged; he turned the wheel to port to close the enemy but it spun uselessly. Glancing aft he saw the boat to be under control from there and hoped that 232's sting had not been completely drawn, but just then Douglas came forward to tell him that the starboard engine would only run at half speed and the port had failed entirely. Poor chap, his fighting spirit deserved better luck, but now he had no option but to take his crippled boat and wounded captain home. Even that was no mean task, placed as he was on the wrong side of the enemy, and when another harbinger of woe arrived to say that the starboard engine had finally seized through lack of oil his cup of bitterness was full.

All First Lieutenants worthy of their salt pray for the day when they shall find themselves in command. The nicer ones wish their captains no positive harm in the manner of their going; but when they do so the reality of lording it over everyone becomes not the pleasure it had had seemed but a singularly onerous duty. Faces look up to ask mutely, "What do you want us to do? Just say the word and we'll do it," and then one also is dumb except to cry with one's whole heart, "Come back, O my Captain!" Chaffey could hardly have had greatness thrust upon him in more trying circumstances but he squared his shoulders and bore it, considerably helped I suspect by Douglas Gill. With palpitating doubt for the welfare of the last remaining engine which might succumb to the effects of any of the many hits all over the boat at any moment, and with a gauntlet to run ahead, 232 set off purposefully at her full 15 knots.

241 was all right. Mac had turned in *237*'s wake and then pulled out to port, choosing as his target the second ship in the enemy's line. From the first he was doubtful whether they were proper targets for his torpedoes, which cost as much each as a Rolls Royce and must not be wasted on anything so insignificant as an auxiliary mine-sweeper. When his enemy started shooting he observed her coolly, being a cool customer—and a cool seller too when he found himself on the other side of the counter—but now he saw her to be very small and definitely unworthy of his torpedoes. She is likely to have been *M 3821* from his description; the much larger *M 3800* was beyond and hidden by the tracer.

Mac took *241* away to the northwest at full speed to probe the enemy at another point, and almost immediately found himself crossing *RA 2*'s bows at an acute angle. The encounter was a surprise to both though that did not prevent either from engaging; and since *RA 2* was equipped with six guns of up to 37mm caliber against *241*'s twin machine-guns, and the range was 70 yards closing, logic would suggest that the latter should have been taken apart like *232* and *237*. She emerged however without a scratch in strangely interesting circumstances. To quote *RA 2*'s report:

I found myself in the middle of eight S-Boats*; three boats making fairly thick smoke ran past my star-board side (presumably *232* and *237*). Five others suddenly appeared on the port side and moved towards my stern in line astern but two abreast; *RA 2* engaged all these five boats with her port weapons and good hits were seen.

Perhaps Mac's strength was as the strength of five because his heart was reasonably pure, it also seems that he was miraculously endowed with the power to split his image, for the real *241* was only engaged with a part of *RA 2*'s potential frightfulness, and that was well within the scope of Able Seaman, Seaman Gunner "Ginger" Harry in the 0.5-inch turret. He was an old, old man of forty-seven who sat hunched between the barrels, clench-ing between his no doubt toothless gums an old clay pipe;

*Schnellboote = MTBs.

the bowl was downwards and it was unlit, not because he
scorned to smoke it but because Edwin "Knocker" White,
the Coxswain, Welsh and a regular Petty Officer, made
very sure he did not, perched as he was on top of a petrol
tank.

Harry let fly, rock steady and impervious to the enemy's
tracer, which is the only way to shoot straight when someone is shooting at you. He hit *RA 2* ten times, wounded
one man badly and one slightly, caused her gunner's aim to
falter, and perhaps was the reason for her ceasing fire
altogether. At 40 knots *241* was soon out of danger,
perhaps even before the crew fully realized they were in
it. White told me, "It was very enjoyable that night when
old Harry got going with his point fives."

Nineteen-year-old Midshipman Henry Franklin was
large, ebullient, looked much older than his captain from
whom he differed in almost every particular except mutual
esteem, also enjoyed excitement. Unlike Gaunt and Chaffey who rightly stayed in their wheelhouse in increasingly
trying circumstances to keep their plots going, Henry's
custom was to draw a ring round his present position on
the chart when an action started, and go on deck to take
part if he could; assuming, when he returned below, that
the boat would still be in the circle irrespective of where
she may have moved at 40 knots or two-thirds of a mile
a minute. That is but one of the interesting practices in
my flotilla which I now discovered for the first time. Had I
been Mac I should have considered keeping Henry in
after school to write out 100 times, "I must not run my
boat ashore"; even though it was never particularly easy
to keep Henry in after school. This time he manned the
stripped Lewis gun and supported Ginger Harry vigor-
ously; after all, the shore was at least two miles away,
dead ahead.

Euphoria is often short-lived when in the presence of
the enemy. Clear of the turmoil Mac sighted *237* steering
a parallel course two cables on his port bow, and she was
on fire.

It was comforting to see *241* in close company when I
glanced back for the first time, because disquieting reports
were arriving on *237*'s bridge. The radio cabin was well
alight and so was the galley next to it. That did not seem
too bad after all the punishment we had taken, and Gaunt
was already below with a team of fire-fighters; but then

Twin Browning .50's

Guy and I realized with a jerk that both these rooms
shared a bulkhead with the forward petrol compartment
which contained 1,500 gallons in three huge tanks.

We stopped well clear of the enemy, and I told Mac
airily that we should soon be all right, adding that he had
better keep his eyes open in case of interference. At first
Gaunt seemed to be winning, but then the Motor Mechanic saw flames in the petrol compartment through the
forward bulkhead of the engine-room; he very promptly
flooded the space with methyl-bromide gas and again the
fire appeared to be under control.

Extinguisher after extinguisher was emptied into the
forward blaze with no further effect however, and we
shouted to *241* for hers. Again the situation seemed to
improve and Guy ordered main engines to be started. That
did it; the breeze fanned the fire, and I had no doubt
then that we had lost the boat. Tongues of flame licked

out through the hole in the wheelhouse, and I could hear
a roaring, hissing noise below the petrol compartment
hatch which started to lift and buckle as I stared at it
compulsively. Frightened now, I looked around for *241*
but she was nowhere to be seen.

Mac had done precisely as I had told him so I had no
cause for complaint. He had heard engines to the southwest and headed quietly in that direction to investigate;
sure enough there was a blurred shadow and if it was
not *232* I should be very much surprised, but no further
contact was made for the very good reason that neither
boat wanted it. The slightest hint of anything was enough
to send Chaffey scurrying in another direction, quite
rightly; and Mac had to keep glancing over his shoulder
at *237*, his first responsibility unless something of overriding importance should turn up. The next time he did
so settled the question of whether there was to be an
encounter; *237* had blown her top.

We were lucky beyond belief; petrol is unpredictable,
and although its ignition can be as violent as high explosive the right amount of oxygen must be present in the
vapor. Only last night Christopher Dreyer, an officer of
more than ordinary gallantry, had decided that his badly
damaged boat must be destroyed in the presence of the
enemy, so he flooded the engine-room with petrol and fired
a Verey light down the hatch. Not having been experienced in the role of human cannon ball, he is not sure
whether he was hurled twenty yards or eighty; but he can
say with assurance that the petrol/oxygen mixture was correct. *237*'s tank space contained only a small volume of
air, so that the explosion itself was not catastrophic and
"Fish" Salmon, poor chap, was lifted only a few feet into
the air. He came down on the mast-rigging and was cut
painfully, though not seriously. Guy and others were
thrown to the deck, but I do not even remember the oc-
currence, having, I rather think, removed myself as far
from the threatened holocaust as was possible in a seventy-
foot boat.

Some think the explosion was vented mainly through
the two bulkheads below and thereby sealed the boat's fate;
although the first bright flame soon subsided and I could
peer cautiously down past the wrecked hatch-cover, what
I saw was a self-perpetuating white heat. I seized what was
probably the last extinguisher and emptied it round the

tanks without even momentary effect. Whether I told Guy to abandon ship before the remaining tanks blew, or he urged me to do so, I cannot remember, but there was no divergence of opinion and the crew was soon on the forecastle being mustered by the coxswain.

Last to emerge from his fire-fighting was Bob Gaunt, almost overcome having struggled to the very end in a hell of heat, smoke, gas, and acute confinement. In the little ceremony I realized I was witnessing a very traditional scene; one indeed of which I could truly report that it was in the best traditions of the Service, so calm and steady were the men. I drew strength from them, guilt-ridden as I was for leading them into this profitless disaster; though not enough to prevent me now committing an act of almost criminal folly and leaving behind my binoculars, Pattern 1900, pairs, one. Those glasses were worth their weight in gold; at least two pairs a boat were needed for look-out efficiency, but only one was allowed and more could not be obtained for love—for the Stores Chief Petty Officer's Wren—or money. That pair was subsequently written off as "Lost by enemy action"; as would also have been the case had they still hung round my neck, from the purest motives of tactical flexibility of course.

The parade being dismissed we all took three paces smartly to our front and were on board *241*, dry shod. One of Mac's many admirable qualities was his thoughtfulness; a young man of few words and none of them unnecessary, he brought calm judgment to bear whatever the distractions and usually turned up in the right place at the right time. He had done so now, when *237* was becoming warm underfoot.

The fire flared up brightly for all to see, and among those who did so were soldiers Fischer, Heckmann and Dinkhoff on look-out duty ashore. They noted every event, but all they or their seniors could do was try to illuminate us with a searchlight. In that they failed because the range was a good two miles, give or take a soupçon for any possible error in Henry's navigation, although at our end it was bright enough to read by. We felt naked, so Harry directed a stream of tracer up the beam and persuaded the Germans to switch it off; they tried it again at intervals but always with the same result.

Our old enemy also saw our two boats, more clearly because the searchlight made a backdrop for our silhouettes, and debated what to do. Wunderlich was all for going back, reasoning that the Group was not protecting a convoy which it would have been wrong to leave. However the Senior Officer expected further attack, thinking there were eight of us; and did not want to risk air attack by being caught out in daylight for the sake of an uncertain prize, which might well have vanished by the time his slow minesweepers could reach it.

To attack again was my first thought too; though to suppose I could overtake the enemy on main engines and then torpedo him successfully with but a single boat was a pathetic attempt to salvage something from my wrecked conscience rather than practical tactics. "Let's destroy 237 quickly," I told Mac; but even that proved easier said than done.

We dropped a depth charge close alongside so as to break her back, but all it did was apparently to douse the flames with its watery plume. Laughing happily we prepared to tow, but alas the water had not penetrated to the seat of the fire which soon blazed up again. Then we tried shooting at the after tanks, to the Germans' mystification, but although 237 burned from end to end it was a whole hour before I felt justified in leaving her; and not until an hour after that did Dinkhoff's relief, Durck, see the last feeble flicker, after which she must have sunk, for her remains were never found.

We came home fast; the healthy roar of the engines, the rush of air and the fact that we were leaving hostile territory at last were all satisfying, though nagging concern for 232 predominated in my mind. Eventually however, her Telegraphist having managed to repair the transmitter, Chaffey sent a signal saying, "Attack completed, unsuccessful, three casualties," so that was a partial relief. His last unpleasant adventure had been an exhaust leak into the engine room which gassed two of the crew badly, and that is a particularly nauseating form of gassing; but the center engine chugged faithfully on, which was the main thing.

All my immediate cares being over, I occupied the last few miles home in trying to remember the Articles of War which might apply to my vulnerable situation. There was one which made me distinctly uneasy:

Any person subject to this Act who, through negligence or other default, shall strand, lose or hazard, or suffer to be lost, stranded or hazarded, any of His Majesty's ships or aircraft shall be dismissed from His Majesty's Service with Disgrace, or suffer such other punishment as is hereinafter mentioned.

When therefore *241* slid gently alongside at HMS *Hornet*, the Coastal Force base up Haslar Creek in Gosport, and the slumbering sentry batted not an eyelid, I delighted to find someone else in dereliction of his duty; and with no logic, less fellow-feeling, but a most satisfying relief, I put the metaphorical boot in accordingly. Sweeping on into the building with self-unrighteous ire I dealt similarly with the equally unconscious Officer of the Day, to his goggle-eyed alarm, and then, gathering momentum, strode to the Captain's cabin itself and thrust open the door a split second after the most perfunctory knock. The poor man dashed the sleep from his eyes with the sleeve of his pajamas which were woollen and of an off-white hue.

"Sir," I snorted; and it is a fact that never before nor since did I presume to snort at so vastly senior an officer, having been born of a timorous nature and subjected to naval discipline from that moment on. "We have fought a battle against the enemy, one boat has been lost, another is still at sea probably badly damaged and with three casualties serious enough to make a signal about, and not a soul in this benighted dump gives a damn!"

If I had not rendered myself liable to Court Martial before, I did so then; but all was well, the worthy veteran hummed then buzzed, and in a twinkling of an eye a veritable hornet's nest swarmed about our ears. But we were the only ones who were not stung.

"I was pretty sore for a bit," was Ian's way of describing his troubles. His nurses' first task was to peel off the fancy shirt he was wearing, for he had been on his way ashore the previous evening on an entirely different mission when he was recalled for the operation; then they started to pick the pieces out of his side, and he cannot be sure that he is free of the last one yet. He endured much, for many months, and of course was lost to my flotilla so that I felt that a prop had been knocked from under me. Worse, I myself had done the knocking and included Guy Fison, Bob Gaunt and all *237*'s crew in the clumsy swipe.

What a beginning! Yet failure proved the best and quick-

est teacher. To have plunged into the fiery furnace—and
reemerged through the intervention of who knows what
agency, certainly not my leadership—was to have experienced both flame and heat with an intimacy that
branded us with the mark of the warrior in one quick siz-
zle. Before the battle there had been so many uncertainties
as I took my place in proud though tentative command,
and I could not but echo the Breton fishermen's prayer,
"O God be good to me, thy sea is so wide, my boat is so
small." Then equally inevitably I added my own rider,
"and my enemy is so big," because in theory a 50-ton
MTB could sink a 40,000-ton battleship; and although I
thrilled to the prospect of earning glory for us all beyond
the dreams of vanity while also furthering the war-effort
not a little, I was uncomfortably aware that such an un-
dertaking would not be easy.

My disquiet was of two kinds. The first was animal fear,
which apparently afflicted me alone among my carefree,
jesting companions; all of which felt exactly the same as
I later discovered. The second was fear of the unknown,
of a particular kind whereby the uncertain factor lay within myself; I had to *do* something but did not know what.
I felt like the man who answered an advertisement for an
infallible rat-killer and received two wooden blocks with
the instruction, "Place rat on 'A' and strike smartly with
'B.'" The idea seemed good as far as it went but hardly
described the complete process; a part, perhaps even the
more difficult part, had surely been glossed over.

The equivalent to placing the rat on block "A" was to
maneuver one's MTB into a position on the battleship's
beam at half a mile's range; once there the enemy's clumsy
bulk would require him to hold more or less still while the
torpedoes, block "B," were wielded with good prospects of
breaking his back. But how to get there in one piece in the
face of that bristling pin-cushion of guns? A stand-up fight
with such a mighty adversary must be avoided with that
discretion which is truly and honorably the better part of
valor, as not all discretion in battle is seen in practice to
be, and was probably best done by using the boat's small
size as an asset to conceal her approach. She must come
in quietly therefore, slowly to show no wake, and point
her bows at the enemy to present the smallest possible
silhouette.

So much was obvious; but what if we were seen too

early just the same? Would it be possible to use our full forty knots to press in closer, jinking like snipe to offer difficult targets? Should I concentrate my boats and risk them all being discovered together, or disperse them and have them picked off one by one? The answers to such questions depended upon a host of others: At what range would a boat be seen in given conditions of visibility When would enemy gunnery become dangerous? Wha punishment could a boat suffer and still be fit to fire torpedoes? How much could one see to maneuver and attack while being engaged? There had been no means of knowing these things but now we had been initiated; and never mind if Wunderlich's flotilla of armed auxiliaries fell some degrees short of being the *Tirpitz*, we could extrapolate. Less precisely but even more important we knew what close action felt like, and it really was not too bad.

tively attentive in times of inactivity, only when
granted my objectives and their obedience did I ...
and in ... ... and manage to sound ...

II

CONDITIONING FOR WAR

My apprenticeship started without delay for I was born
into the Navy. Certainly no pressure was brought to bear
on me to join, nor was it needed; and the only serious
question having to be decided by my father and their Lordships of the Admiralty was whether I was worthy of the
honor. For it was, "On the Navy, under the Good Providence of God, that our Wealth, Prosperity and Peace did
chiefly depend." That precept, arrogant if you like and
certainly uncompromising, had nevertheless stood the test
of centuries and was probably truer than most. Those disposed to censure the apparent blasphemy that God Himself - had delegated to the Royal Navy the task of
maintaining His prime requirement, peace, would do well
to contrast its peace-keeping record with that of other
agencies, including—certainly including—the Christian
Churches. I wonder if my mother was any more confused
about the nature of God than most of us when, admittedly
distracted, she wrote "RN" in the space for Religion on
the hospital form for my father's last illness.

I grew up in the shadow of the great fleets. Sometimes
I could even see one from the bathroom window, as at
Hong Kong at the age of six when I was allowed my first
day at sea in "Daddy's ship." Being as yet imperfectly
disciplined, I idly tried all the knobs on the bridge until I
came to the one which summoned the ship's company to
action stations with fearful clamor. As the men tumbled
up from below and cast loose the guns with fierce, incomprehensible cries I was terrified, and it was only later that
I realized how delicious it was to have exerted such power
with one small button.

Yet I was not a power seeker by nature, and feared
responsibility at the same time as seeking it. I tried to
dominate my juniors because there was no other way of

running a fighting service, but lacked the necessary urge and was not very effective in times of inactivity; only when the task demanded my decision and their obedience did I feel justified in pulling it over them and manage to sound convincing. I only realized this fully the day I left the Navy, which promised to be one of profound gloom but was tempered with an astonished relief that no one, ever again, would have to salute me or call me Sir.

After that admission it may seem illogical that my over-riding aspiration was to command a ship at the earliest possible age, but that seemed to me what the Navy was all about. I recognized that there was much to learn before I could be entrusted with a ship, though not how much, which might have been daunting; yet the wish to command and one's blind assurance at that age which supported the wish, were tremendous assets when the appointment came, for they gave confidence and this, however irrationally, in turn begets loyalty from one's team. It therefore became important to evade official pressure to specialize, for that would delay command until one was at least a Commander, which to me then was forever. Fortunately most of my contemporaries acceded willingly as specialization was held to enhance promotion prospects; each trade carried a different career rating, from Anti-Submarine well at the bottom—though experience soon forced it to be, with Aviation, the most important of all—to the Gunnery branch which thought it was. Besides, my father had taught me to mistrust all "super-plumbers" as narrow-minded bigots; "nuts and bolts" were no foundation for sound judgment in command.

Luckily, perhaps understandably, no branches competed for my allegiance and I was allowed to follow my father as a nonspecialist or "Salt Horse." Although the super-plumbers saw us as perpetual officers of the watch on battle-ships' quarterdecks, there being nothing more testing for us to do, there was in fact an infinitely more desirable alternative for one who loftily disdained the career advantage of living in the shadow of captains and admirals in big ships. Small ships offered intimate wardrooms, scope for learning all trades and keeping them in balance, far greater responsibility for a junior officer, and a shorter road to command. There was nothing to prevent me asking for one and, lucky again, I joined the Tribal Class destroyer *Somali* in 1938 as Sub-Lieutenant.

The Sub-Lieutenant; it was not just a rank but a title
of euphoric grandeur, and if it ever occurred to me that
I was also the most junior and least useful officer on board
by a wide margin, I was by no means cast down by the
reflection. The Captain observing that deflation was unlikely to be self-administered saw his duty, and choosing his
moment and his words carefully asked, "What's the good
of you?" A reply did not spring readily to mind.

Somali was ready for the coming war. She was an
efficient and a happy ship, and we saw in this war a clear-
cut confrontation between good and evil. I took what was
for me an important decision, to *wage* war, not just endure it like Neville Chamberlain; I knew we had to win.
I knew also that war would be a full-time job, twenty-four
hours a day in a seven-day week, demanding a degree of
commitment and endurance which strength of character
alone would not provide. The human instincts for aggression, adventure and protectiveness had to be called in as
reinforcements, not in fulfillment of some tyrant's barbaric
ambitions, but to guard civilization from dissolution.

I believed, and still believe, that the greatest British contribution to civilized existence has been our unwillingness
to fight until the justice and inevitability of doing so are
clearly seen. If this reluctance on occasion loses us the
first round, it certainly strengthens our purpose with
startling force.

The right conditions being met, the propect of war in
1939 to a young, untried man was rather fun. I am not
ashamed to admit it, and started with a reserve of moral
buoyancy that kept me afloat through the long dark years
of recurrent disaster. But now I had to begin learning the
complex professional business of war, and to master fear
which, uncontrolled, would distort judgment and inhibit
action.

Norway was our first real battle, but even that humiliat-
ing reverse to British arms could not shake my youthful
mood of supreme confidence. The setting was breathtakingly romantic; great mountains rose from the depths,
breaking the glittering sea into fjords, and then leaped ever
upwards into the brilliant sky. Cold, crisp air dilated the
nostrils and filled the breast with manliness, as the little
ship raced through the waterways like a toy boat in a
bath, dwarfed by the crags, in pursuit of German warships
which might lurk round every corner. None did however

and I was taught, but did not fully learn, my first lesson in sea warfare; when one expects the enemy to appear he rarely does, and when one relaxes there he is approaching from the wrong direction and in unanticipated guise.

"The readiness is all," my father used to quote; and although I paid little attention to such maxims at the time I found them comforting when they began to accord with my own experiences, for they helped me to absorb the lessons reasonably quickly. However cold and tired one had to be ready, both physically at one's action stations, and mentally prepared with countermeasures to likely forms of attack, yet with a mind open for the unexpected. Pigeon-shooting is a good apprenticeship; if one does not keep one's eyes constantly moving a bird will surely come from behind and when, flustered, one has missed it, another will fly out from the very tree under which one is standing—but one's gun is broken for re-loading.

In Norway the enemy came from over the mountain peaks; and I, as Gun Control Officer, delivered myself of the sanguine cry, "Switch to High Angle!" which initiated a series of control orders from my gun-director's crew that were reminiscent of the Peninsular War. Indeed, "Load your muskets!" "Present your muskets!" "FIRE your muskets!" would have been no less effective against the German bombers than the barrage we actually put up; and even so our guns were silent most of the time because they would not elevate above 40°. To pull the legs of the poor gunnery people may seem cruel as they were so earnest and dedicated; yet it remains true that the bolts with which those sons of thunder have equipped the fleet from Jutland onwards have too often been ill-adapted to the functions they were actually called upon to perform. On the other side of the coin, however, the bombs which exploded on the water with splashes several times the height of our lofty director seemed more than adequate to their task.

Thus the next warlike lesson could be learned, how I personally reacted to battle. One cannot know in advance because others' experiences apply only to themselves, so that one approaches the trial with the twin fears of unaccustomed danger and of revealing oneself as a coward. But to show fear was the ultimate degradation in the officer's code to which I had been trained, far worse than seducing the Colonel's wife or making off with the mess funds, and it gradually became apparent that the dictum was wiser than it seemed. The greater fear of seeming afraid overrode the lesser, physical fear, and the astonishing truth emerged that though one's bowels might have turned to water those around need not know so long as one kept a stiff lower lip, that being the one most liable to wobble. Then they, probably just as incapacitated, said to themselves, "If he can take it so can we"; so that by a process of moral leap-frog based apparently on a vacuum of courage, the team soon felt itself to be quite brave which is the same thing as actually being so.

We were lucky to be inoculated against violence in a course of tolerable doses; high-level bombing was really not very dangerous as it allowed time to watch the bombs' trajectories and move the ship out of the way. But when we came within range of Stuka dive-bombers, whose near approach permitted much greater accuracy without giving us time to dodge, I began to doubt whether the ship could long survive. That was frightening, but I could feel the previous vaccine working and found no particular difficulty in keeping outwardly calm. Curiously it was a help being forced to sit in that director between bomb and ship, with absolutely nothing to do, the dive-bombers being well above our limiting angle of fire. The crew and I observed the aerobatics from our superb vantage point, and discussed them with the appreciation of sports fans:

"Too steep that one; he'll never get his nose down—there you are, right over the top."

"Don't like the look of this," when the bomb appeared to hang, perfectly circular but growing larger in diameter. "No it's all right, bombs don't travel in straight lines." And sure enough it would fall short.

On one occasion we actually applauded a pilot who approached in a seventy-degree dive from the port beam, crossed over the ship and, still in his dive, flicked his aircraft round through 180 degrees and made his aiming run from starboard. To have something positive to do is best; to have nothing is bearable if duty is thereby satisfied; but to feel one ought to do something without knowing what is conducive to dithering and loss of self-control.

Constant and prolonged action was the next trial. For the five weeks of our Norwegian operations we searched for enemy ships, landed troops, evacuated them again, and bombarded enemy positions ashore; but whatever we did we were always under threat of air attack without effective defense of our own nor any fighters that we ever saw, and with every near-miss the bomb with our number on it came mathematically closer. I could feel tiredness sap my resolution, and learned that physical well-being is important in maintaining moral strength. This well-being is not however predominant, especially in a defensive situation where one has only to react to the enemy's initiative; I found later that to maintain offensive pressure when dog-tired and depressed took far more doing.

Awareness of the enemy as a man who was doing his best to kill—us—was novel and chilling; though being a man he was also liable to weakness, and we could tell by his behavior in the air that he was often as timorous as we were. By no means every pilot pressed his attack home to point-blank range; some even dodged behind the mountains never to close at all, no doubt devising plausible heroic yarns to spin on their return to base. We saw we were as good as they were if not better, and our sense of a just cause was an important factor in sustaining us. If only our guns had been some use!

Junkers Ju 87 "Stuka"

The final lesson from Norway was the crunch. That particular attack seemed like any other, though with per-

haps an indefinable hint of extra determination in the rock-
steady, end-on silhouette of the Stuka with its menacingly
crooked wings. I realized only slowly that the bomb, having
left the aircraft slightly obliquely from my viewpoint, was
growing more nearly circular as it fell until at mast-height
it became a huge, black shrieking orb that must surely carry
me down with it. All thought and movement froze; but a
milli-second later I became aware of the thing flicking
over the director, then the bridge, and missing the side of
the forecastle by what looked like inches.

> The lights went out! The windows broke!
> The room was filled with reeking smoke.
> And in the darkness shrieks and yells
> Were mingled with electric bells.

The immortal words of Hilaire Belloc, one of the few
poets who had made any impact on my unimaginative soul,
sprang instantly to mind to comfort and sustain me as the
ship plunged into the hole scoured by the explosion, and a
wall of dirty water rose to engulf her, even the director.
I thought we were under the surface, diving.

Not at all; we were practically unscathed with just a
couple of minor compartments flooded. These were soon
isolated and shored, but since it would have been hazardous
to steam the ship at high speed in that condition we were
ordered home for repairs. I was unashamedly delighted.

Thus I was blooded and felt all the better for it. Later
I should have to learn how to take the initiative in action
so as to impose my will on the enemy, for I felt sure the
chance would come. The command for which I yearned
would bring it, yet my stomach shrank at the pospect; why
go deliberately looking for trouble? it asked.

The *Somali* had scarcely berthed at Liverpool when I
was handed an Admiralty message ordering me personally
to report to Chatham Barracks. Why? I wondered, but was
told, "get moving!" In Kent they seemed relieved to see
me (and hundreds of others) and said, "Go with these
sailors to London Docks, take over the Schuyt *Doggersbank* from her Dutch crew and make your way to Sheerness."

"Why?"

"The lorry's outside, don't hang around."

Whatever the *Doggersbank* might be, and whatever we were going to do, my heart leaped at the prospect of command; but that was not yet to be as I was joined by a delightful Lieutenant, Donald McBarnet, who was my senior by a dog-watch. At Sheerness we were told, "Here are blankets, cigarettes, rum and other necessaries; get them on board at once and sail for Dunkirk."

"Why?"

"You'll find out when you get there."

There was nothing apparently to be happy about at Dunkirk, yet I was. The Army had been defeated, incredibly, and I half believed we had lost the war as well. 350 soldiers stumbled and lurched on board the little coaster, spent and weaponless, to lower themselves down the single vertical ladder to the hold where they collapsed. I shuddered as I watched, imagining the carnage should the ship be hit or the writhing, groping hands if she were to sink. Their spirit was wonderful but the ambience depressing, and the wounded did nothing to enliven it; I remember one man—no, never mind the detail.

There was no animal satisfaction to be had from male aggression for we were unarmed and must submit to constant dive-bombing and strafing, unsure whether we were sailing over minefields. The limitless task was to take off as many soldiers as possible, and they were as, and on, the sands of the sea-shore, innumerable. Every moment had to be filled with activity and fatigue built up; but we could see we were doing a supremely worthwhile job and the sense of purpose lifted our hearts and deferred exhaustion. Before I saw the soldiers I had scorned them for being defeated; but now it was, "poor devils!" followed by astonished admiration for the trials they had undergone and survived. Finally I was surprised by an unexpectedly brisk clatter on the steel deck.

"Atten*tion!*" A line of left legs were raised as one, then crashed to the deck and sounded the hollow hold below with a cheerful boom. Heads were high, eyes bright, shoulders square to the front, and the young officer gave me a rotary, vibrating salute that bidded fair to carry away a signal halyard.

"So-and-so Unit, Royal Horse Artillery; we have four automatic weapons, request permission to mount them—SIR!"

I grinned with pleasure but my eyes were moist, and

from that moment my loyalty to the Army has never wavered.

Carefree adventures followed one another. McBarnet bravely solved the exhaustion problem by going below and instructing me *not* to call him for any reason other than the ship actually sinking; so I was in command at last, if only for a few hours at a time. I honestly forget whether it was McBarnet or I who put the ship aground on a falling tide because it seemed a matter of small moment; indeed it worked out very neatly for it was evening, the soldiers waded out to the ship at low water, and the tide came in again before dawn. During my watch some French soldiers arrived with cognac in their water bottles; and in a remarkably short time I was monarch of all I surveyed in very sooth, there being no one left capable of either disputing my right or doing my bidding. I steered the ship towards the beach, yanked the great gear-lever to stop, then astern, leaped like a stag for the forecastle, let go the anchor, and prepared to receive the next load of troops.

It was all great fun; and I am sure that was because we were all doing our job to the utmost. I am strengthened in this belief by the fact that the only time I came off the peak was when I may not have lived up to the high purpose. On our last trip home from the beaches with only half a load of troops, all we could find, we had to pass Dunkirk itself and I wondered whether we should enter the harbor and fill up. There were arguments both ways but I inclined to the view that we should; and did not. The memory is still painful. Those who would expunge the word duty from from our vocabulary not only attack our moral fiber, they cruelly detract from human happiness.

I met my brother Claud on Margate Pier, totally unexpectedly, and since it was my birthday we put away a bottle of sherry, all we had between us. Not yet twenty, he had been sent off in a Dockyard craft with its civilian crew, and owing to a trifling error of navigation brought about by the compass not having been adjusted within living memory, arrived at dawn off Gravelines which chanced to be in German hands. Pursued by shot and shell he fled at his full speed of 6½ knots, and was then further discomfited by a delegation from the crew who complained that nothing in their articles compelled them to endure such goings on, and demanded to return home instantly. Claud sought to quell the mutiny by reaching for his pistol but, thank heavens, had mislaid it and was forced to cajole, persuade or bully the men into continuing to Dunkirk. He succeeded and embarked a full load of troops.

A fortnight's "Dunkirk" leave and never had our Wiltshire farm seemed more lovely and precious. The primroses were over and I had to imagine them for they were my prime symbol of love for home and country. But I could also see them being ground under a jack-boot and was afraid, because I truly did not know whether we were beaten or not. I was one of those feeble creatures who had to be told by Churchill, "We shall never surrender"; which I believe to have been more than just the roar of an indomitable British Lion. It had to be said.

The family was reunited and we all told our tales, not the least exciting being Father's. Aged sixty, retired and recalled, he had been in Holland as Naval Attaché; and having got the Queen and many others away he tried to telephone London, only to be answered from the Hague exchange by a very rude German. "Get off the line, you bloody Hun," he retorted with that commanding authority to which I was well accustomed and invariably deferred, but this time it failed. With the good offices of the American Embassy however he got through to the Admiralty:

"Quick," he said, "I'll tell you the situation in Holland."

"You can't do that," they replied, "it's secret."

Then, seeing German soldiers swarming over the garden wall, he thought it time to get himself away and drove in the ambassadorial Rolls to The Hook, embarked in the lifeboat and was picked up by a British destroyer.

Mother listened to our yarns which lost nothing in the telling, cooked bountifully, made heroes of us and covered us with love. Whether I wondered if life for her, alone and isolated in the country while all these things were happening to three of her men, might have been just a little trying I cannot recall; but I doubt it.

Among the many valuable experiences I underwent at Dunkirk was the introduction to operating among the shoals, tides, wrecks and minefields of the southern North Sea. Now the lesson was continued as though in preparation for Coastal Forces when I was appointed to HMS *Cotswold*, a little Hunt Class escort destroyer which was to operate on the East Coast; my chief thrill at the time

however was because I was to be First Lieutenant and
Second-in-Command, a vital rung in the ladder to my
cherished aim. Peter Knowling was the Captain and I became very attached to him. He rode my enthusiasm with
a light rein and indeed the *Cotswold* was the happiest ship
I ever served in; I should like to linger with her but must
discipline myself to picking out only those aspects which
bore on the future.

Hunt Class Destroyer

Our job was to defend the convoys, the greater proportion of whose ships carried the coal on which London
absolutely depended; the Germans did their best to thwart
us with aircraft, E-boats* and mines, and business was
brisk. Air attack in the North Sea was like air attack anywhere else, but E-boats were peculiar to the area and
presented us with new problems in tactics and gunnery.
We often heard and saw them as they strove to close our
convoys, but to take a damaging shot at the ghostly shadows

---

*The E-boat was the British name for the German MTBs—Schnell-
boote. (See Appendix III for details.)

while they shimmered fleetingly in and out of our ken seemed beyond the capability of our ponderous control system. That a fast craft could maneuver with comparative safety within 1,000 yards of a warship many times her size was of course a valuable lesson for the future; but now I was concerned to hit and failed to do so, despite having appointed myself Gunnery Officer and inventing my own unorthodox method of fire control.

Nevertheless our lack of success was not only caused by the inadequacy of British gunnery but also by the E-boats not coming close enough; I really could not bring myself to be very impressed with their performance even at the

time, but later when I was in their shoes I was astonished
that they had not pulled off the biggest bonanza ever
offered to Coastal Forces. There were usually about forty
ships in our convoys and one ran in each direction every
night; because of the mine threat ships had to stay rigidly
in the narrow swept channel strung out in two columns
perhaps ten miles long, and to protect them we rarely had
more than two destroyers and a few motor launches (see
Appendix I) so that the long flanks were utterly vulnerable.
Contrast that with the weakest enemy convoy we ever met
in the 21st MTB Flotilla, eight merchant ships and five
escorts.

No one would accuse the Germans of timidity, their
Army, Air Force and U-boats ridicule such a thought; but
their surface fleet from the *Bismarck* to the E-boats always
kept a wary eye open for trouble when acting offensively.
I suspect that the fundamental reason was the German
navy's perpetual strategical and numerical inferiority to
ours ever since Germany emerged as a great power; the
loss of a ship was therefore of great moment and commanders afloat were always urged to be careful. I believe
too that the morale side was just as significant, and the
almost mystical awe in which the Royal Navy was held
acknowledged its outstanding quality.

The E-boat threat could not be taken lightly however,
and the Commander-in-Chief The Nore was active in seeking every effective means of combating it. The evolution of
the Motor Gunboat (MGB—See Appendix I), which
could safely override minefields and position herself to
intercept the enemy well to seaward of the convoy route,
was one such. Another was the exploitation of the German's
propensity for chattering on voice radio, to intercept which
a chain of listening stations was established along the East
Anglican coast; its efficiency was remarkable, and not
despite its being manned entirely by women but largely
because of that, the brightest girls and best linguists being
concentrated in the team.

The only snag was the short range at which a shore
station could detect a transmission, only just beyond the
convoy route, and despite the girls' quicksilver reaction
warning was often minimal. We were therefore joined on
board by a young German graduate Jew whose parents
had gone the way of Auschwitz and whose first and only

aim was to help bring about the Nazis' downfall by any means within his power. We called him Wolfgang. His English was basic, and nautical jargon which is esoteric in any tongue was a closed book; but we were delighted to have him.

Wolfgang found, as we all did, that the greater part of war is spent in trying to maintain intense concentration in the face of unutterable boredom. Twiddling the knobs in his stuffy little office night after night in the very remote chance of hearing a crackle in his native tongue must have been testing beyond belief, yet his hate sustained him and he had his reward.

"It is German speaking."

Every nerve on the bridge twitched and the Captain ordered, "Stand to!"

Another officer was on the voice-pipe, shouting, "Headache Office!" (For some obscure reason the system was called "Headache"—so that it should remain obscure.) "What does he say? Quick!"

That was no way to treat Wolfgang; fluster him and all must be lost, so I took over. "Take your time," I soothed, "and tell me all you hear."

"It is about torpedoes; I think he say, 'Prepare to fire.'"

The captain said, "Make an enemy report to Nore and all ships."

"I think," resumed Wolfgang, slowly as an academic seeks absolute precision, "it is not 'prepare to fire' but 'fire now.'"

We were on independent patrol that night and the nearest convoy was ten miles astern.

"They're probably attacking the convoy," reasoned the captain. "We'll go and augment the escort. Hard-a-starboard, full ahead both engines."

The ship shuddered as the propellers bit, and listed with the turn.

"Ach!"

"Y—e—s?" I encouraged gently.

"He is swearing; he says, 'Der Kerl hat Kurs geändert,' the—in English I do not know how you say?—his course is changing."

The full impact of a profound observation is often not felt for a moment or two—then,

"Whoops!" whistled one.

"Ow!" cringed another.

"Midships!" snapped the captain. 'Hard-a-port! Fire starshell all round!"

This was one of our patent drills and was well rehearsed. As the captain threw the ship from side to side to avoid the torpedoes which were presumably even then running towards us, we surrounded ourselves with a halo of light which revealed—absolutely nothing.

My ear went back to the voice-pipe. 'The swear it is very bad; he say, 'The enemy is awake now, stop the attack.' "

"Wolfgang," I cried, "you've saved the ship."

"What is that please? I do not understand." And of course he did not; how could he?

The E-boats had evidently spread for their attack and were then scattered by our starshell, because they could not find each other again and the Senior Officer became more and more vocally exasperated. Finally he could bear his unit's truancy no longer and ordered, "Join me instantly; I am about to fire a green flare—stand by—green flare—now."

And there it was; all we ever had to show that the battle we had almost fought was not just a vivid dream. But it was enough to do that, and also to emphasize with great cogency the importance of security in tactical communications.

When Officer of the Watch one evening, I sliced through one of our minesweeping trawlers and sank her like a brick, though by great good fortune all her crew were saved. She had come from our convoy's beam and steered an unwavering course for her home at Grimsby, dreaming no doubt of the fleshpots ahead and remaining impervious to present reality. It was all her fault, say I, and if I had not hit her she could not possibly have traversed the convoy without someone else doing so; but Their Lordships took a different view, and expressed it as only they could: "I am to request you to convey to Lieutenant Dickens an award of My Lord's displeasure."

Oh well, fair enough! One must not run children down even though they ought not to dash across the road. While not being unduly disheartened, indeed I had earned the ship's company's approbation for getting them three weeks' leave while the crumpled bow was ironed smooth, I nevertheless made a solemn resolution to do something positive which would redeem both the trawler and the indictment.

In two years on the East Coast we sank only one ship and shepherded many safely, becoming ever more at home in those muddy, fogbound waters where every mile contained its hazard. Like Kipling we warmed to shoal-names like the Gabbard, Galloper, Sunk, Haisborough, Dowsing; and laughed at our friends from the great oceans who told us it was there that the real war was being fought, although they ventured into our cold lairs only when they must, and with pale faces when they saw our wreck-studded charts.

Many lessons of war having been presented, and some learned, my preparatory schooling came to an end quite suddenly on April 20, 1942. Returning from patrol in a calm and beautiful spring dawn, I said to the signalman on the bridge by way of conversation, "This must be about where those E-boats were last night; I wonder if they laid any mines?"

"The lights went out...," the compass binnacle rose up and struck me sharply under the chin, and all the Cotswolds became eligible for a change of appointment. Despite a 40-foot hole in the bottom and round both sides we remained in one piece by virtue of the upper deck, but you could feel the two halves moving differently if you stood with a foot each side of the hinge. Mercifully our casualties were few, though of them most were pitifully burned when a fuel tank ignited. We asked for help to take them ashore, and three motor gunboats speedily arrived under their already renowned leader Robert Hichens.

That was my first intimate contact with Coastal Forces and I fear I did not welcome them too graciously. Pre-occupied with organizing a team to bail out the fore part of the ship with buckets, fighting a fire in the after boiler-room, trying to extract a man trapped in fetid air among the blistering serpentine pipes of the flooded forward boiler-room—failing—and being deservedly humiliated by seeing him brought out by Chief Stoker Wigfall five minutes later, I told Hitch to switch off his thundering, ear-blasting engines so that we could all hear ourselves think. I never dared to speak to him like that again, though neither did I ever want to. Two nights later he went over to Ostend and repaid those E-boats in kind.

The *Cotswold* lived to fight again, but only after major surgery. I went home, and this time the primroses were out; I picked them with my fingernail pressed into the heart of the plant so that the stems would be as long as possible, and in great numbers so that I could thrust my face into the mass and breathe the very essence of purity. Mother helped pick, of course.

III

COASTAL FORCES

We were encouraged to visit the Admiralty to discuss our next job, and so I did; but not until I had lain low for the 14 days of survivor's leave to which I was entitled, and slept the sleep of the just which war experience had taught me would occupy about 16 hours in every 24. The appointments officer in question was always most charming, and although he might not actually accede to your request would, while sending you to the Black Hole of Calcutta, make you feel that the surroundings would be delightful, the job supremely important, and that you and only you could do it.

Peter Knowling's many kindnesses to me are a grateful memory, and his last act on paying off the *Cotswold* had been to recommend me for command. Even so I did not expect that at twenty-four I could yet be given a destroyer, even a little "Hunt," but the final rung of a big fleet destroyer as First Lieutenant seemed attainable and for that I boldly asked. The request was not disdained, I thought because the Commander had already resolved to do just that with me; but then he paused and eyed me as though he really wanted to hear my answer to his next question.

"I've just had a request for a Lieutenant to command a new MTB Flotilla; I wonder if that's your cup of tea?"

Command! The word rang in my ears; but then I thought of those scruffy boats of which I had heard little except that they usually broke down when in the presence of the enemy and at most other times too. Still, Hichens's MTBs had been faultlessly efficient; but on the other hand, were not MTBs rather outside the mainstream of the Navy proper? Conflicting emotions must have chased each other across my face, for the Commander told me to think about it over lunch and give him my answer in the afternoon.

I found a congenial listener and marshalled all possible arguments in favor of accepting my first command, entirely subjectively. My boats being new would surely work; there were eight of them so I would be not just a Captain but a mini-Admiral; they were offensive by their very nature and we should "seek out and destroy the enemy" as nothing else except submarines habitually did; and as for not being in the main stream, pooh to that! Had not Father taught me that the true Nelson tradition was, "I always act as I think right without regard to custom"? The step was inevitable, and I took it quickly before my heart could fail at the enormity of the task.

MTBs broke down because they were too hastily designed and thrown together; but that was much less the fault of those who built them than the Navy's own. The Establishment, and I use the word without a sneer because it is both necessary and inevitable, had in its human fallibility omitted to consider the problem of disputing narrow waters in war, and in particular the stretch between our homeland and the continent of Europe. Strange as that may seem it becomes even stranger when it is recalled that in 1914 the German Army had, against all our military predictions, reached the Channel coast and forced us at short notice to invest in a whole new armory of monitors, minelayers and sweepers, fast torpedo craft, aircraft, and a host of other activities. The Establishment clearly did not like such things for they vanished almost without trace or memory after the war; so that in 1940, after it had again been thought impossible that the Germans could reach the sea, the whole distasteful business had to be started all over again, and quickly.

It may have been argued superficially that narrow waters demanded small-scale effort which could easily be improvised should the need arise, and left at that. But deeper study would have shown that ships and aircraft designed for ocean warfare would either be ineffective in enclosed seas or far too vulnerable, and that requisitioned fishing and coastal craft were by no means suited to front-line fighting. The environment was specialized and demanded study, research, development and practice, all of which steps had eventually to be taken in the stress of actual war; and it was not until three years after the start that our forces and organization began to be geared to their tasks.

I doubt myself whether the subject was much discussed at all, partly because our coastal nakedness bears a strange resemblance to at least one other aspect of war at sea of greater and more obvious importance which was similarly thrust out of sight: the protection of merchant shipping. Our suicidal neglect of this vital function cannot be explained by mere obtuseness, and I am inclined to think that the failure sprang to some extent from the way the power game was played at the Admiralty. Each specialization had its School, once a specialist always a specialist, like an Old Etonian, and after centuries with the gun as the Navy's principal weapon its exponents had been able to entrench themselves, with the most honorable motives and unquestioned integrity in execution, as the Establishment. There were no specializations for Trade Protection or Narrow Waters and, perhaps consequently, virtually no escort or coastal forces.

The chief creators of such craft as existed at the outbreak of war were Hubert Scott-Paine of British Power Boats, and Peter Du Cane of Vospers, and they suffered more than usual frustration in dealing with the Admiralty. Du Cane's boat was designed round the best engine he could find, the Italian Isotta-Frascini, and he went to great trouble to negotiate a license to build it in England and a factory in which to do so. He was not allowed to go ahead because the Admiralty said we were unlikely to fight Italy, but if we did we could always use Rolls Royce Merlins. It may be imagined that the RAF had few of those to spare after the Battle of Britain.

Scott-Paine became disenchanted and took most of his business to the United States where he found a readier market; and it came about that the American Navy's Patrol Torpedo-boat and its Packard engines were of basically British design.

Du Cane struggled on and produced a beautiful 70-foot hull; but of course his Isottas were soon denied him and various other engines were pressed into service. Such makeshifts were far from satisfactory as was to be expected, for in a high-performance craft the hull and engines must be married for love and not convenience. My hope that by 1942 the troubles would be over was reasonable but alas

premature. The urgency of expanding Coastal Forces having been strongly advocated by the enemy, Their Lordships
had at last acceded; but as time did not permit re-designing
the latest Vosper hull around the Packard engine, which
was now available under Lease-Lend, yet another incom-
patible union resulted. The beautiful engine lay on the
wrong-sized bed at an uncomfortable angle, uncertain, coy
and hard to please despite passionate titillation—the pout-
ing cause of intolerable frustration.

The boats were lovely to look at, and claimed my devotion from the moment I first saw them. That beauty is
fundamentally important to the human race should not be
denied, though it often is in functional design, but neither
Du Cane nor Scott-Paine could be faulted. As businessmen
and artists they knew that beauty was both a good selling-
point and a help to the fighting sailor in achieving high
morale through pride in his ship. Function comes before
appearance, but the two are wonderfully interrelated by the
most gracious dispensation of providence which is illus-
trated by the whole of nature.

One last dig at Their big-ship, gunnery-oriented Lordships; they were unmoved by art and did not like us for
ourselves, even though they had called us into being. Flashy
fast craft, piratical young officers and scruffy men, who
dashed in small units at great speed all over the ocean and
away from the restraining hand of authority, to indulge in
who could tell what abhorrent deviations from the conventional norms of discipline, were anathema. They acknowledged our existence reluctantly, placed us at the very bottom of the priority list for scarce equipment, and did their
very best to forget us. In all this they had a point; but
their conclusion was feeble and unworthy for if we were
needed at all we could easily have been made to pull our
full weight.

My first glance at the boats having convinced me that
they were lovely, my second showed clearly that the sailors
were not and my duty was plain. My Horse Gunners had
shown how men increased their stature by being smart
and I saw no reason why an MTB should not be as smart
as a battleship. I debated whether to start with a bang and
would have done so, had I not realized just in time that
pitfalls gaped before the newcomer who tries to put it
across old hands. For instance the Packard engines had

superchargers in which was concealed something called boost; you could see how much there was by a small dial and it seemed obvious to me that the more you had the better, indeed we could all do with boost and plenty of it. Then Ian Trelawny of *232*, sensitive and loyal as always, led me aside and explained that boost was bad; if it was plus one (one what? Tigers? as my math master had used to ask) you cocked an eye and watched it, if plus two you fussed, and at plus three things flew off and the engine stopped with a horrid crunch. That was "nuts and bolts" to my father's son, and I took some time to discover why we went to such pains to acquire boost and then wished it would go away. I trod warily then; but persisted too.

If ever there was a piratical young captain it was Jamie Fraser of *233;* dark, slight, wiry and lively, he was imbued with dash and a consuming desire to get at the enemy that would have gladdened the heart of Henry Morgan. It certainly gladdened mine, but Jamie was a Scot which meant —and it has been my privilege to observe that decisive race at close quarters over many years—that he was always right. That is certainly a most useful quality, though not invariably an endearing one and I, English and a prey to doubt, wondered wistfully where I was to fit into Jamie's world; even whether I had a useful part to play in it at all.

One does not argue with a Scot like Jamie because one will lose. Having tied one hand behind one's back by acknowledging that there may be two sides to a question, and that part of the pleasure and value of an argument is to learn from one's opponent, one is annihilated by both hands and a pair of tacketty boots to whom such an approach is bumbling, unheroic and indeed incomprehensible. There are few gray tones to the Scots, which is a huge advantage in the field of leadership and it was no accident that they usually ruled both England and the Empire. But when one of them apparently essayed to rule the 21st Flotilla I had to do something if I was to keep my job, and to do it so that Jamie would understand, the Scots way.

Mac of *241* was also dark like Jamie but heavily muscular (a superb swimmer), slower to thought and action, and very, very sure. I thought I recognized that sureness, and then the significance of his name, Macdonald, advocated wariness; for although he was a proud and fully

assimilated New Zealander of the third generation I had
the strongest suspicion that masterful Scottish blood was
not so easily eradicated.

Of course these young warriors were naturally, indeed
properly, sizing up their new chief who was to lead them
into battle, or so they devoutly hoped, and with luck out
again. Ian Trelawny of *232* must have been doing the same
but he never showed it, and only gradually did I perceive
something of his true worth for he took care never to push
himself. He was one of those who is truly born free; at
fifteen he had sailed a dinghy by himself from his native
Cornwall to the Channel Islands instead of going to school;
and later, rather than remain one of fifty clerks on a row
of high stools, he had set up in one-man enterprises in
which an entire absence of capital was more than counter-
balanced by enthusiasm and initiative. It was therefore
wonderful how apparently naturally he joined a team and
accepted discipline; he went out of his way to make me
welcome, we were of an age, and although I had not yet
done anything adventurous I keenly wanted to, so that I
spent many hours in his wardroom picking his brains and
planning our future, while staring at a stupid motto on the
bulkhead which read, "There's no fuel like an oiled
fuel."

It was daunting to realize that I must learn to lead these
three strong characters, and four more captains who would
eventually join to complete the flotilla. I knew that my
status as Senior Officer would do little more than tide me
over until I asserted real authority, if I could, so how
should I begin? Leadership being an officer's stock in trade
I had been subjected to many lectures on the subject, and
how dull and unconvincing they were. Few can expound
the art, even those who have mastered it. John Buchan
for instance, a much-quoted authority, held that leadership
depends primarily on moral endowments, by which he
meant the elevated, God-fearing morals of the English
gentleman; but clearly that took no account of Hitler, who
led the Germans brilliantly to act in ways that they themselves can now hardly believe possible, and he was certainly no gentleman.

My father's upbringing returned to help me. If the Navy
was his religion Nelson was its High Priest, and one need
look no further than him for an example; the real man of
course, not the image of tradition. Lesser men cannot ex-

pect to achieve his results just by aping his techniques, because he was unique. But all can learn from him, and not least the aim of perfect discipline which is to create a team with a common purpose to which each contributes his utmost in his own way and obeys his leader because he wants to. First establish authority, then take care that it is not too rigid or initiative will be crushed—for one is leading men who must think as well as obey, not driving a yoke of oxen—and finally work towards the highest peak of excellence whereby the junior not only obeys and thinks, but anticipates. Being inside his leader's mind and trusting him, each will decide his course of action as he feels his leader would were he present, and act with the same determination and loyalty as if he had actually been given an order; that generates a force which little can withstand. I must therefore set about inspiring obedience and trust; but oh dear, I was no Nelson and the task wearied me before it began, though at least I knew where I was heading.

I could not entertain Ian in my wardroom because I did not have one. *232, 233* and *241* were the first boats to form the Flotilla's nucleus, and I met the first two at Weymouth where they were being "worked up" by HMS *Bee*, the base established for that purpose under the command of a retired old swashbuckler called Roland Swinley. His methods were unconventional, and he kept one drinking and yarning until the not so small hours which did nothing to increase my efficiency, but no young RNVR officer could accuse him of hidebound RN pomposity and he and his team trained us well to think and act on our own initiative.

Officers and men were instructed and drilled in their jobs, and boats were exercised incessantly both individually and collectively. We "sank" the old Bob-a-nob-round-the-Fleet paddle steamer time and time again, after which our performance was critically examined by Lieutenant Commander Younghusband who judgment at the beginning was likely to be, "You might as well try to manure a 40 acre field with a fart"; for he was a man given to pungent imagery. The program was fixed by Jimmie Matheson so that there was never a spare moment, and de Labalmondiere, Wood, Hey, Long, Church, Smith, Hood, Bickerton and others were tireless in their respective skills so that under their tutelage we could not but improve.

237 was to be my boat but she was not ready, so I was able to watch and learn without having publicly to reveal my ignorance of boost and all the many differences between a small gasoline-driven planing craft and the displacement-hulled steamships to which I was accustomed. I applied myself particularly to the techniques of controlling a formation of boats, my first practical task as Senior Officer.

The hulls were nearly one-third as wide as they were long, like the medieval "round ships" which were probably the slowest craft ever to take the sea, but there the comparison ended; their bottoms formed broad V's forward which splayed to almost flat at the sterns, and turned up sharply at the edges, or "chines." At slow speed a boat could be maneuvered in company like any other type, except that she tended to blow sideways in winds of any strength. As engine-power was increased the bows rose, the stern tucked down, and the wide beam pushed a foaming mass of water ahead which caused turbulence past the two rudders (making steering difficult), strain on the engines and excessive fuel consumption; the whole attitude of the boat felt and looked unnatural and ugly, and speeds between 15 and 22 knots were therefore best avoided. A little faster and the stern lifted to begin the planing motion, the water under the hull flowed smoothly and the boat felt contented. 25 knots was a good cruising speed; I doubt whether it was the most theoretically economical in miles per gallon and suspect that 30 knots would have been better, the hull then being even freer of the water's drag. But from the earliest days our engines' waywardness forced us to cosset them by never going faster than we had to, especially for long periods.

At 25 knots the V-shaped wakes became important to the formation of a unit, because the amplitude of the curling waves was huge compared to the size of the craft, and a following boat who unwisely tried to ride them was tossed, cork-like and uncontrollable. There were thus two choices for cruising formation; line ahead was flexible in that the leader could turn as he wished without signal, but we had to keep well closed up so as to be ready for any emergency and to avoid having to use bright lights for signalling, and that was not easy on a dark night when distance apart was hard to judge and a concertina effect down the line difficult to avoid. The most comfortable position for a following boat was on her leader's quarter just forward of the wake. Being in undisturbed water the boat could be steered precisely, and so close to the next ahead that even a gesture on her bridge was enough to convey alertness; and that was important because although the leader should obviously not alter course without warning, the circumstances of high-speed navigation and war might allow him to give very little warning indeed. "Quarterline" and "Arrowhead" formations thus became conventional.

At 30 knots Archimedes' "Eureka" Law, in which he shows that, "If a body floats in a liquid the weight of the liquid displaced is equal to the weight of the body," was set aside by the MTB Law which states that if a flat-bottomed boat was driven fast enough she would be thrust bodily upwards by the flow of water and displace far less than she did at rest. Consequently the drag would also be less, also the proportional engine-power needed to maintain the speed and increase it further. At about 33 knots she finally shook herself free with a little leap that was like an automatic car changing into a higher gear, and imparted a thrill which to me was always fresh. She steered sweetly at high speed, but her turning circle was rather wide and that made me slightly uneasy.

From the beginning, I drilled my people in close-station maneuvering at all speeds. Whether that would have any great tactical significance I could not then tell though I thought it likely, but I had learned in destroyers that its training value was great. To be good one had to know one's boat like a favorite horse and have her under finger-tip control; to remain instantly alert for signals and the slightest deviation by others; to have developed an instinct for assessing the relative movement of independently moving bodies; to react instantly to orders and a constantly changing environment; and to develop a cool, controlled courage in the knowledge that collision could be catastrophic in view of the great kinetic energy locked up in even a little MTB at speed, and that the least slip could cause one.

It also occurred to me that the cause of discipline would be furthered by this exercise; for should there be any young officer who thought he knew all the answers and then revealed publicly that he fell an iota short of perfection in an unarguably professional skill, there was little

he could do but shut his big mouth, walk humbly, and try
to improve. When Officer of the Watch in the *Somali*,
leading the flotilla at 15 knots, the signal was made for 20
and I rang down to the engine room revolutions for 10;
oh, just a momentary aberration, figures get so easily trans-
posed, very natural! Then seven great ships with shrieking sirens were about my ears on either side, going full
ahead, full astern, hard-a-port, hard-a-starboard, so that
I first opened my eyes wide with astonished horror, and
then shut them tight. In harbor later my Captain sent me
to apologize to all the other Captains, dressed in the garb
of penitence, frock coat and sword. They were charming,
having erred similarly in their own younger days, and I returned less chastened than I deserved to be with seven gins
inside; but the lesson stuck.

While still learning the basic trade I looked ahead to my
task as tactical leader, and sought enlightenment on the
experience gained by others in the key problem of attaining
a torpedo firing position; but there was very little advice to
be had. One closed the enemy on auxiliary engines to 500
yards, fired unobserved, crash-started mains, and pushed
off; but to the question of what to do if one *was* observed
there was really no answer and I was both amazed and disturbed. I even asked the Admiralty for any lessons passed
down from World War I; they had nothing of course, which
reinforced my theory that fast craft were abhorrent to the
higher ranks of the service and all mention of them had
been struck from the rolls. Finally I cheered up, thinking
that if no one had tried any clever stuff the enemy would
not be expecting it, and that there would be honor for
him who did. The trouble was that I could not think of anything to try, both through lack of imagination and because
I felt instinctively that I might stray from reality by taking
too many steps without having experienced the authentic
feel of battle. That would come, of course, at Barfleur.

Being always a passenger in someone else's boat soon
palled; I badly needed to handle my own craft and become expert, and a flagship from which to lead and set
that example which I myself believed to be the right one.
237's completion date was slipping; but the next in line,
234, was ready and her I stole, dictatorially and shame-
lessly from John "Polly" Perkins who had supervised her
building and brought her through her trials with ship's-
husbandly devotion, and was as eager and aggressive as

any of us. I am glad to say that he was soon given another boat, but the loss was mine as that one was destined for a different flotilla. When we sailed from Portsmouth to Weymouth on May 29, 1942 I was at last truly in command; the crew was marvellous, the boat was marvellous (indeed she did not break down), the future was marvellous; and when Younghusband asked on our arrival at HMS *Bee*, "What's that bag of rust you've got there?" it was the wrong thing to say.

I gave *234* a bare fortnight to work up so that we should lose no time in joining the other three boats and getting on with the war, at least partly because I did not want them to form habits and customs on their own which might not necessarily be mine. We worked ourselves hard in *234* therefore, and got to know each other as we did so.

The crew began the process by putting its collective toe into the disciplinary water to test the temperature. That was natural and proper, for no man worth his salt, or woman either, must feebly submit to domination by however lawfully constituted an authority, and there came a tremendous furor of whistling, singing and general manifestations of excessive license from the messdeck. Fear of the mob is with good reason a basic fear, but I kept my weakness well out of sight and the men never had a chance to realize their strength for I soon showed them that I could make as much noise as all of them put together. The toe was withdrawn, it was too cold.

I was pleased to find, without really understanding why, that the outcome of that little confrontation gave satisfaction to everyone. It certainly did so to Alan Jensen, the First Lieutenant, whose prime characteristic was intense and meticulous concentration on the task, disliking such distractions. To "Gentleman" Jensen life was meant to be quiet and orderly, and he took these qualities with him into the lion's den. When he once thought that I intended to board and capture an enemy craft, a rash expedient which if it ever flitted into my mind soon scurried out again, he appeared from below in his tin hat and said," You may need your revolver, sir." A silver tray was all that the occasion lacked.

Alan, well into his civilian career as Personnel Officer to Imperial Airways, was five years older than I, and I hope he will excuse me for having wondered how on earth

he came to be First Lieutenant of an MTB. The reason
however was quite simple, he wanted to be; and that indeed was the first essential qualification because as the
hundreds of new officers emerged from the training machine they divided themselves quite naturally into three
streams. There were those who for one reason or another
were unfitted for the front line. Others would accept
what Their Lordships called "the exigencies of the Service" with enthusiasm and devotion; and they found themselves in the great bulk of the Navy from battleships to
motor launches whose task, apart from the occasional offensive operation, was to react to what the enemy might
do and who consequently spent the greater part of their
time waiting, watching and enduring.

The third category knew that it must get to grips with
the enemy; and begged, made nuisances of themselves and
crammed for exams so that they might join a branch
whose main purpose was to do so, because they would be
lucky to achieve their goal in General Service. One might
of course find oneself with one of the great leaders in the
Battle of the Atlantic such as Walker,[1] Gretton or Macintyre,[2] whose aggressive professionalism was so well
developed that they seemed magnetically attracted to the
U-boats lurking in the ocean depths; or with someone like
Hichens or Richards in Motor Gunboats who escaped
from their designated task of guarding the convoy routes
whenever possible, and took their aggression to the enemy
on his own coast. But one would have to be lucky because most men are not like that; and the only way of
being certain of battle in the floating Navy was to join submarines or MTBs.

That was a healthy process of natural selection, and it
was continued by the aggressive faction being greatly over-
subscribed. But not all those who thought they wanted to
meet the enemy found the encounter so glamorous in the
event, and decreasingly so if the acquaintance was constantly renewed. The sifting was thus drastic, but Alan
Jensen like all my officers had forced himself through.
Having reached the front line he knew that his place in

---

[1]For the full story of Capt. Frederick John Walker read *Escort
Commander* by Terence Robertson, another volume in the Bantam
War Book Series.

[2]Read *U-Boat Killer*, Donald Macintyre's own story of The Battle
of the Atlantic. Also in the Bantam War Book Series.

it much be as second-in-command and not as Captain, despite his great age, and it is a wise man who knows himself to that extent; not all who were captains should have been, and many who aspired to command did not make the best First Lieutenants. Alan ran *234* for me with complete loyalty; though he took his own decisions too which was important, for although she was mine and I loved her I must not be seen by the other crews to be giving her more attention than their boats. His almost passionate pursuit of accuracy made him into that other, vital, aid to a Flotilla Leader, an outstanding navigator.

"I remember him sharpening his pencil; point like a drawing pin and he had several. One of those blokes who always had the right gear."

So Alan Jensen by Leading Seaman Jim Saunders. I wondered about him too, and how he had managed to become my Coxswain when most boats had regular Petty Officers; his claiming to be as nervous as a kitten at the first sign of danger also seemed unpromising.

"The reason I volunteered for Coastal Forces was two shillings a day extra and then another dollar for being Coxswain; I was married and needed all the money I could get."

Personally I doubted whether that was the whole story and soon had cause to thank whoever picked him out and sent him to me. The Coxswain's was a key job and sometimes a lonely one; as senior rating he was with the lower-deck but not of it, and neither did he belong in the wardroom yet must consort with officers with the nicest blend of respect and intimacy. But he can describe his problems better than I:

I had some trouble with the crew at the beginning; maybe it was my fault because I had no experience in taking charge. There was that Eric Mayers, the Gunner; now he was a lower-deck lawyer, always knew everything. Jimmy [the First Lieutenant] said, "If anything goes wrong you can put them in the report." Well Mayers was a bit stroppy, came from Nottingham, so I said something silly like, "Put your hat on square"; and he said, "Get knotted." "Right," I says, "First Lieutenant's report"; though I'd as soon give him a right-hander. He got 14 days stoppage of leave and that was the turning point because I found the officers were working with me, and the crew was quite different. Mayers and I turned out the best of friends.

Some Coxswains would go drinking with their crews but that was slap-happy. When we went ashore the Coxswains used the Saloon Bar and the crew the Public; we'd see them through the hatch and if it was our crew we'd send them in a beer all round, and they'd poke their heads through and say, "Cheerio Swain." Then they'd send me in a large rum.

Saunders's "oppo" or brother Senior Rating, the Petty Officer Motor Mechanic, with whom he shared a tiny cabin, he describes thus:

Cuthbert, he was a case! Proper grease-monkey, covered in it and used to bring it into the cabin, and I used to sling his gear out into the alleyway. Proper up-and-downers we used to have, even though we were townies from Walthamstow. Good fellow though, knew his job first class; and he was conscientious, irrespective about his tidiness. Many a time we'd be turned in and he'd still be in the boat making sure it was all right for the night.

Cuthbert was indeed a stalwart, as were all nine of them. Leading Telegraphist Churcher (later to go to the Mediterranean and be replaced by Traves), Leading Stoker "Nobby" Clarke ("He could fight, specially with the RAF; he was a good hand."), Able Seaman, Seaman Torpedoman Jolly ("That's right!"), Ordinary Signalman Haynes ("Very good bunting-tosser, on the bridge all the time. Another sea-lawyer but discreet; make a good shop-steward."), Stoker Gilbert and Ordinary Seaman Herring ("Very young but hearts in the right place."). How different we were from each other, yet very much of one company; 234 belonged to us and we to her, ashore or afloat, and another crew would question her excellence at some risk.

I felt the men to be friends, at least from my side; and if that seems a romantic exaggeration I should make clear that if anyone had not been more than just acceptable he would have been out on his ear. I certainly felt—outrageous admission—paternal towards them, especially when I took them into danger that was none of their seeking; though I fear that their regard for me as expressed by Jim Saunders was somewhat different; "A rating was a rating and don't you forget it like; the Captain or First Lieutenant never spoke to the crew, the Coxswain had to be the go-between."

"Oh come," I pleaded, "surely I said 'Good morning'?"

"Well I don't know, you had so much on your mind. The officers treated ratings like ratings so as to keep them in their place; 'Put your hat on square,' and all that."

The indictment is damning; but the men, apparently, strangely did not seem to mind and then went on to "conduct themselves to my entire satisfaction."

234 and her engines played the game well so that we were able to fill our short time at Weymouth with training value. I had the sense to fire torpedo after torpedo; they were the reasons for our existence and their successful use depended on the techniques being practiced until they became instinctive, after which intuition born of experience would raise the process to the level of skill, as with a sport. (See Appendix I for details of torpedoes and firing arrangements.)

The torpedo had to be ponderous in order to carry its massive 500-lb warhead, and everything about it was slow. That was an important point to grasp, for events usually moved extremely fast when the opportunity came to fire, but a snap shot from the hip was useless with a torpedo. Its speed being not very much greater than a ship's there was little chance of hitting unless either the target could be kept in ignorance of its approach or the range was so short that he could not get out of the way; but even if he cooperated by holding his course and speed there was little point in firing from fine angles on his bow or quarter, as the small are subtended by the target allowed no margin for error and the torpedo was not built for such accuracy. The aim was to hit at right angles, from the beam, which meant firing from broad on the bow to allow for the aim-off angle; so that before ever the technical business of aiming and firing could start, the captain was wholly preoccupied in getting his boat to the best position despite the enemy's attempts to thwart him.

The enemy's course and speed had to be assessed roughly for the approach, and then as precisely as possible so as to set them on the sight. A darkened ship at night gave little away, though one could improve one's judgment by forcing oneself to size up every ship one met as a matter of habit; but what one thought one saw had usually to be modified by what one imagined the enemy would be doing in the tactical circumstances at the time, and if he had sighted his attacker he would be most ill-advised not to do something because no ship however large could afford to be hit by a torpedo. The scope for guesswork, intuition, art, and the invocation of providence was thus considerable.

Having set his sight the captain squinted along it, in which crouching position his head was close to his coxswain's and their bodies touched. I gave the necessary helm orders to bring the backsight, foresight and target into line, and Saunders strove to steer with minute precision. He had his problems:

> We used to steer by compass right up to the last, and you'd say, "Bring her three degrees to port," or something; of course I could only concentrate on that and nothing outside the boat, you could have rammed the enemy for all I'd have known about it. You used to get down and put your hat on the back of your head, right down as though you were going to take a billiard shot, as though your life depended on it, you *had* to sink that ship. I didn't take any notice of that, I was looking at my work; and when you were concentrating I'd turn up the light a bit because I couldn't see the compass, but if you rumbled it you'd say, "Turn down that bloody light" because you couldn't see the enemy. She was very sensitive on the steering when a wave or a gust of wind hit her.

Those few seconds of intensely concentrated intimacy, repeated many times and always in an atmosphere of great excitement, formed a bond between us that was usually unspoken but which we both now know will last all our lives. When the sights were as nearly on as they would ever be I pulled the triggers, the impulse cartridges burst with muffled explosions, pressure built up in the expansion chambers, and the two great fish lumbered out of their tubes with their propellers whirring and wreathed in smoke. Like penguins they flopped inelegantly into their proper element and immediately acquired a sinister grace; diving at first, then often nosing the surface with a roar as the engines momentarily exhausted into air, and finally taking their set depths to leave straight, purposeful tracks that were soon swallowed by the darkness. The deed being done it was irrevocable; these were no guided missiles, we carried no re-loads, and a miss robbed our very existence of relevance. No wonder the running time of perhaps 25 seconds seemed interminable.

Guns, depth charges, smoke-making apparatus, signalling, radio, damage-control, first-aid, towing, and above all engines, were exercised time and again in all their functions and aspects, and after every conceivable breakdown. There is a trusting facet of human nature which confides, "It was all right last week so it ought to work." "Maybe," one replies cynically, "but have you actually tried it?" In a small boat with simple equipment there was no need to leave anything to chance, and every reason why the men should handle their gear like experts and be so sensitive to its every mood that instant diagnosis and repair of a fault was also second nature. To that end we progressed, and also began to introduce a policy of exercising everybody in the boat in everybody else's job, so that a Gunner could start and operate an engine and a Stoker prepare a torpedo for firing. Everybody that is except me, for I am both idle by nature and sneakingly uphold the much-derided exhortation, "Don't do as I do, do as I tell you." If an officer tries to uphold the old convention of trying to do everything a man can do only better, he will probably both fail and be an interfering nuisance. A man will give of his best if he knows he has full responsibility for his part of the ship. All the same I should have done well to imagine myself the last man alive and upholding the honor of the flag to the last round, or conceivably running away on the last engine.

Alan Jensen supervised all these things and took his own skill at navigation a stage further. There were frequent plotting exercises in which the boat was more and more often where he said she was, as the result of his painstaking accuracy, calculation of tidal streams, chart-corrections, build-up of data concerning the boat such as engine revolutions per knot, deviation of the magnetic compass (which changed with each new torpedo), steering inaccuracies, leeway in given wind-strengths, and so on indefinitely. There is no short cut to proficiency at navigation, and although the minutiae might have proved irksome to such as *241*'s Henry Franklin whose talents lay in more active directions, Alan loved it all, and I loved the sense of security which his skill imparted to me.

There is no such thing as a fully worked-up ship, but we left Weymouth on June 15 just the same with Young-husband's parting blessing, "Off you go and do your worst; Ali Baba and the forty garage proprietors."

IV

GETTING THE HANG OF IT

The day was upon us when I should be expected to lead my team out to seek the enemy; between him and us all barriers of time, space and circumstance had one by one been drawn aside and there he lurked, sharing the very sea that lapped our boats in Felixstowe Dock. I felt terrible; fear of him, fear of being afraid, fear of proving incompetent, fear of the unknown, each drained a part of what little vital force I naturally possessed until I felt like a woven husk of stringy nerves enclosing absolutely noththing. "I have the heart and stomach of a King," boasted the Great Queen, and I gave her best because I seemed to have no guts at all; an overpowering lassitude overcame me as it might a human sacrifice on his final, hopeless steps to the altar, easing the task of the executioner.

With what little energy was left to me I acted the lie that it was wonderful to be poised at last to begin our great adventure, with varying degrees of success. When I confessed afterwards to Saunders how scared I was, he asserted in total disbelief, "No you weren't."

My captains were not so easily fooled, if fooled they were at all; but whatever they were really thinking I imagined Jamie and Mac as ready to condemn any overt weakness without mercy, and that did me all the good in the world. That they might have been afraid too and needed my sympathy and encouragement I cannot remember considering.

Tommy Kerr was the wise and kindly captain of HMS *Beehive*, and he needed no X-ray to pierce my emptiness. While endorsing my fictional bravado with outward heartiness, he drew on his World War I experience in submarines and life-long study of people to convey with infinite subtlety that he understood, that everyone feels like that, and that the bold face one was putting on it

could, if persisted in, cease to be a veneer and become
part of the living flesh. I would have followed him anywhere, but that was just the trouble because I had no
one to follow, and very nearly broke the taboo by cling-
ing desperately to the apron-strings of Chippy Leigh, his
Staff Officer Operations, also charming and middle-aged.
When he had told me all he knew, the Operation Orders,
Enemy Intelligence, recent experiences and so on, I could
not bear him to stop and asked yet another question to
which his only possible reply was a gentle, "That's up to
you, isn't it?" as indeed it was.

Right, buck up! What the hell do I matter anyway unless
I do my stuff? And very soon I saw my enemy for the
first time. The blurred horizon was the visual image of
my fear which flooded back; but as we drew nearer and
the outlines sharpened, I recognized them as small craft
which looked very ordinary and innocuous.

Of all the possible causes of fear, that of the unknown
is the worst; and very often, usually in fact, it is a complete waste of time and energy. The great unknown,
death, is often surprisingly easily borne by those not
hitherto conspicuously brave, because a highly competent
providence fits the appropriate mental attitude to physical
circumstances; and since the nature of our existence dic-
tates that when we rise each morning we cannot be sure
that we shall survive to eat our breakfast, it is well for our
appreciation of life and our usefulness that we learn to
stop fussing about an infinite number of frightful con-
tingencies, and use our benign instinct of animal fear to
warn of danger, to set the adrenalin flowing so that
senses are alerted and awareness heightened, and *do*
something.

That encounter came to nothing because the enemy
craft were certainly not torpedo targets; but we were
able to watch them for several minutes until their near
presence ceased gradually to seem climacteric, exceptional
and awe-inspiring, and started to become what I now
saw it must if we were to succeed at our task, our natural
environment.

The next night, June 21, we were out again off the
Belgian coast. *234* had over-exerted herself and pulled
a muscle so I went with Mac in *241;* she indeed was the
only 21st Flotilla boat running and I was extremely
annoyed, not yet anticipating the bitter frustration and

near-despair to which my boats' appalling unreliability would subject me. To form a unit of two I had to be lent one of the 4th Flotilla, *72*, which was commanded by Norrie Gardner, a delightful Scot, and a compliant one too which shows there are exceptions to every rule.

In adjacent patrol areas were a unit of the 4th under their Senior Officer "Harpy" Lloyd, Irish and mercurial, and another of Hichens's gunboats. This was because intelligence indicated that a big enemy ship might be on passage, possibly even an ocean raider which would make her very important. After last night's nodding acquaintance with the enemy I felt equal to the task; but all I had really learned was the *need* to be at home in the enemy's company—I had not yet become so—and when things started to happen my mind, boggling as it used to at school when I gazed at an incomprehensible blackboard, darted fitfully in every direction except towards the holy grail of all military operations, the Aim.

There were two small enemy ships, probably armed trawlers and quite obviously not what we were looking for. Nevertheless I had already determined to attack at the earliest opportunity and convince my people and myself that I would and could; so I did, but feeling instinctively that I was wrong, I did it half-heartedly. First I ordered one torpedo only to be fired by each boat because of the small size of these targets and the possibility of the large one appearing, thus reducing the chance of hitting by a factor of at least two and probably more. Then I made an enemy report which I should have known would alert the enemy if he had an intercept organization only half as good as ours. Then I plodded straight towards, despite being in the moon's path so that I was bound to be seen before reaching firing range. Then the enemy challenged, then engaged, our points of aim vanished in the tracer, and I pushed off.

Harpy received my signal and felt bound to investigate, while tut-tutting a bit because he already felt it to have been unnecessary and undesirable. He saw the firing, and at first the enemy's preoccupation with me helped him to close unobserved to a range of 1,000 yards whence he clearly saw the enemy for what he was. Although he was in a good firing position a vision of the big raider filled his mind, and disgusted with these insignificant distractions he disdained to attack and turned away under ineffective fire. I tried to take advantage of this diversion but came racing back again on main engines; but Harpy had gone before I arrived and we again received the enemy's whole attention, with the same result as before. Nothing had been achieved, and less than nothing because now the coast was alert and the raider would be forewarned even if she did not turn into the nearest port.

Such a nice chap, Harpy. Gesticulating frenziedly, with his wild, blond hair agitated as by some galvanic force, he asked later, "But Peter, why ... ?" It was a good question, fully justified, and there was no convincing reply. Tommy Kerr also being a nice chap always tried to forward our action reports to the Commander-in-Chief with some kindly comment. This time he wrote on Harpy's, "The decision to reserve torpedoes for the main target was correct." But with mine his kindness showed itself by not criticizing as he might have done; "Submitted." We were not too cast down however. Fear of the unknown lessened because we were beginning to know, and as it did so we felt justified in persuading each other that next time we should surely hit the enemy for six.

I instituted frequent tactical discussions between the captains as Nelson had done, that being one foundation of his success which it did not seem presumptuous to emulate. Everyone was encouraged to let his imagination roam freely, and I tried to restrain myself from pouring cold water on ideas I had not thought of myself. Jamie threw himself into the exercise, striding about the Flotilla Office while thinking furiously, then dashing to the desk, scattering the ever-ready matchsticks and rearranging them in some fantastic pattern.

After a time I realized that these meetings were beginning to have the most beneficial effect over and above tactics, of introducing our real selves to one another. Knowledge came first, then understanding, and finally trust, based on two tenets which we found we all truly shared; we were going to attack, and we would not let each other down. True, this was only talk; but in the same mental environment as gladiators in the Colosseum's green-rooms one does not talk too big lest one's words be remembered with ignomiry. From such high principles we skipped to the standards to be set in weapon-training, station-keeping, signalling and so on; but in resolving the central core of our problem, tactical ideas that would outwit the enemy, we could not realistically progress without more experience.

There followed a messy period which is best skimmed over. Few operations took place, firstly because our transplanted engines drastically rejected their surroundings. Obscure pieces of ironmongery became household words; the center engine faced forward and its shaft had to be turned backwards under it by means of a "V-Drive," a clever gearing for just so long as it was fed by lubricating oil. Likewise the "thrust blocks" abaft the wing engines, which had to transmit 1,250 horse power from propeller to hull; "V-drive" or "Thrust block running hot" would come the cry, but only if the Motor Mechanic had been quick on the draw; if not it was more likely to be, "Seized solid." Then there was the purolator which was some sort of oil filter that was often found to be in breach of its contract and attracted universal execration. The cylinders were cooled by distilled water which leaked through the jackets, so that no boat was ready for sea without a plentiful supply of leak-sealing gunk which was sometimes obtainable from a local garage; failing that porridge oats would do at a pinch. Neither of these expedients proved invariably successful, however, and the boat's entire supply of fresh water was often poured into the bottomless pit, to be followed by salt of which the supply was assured, but which corroded everything it touched and could also have the distressing effect of boiling, bursting the distilled water tank, and scalding the engine-room crew. I have already touched on the technicalities of boost, and we had plenty of that.

Having become accustomed to a Navy in which every ship was expected to do the work of two, I was unable to understand the absence of pressure from above to do so now. At first I was delighted, for it seemed to mean that I could act like a pirate of old and sally forth to wreak havoc where and when I would. On a memorable afternoon I telephoned the Operations Room at The Nore: "Sir, I have three good boats, the weather's fine, may I go to sea?"

"Good idea, old boy," was the reply. "Where would you like to go?"

On another even more memorable occasion, so memorable indeed that it stands out as unique in my whole naval career, Saunders approached with unusual solemnity and intimated that the men were muttering. The news was chilling.

"What do they want?" I asked grimly.

"Well, sir, it's like this; they want to go to sea more often."

Delighted, I promised to fix them up. But it was not an ideal arrangement after all because the pirates had one transcendent aim, to make their own fortunes, which was denied us so that we needed an equally or more compelling inducement to attack with zest at the risk of our lives. We coveted honor it is true, though not in a vacuum and we certainly took no pleasure in fighting for its own sake. We had to feel part of a grand, benevolent and high-principled purpose. That will be derided by the cynic who cannot see the difference between good and evil as reasons for fighting, but he can be ignored. My own inspiration was beautifully expressed by Captain Michael John Pugh, RA, who himself died in action:

> Gladly they went to war because they knew
> That hesitation would have brought the end
> Of simple goodness which it was their wish
> As well as their high duty to defend.

The Commander-in-Chief The Nore was to us the vicar on earth of Simple Goodness, but it began to seem that we of the MTBs had little or no part to play in his master plan. His all-absorbing concern was the safety of his coastal shipping against constant attrition by mines, aircraft and E-boats, and whereas motor gunboats were one obvious counter to the latter menace and he had pressed for their development and provision in adequate numbers, offensive operations off the enemy's coast seemed to have small relevance either to that, or to war strategy in general which was still almost wholly defensive. Yet it did not seem to need much imagination to reason that free-flowing coastal traffic was probably just as important to the enemy as it was to us, observing that he was maintaining large forces in occupied Western Europe at the end of long land lines of communication through hostile territory and under constant threat of air attack.

More important still, the iron ore from Sweden which

was the very core of the German war economy had to reach the Ruhr at any cost. Far the best route for such a bulk cargo was by sea to Rotterdam and thence by barge up the Rhine; but never once was I urged to engrave the words "iron ore" on my heart, nor promised that to sink a ship full of it would qualify me to enter into the joy of Their Lordships. Only after the war did I stumble on this startling and fundamental truth.

At The Nore therefore there seemed nothing much for the MTBs to do; and little chance of its being done if there had been, for the boats were few in number and hopelessly unreliable. No one considered the factor of morale, which given a great aim and inspired leadership can overcome all difficulties, and we were allowed to realize by default that we were regarded with little favor. The big-ship Establishment's chronic allergy to small craft undoubtedly contributed to this sad and unproductive attitude.

We could compensate for Authority's neglect by our own enthusiasm to some extent; but I knew there must come a time when I should be tempted to withdraw from the brink of some dangerous opportunity because I genuinely should not know whether the risks were commensurate with the possible gains. I could not but envy the Battle of Britain pilots who knew they were doing a vital job because their whole Service and country were behind them and told them so. Had the *Scharnhorst* and *Gneisenau* reappeared in the narrow seas it would have been the same with us; yet all the time the iron ore traffic probably offered us as great or greater war-winning opportunity. I felt that the extra responsibility which had somehow descended upon me was unfair. Nevertheless one cannot remain depressed for very long at twenty-five; if Authority was not over-interested in our activities then neither would it be over-critical, and later when we had put MTBs on the map they would have to take us seriously.

For all these reasons July was dull and frustrating; the more so because Scott-Paine's beautiful new gunboats had been designed round the Packard engine from the start and ran as quietly and reliably as sewing-machines, and in the hands of that master of warfare Robert Hichens were creating an enviable roll of battle honors. We were just not in the same class, and although the blame could fairly be laid at the feet of the Admiralty and The Nore it was Vospers and ourselves who had to take the brick-bats.*

Word came that the German E-boats were now operating in the English Channel, and Hichens was sent there to mark them. We followed at the end of July; I was not told why and the move seemed illogical as we were of little value against E-boats. Perhaps C-in-C Nore wanted to get rid of us; possibly C-in-C Portsmouth needed us desperately, though if so he kept it to himself for he made no sign that he was aware of our arrival. I incline to think however that it was because Hichens had met a small convoy on the 14th, and having no torpedoes had attacked with depth charges and the utmost gallantry, though at considerable cost in damage and casualties.

Even a short coastal passage was a marathon voyage with our temperamental engine-installations. We had to spend two days at Dover, then 233 could get no further than Newhaven, and 234 arrived at Portsmouth with one engine full of salt water. 241 was consistently the best of the bunch, for which credit must be given both to her builders, Morgan Giles, and Motor Mechanic Arthur Dormer, an exceptional engineer who later became an officer.

237 joined, and Barfleur came and went. My fears of being court-martialled proved groundless, for despite our detailed action reports no sign came from above either critical or encouraging, and the affair began to seem like a dream, though a graphic one and we were all the better for it. Our youthful resilience bent to the fact of failure and sprang upright again unabashed; we had been taught to know each other and the enemy under stress, and the balance seemed however illogically to be on our side so that next time we should win.

We had learned so many tactical lessons that our discussions were long and lively as we chewed them over. Undoubtedly our most serious fault had been not to sight the enemy at maximum visibility range; how obviously stupid it now seemed to imagine that one could ever predict with certainty where he would appear. Had we done so we could have turned towards, end-on, before he had any chance of sighting us, and might well have pulled

*Criticisms.

off an unobserved attack. Separating the three boats had been logical, and had it been done earlier one or two might have had an unharassed approach while another accepted the brunt of the enemy's gunnery; but that was clearly not the whole answer, especially in view of the other major lesson that if the whole of an enemy force was concentrating its fire in your direction it ceased to be a torpedo target however brave you were, because you just could not see the individual ships to aim at.

Then circumstances provided a solution with blinding clarity. We were to join Hichens, perhaps because he wanted torpedo-boats, but of course we wanted gunboats just as much! If unobserved torpedo attack was impracticable the gunboats could go racing off and engage from a different sector, riveting the enemy's attention on themselves while we crept in quietly and dealt the death blow. We could not wait to try this scheme, and surely the gunboats would welcome it as an alternative to closing to the daunting range necessary for mortal damage to be inflicted with small guns. So to Dartmouth where Hichens was based, the sally-port for offensive operations from time immemorial; it was not far, but *234*'s starboard engine stopped on the way with an oil leak from the purolator.

I sat at Hitch's feet, being delightfully entertained by his wife Catherine who had brought their two boys down from Felixstowe, as it might have been for a summer holiday. But there could never be a true holiday for her, poor dear, if by it we mean spiritual relaxation and a temporary discarding of care. Not only did she have to watch from her villa on the Kingswear cliffs as her husband went out nightly to meet death on level terms, but the man himself utterly rejected such gentle yearning for inner security as both impossible of achievement and abhorrent even if it were. Life was a perpetual striving with one achievement serving as a springboard for the next, and the next, and the next; but more than that the striving had to be physically dangerous, because only so would values remain true in this dangerous world. The Le Mans motor race had been his peacetime antidote to the insidious sense of security engendered by his profession of country solicitor; but now danger was normal and so to Hitch life was normal too, though to Catherine and everyone else it could hardly have been less so.

He was devoted to the supreme immediate good of winning the war against the Germans whom he hated, and if ever a man could be called dedicated it was he. And he was strong; like Nelson he viewed the enemy "with the eye of a seaman determined on attack," dominating him; did his boats lack some weapon or equipment which might enhance their fighting efficiency? He stormed the Admiralty and miraculously priorities were altered in his favor. Yet his burning passion was rigidly controlled by the self-discipline of a gentleman; his voice was quiet, his manners courteous and he loved to listen to new ideas, not only to expound them; he was interested personally in every one of his sailors. Add to that a personal magnetism which flowed from his steady eyes and carried strength, courage and in-spiration, and no wonder his officers and men were his, body and soul, and that the 8th Motor Gunboat Flotilla was a mighty little force.

I fell under his spell and never for a moment thought it strange that I, a so-called professional warrior, deferred to a hostilities-only amateur. Neither it should be said did he; for to the RNVR we regulars were "caretakers" who kept the Navy going in peace so as to be able to turn it over to them, the heart, spirit and body of the nation, to use when it was really needed. Nevertheless he liked my scheme for a combined gunboat/torpedo-boat attack and we sailed to-gether for Alderney on August 18 to try it out. He of course led the force, and the shadow of a doubt crossed my mind that he might not find it easy to give us MTBs pride of place should we sight a torpedo target; but I knew that whatever he did it would be intelligent and bold, and to be at sea with him was grand. Alas, all we saw was Alderney.

The next morning we left for Portsmouth again; doubt-less there was a reason, but I was disappointed, since Dart-mouth with Hitch seemed the station for honor. Perhaps it was all for the best though; Henry Franklin of *241* had brought only one shirt and an operational period of five days was above and beyond its call of duty.

Back at *Hornet* and still eager to try a combined attack I asked for gunboats, and was pleasantly surprised when four of them arrived hot-foot from Weymouth; but close co-ordination in action is only likely to succeed with meticulus preparation and intimate understanding. We sighted two small craft which I took to be E-boats and signalled the gunboats to attack, at the same time turning the two MTBs away from the enemy and across the gunboats' bows so as to leave them a clear field. Unhappily the Senior Officer of the gunboats thought I had fouled him and turned away too so that minutes and all surprise were lost. Jamie took ad-

Schnellboot

vantage of the confusion and closed to fire torpedoes, but was halted by the enemy challenging with the letter "G" which was also our challenge that night. Then the gunboats came into action in open order and I followed them to prolong their line, although my puny guns could add little to their fire power.

However the two little enemy craft had no wish to wait all night to be attacked by six of ours, and wisely made smoke and vanished. Seething with fury I increased speed, overtook the gunboats and plunged into the smoke with Jamie following; never mind that our two machineguns were no match for the enemy's 20mm or 40mm, sheer concentrated rage would double their caliber. But we were outwitted for there was nothing to be seen on the far side of the smoke, and I pressed on to Cherbourg which seemed likely to be the enemy's destination, hoping to get there before him. One of the engines gave trouble so we could not make our best speed; but it hardly mattered because I knew in my heart that our efforts now were sour grapes, crying over spilt milk and wild-goose chasing. Jamie and I spent the rest of the night a mile and a half off Cherbourg harbor but nothing turned up.

"Let's go inside," he urged.

"Good idea," I replied, eyeing the massive batteries on the breakwaters and noting the absence of any shipping of consequence, "but no."

We came home with the dawn, filling 234's engines with salt water as usual.

I was strangely unaffected when I found that the gunboat chap was complaining bitterly that I had fouled his attack by turning away. He even committed his thoughts to paper officially, and of course the implication was irresistible that my nerve had failed. But I had no self-doubts and cared little for what anyone else might think, even if they thought anything, which experience had shown to be unlikely in the Portsmouth Command. My team and I were riding the upward slope of a wave believing we knew how to reach the crest, and nothing was going to stop us. It was however a relief to find we were to continue our journey eastwards a couple of days later; not that The Nore had been any more enthusiastic about MTBs than Portsmouth, but I had been at Felixstowe long enough to feel at home there and to know that Tommy Kerr was a man I could work under, on whose support and encouragement I could absolutely rely.

The voyage became the accustomed Odyssey with boats losing their motive power as though Boreas the North Wind had dismasted them, and being lured to strange shores by mysterious forces. Certain it was that 233 could never pass Newhaven, and I just wondered whether there might be something more beguiling inside than an engineering workshop.

Tommy greeted us at Beehive, standing out on the pier as he invariably did with an expansive salute of welcome. Also there to my surprise was Younghusband and it was a pleasure to see him, especially when I learned that he was now Staff Officer Coastal Forces at The Nore. Surely now we should have an enthusiastic mentor to press our case, and indeed it seemed so for he said,

"I've persuaded them to let you have a try right round the corner of Holland where no one has been before, and catch the Hun with his pants down. It's just about as far

as you can go, even from Lowestoft, so take your flying
bedpans up there and stand by."

Curse the man! His description was only too apt;
smooth, streamlined curves with rottenness inside were indeed common to our craft and the lowly article; but wait
and we'll show you what a flying bedpan can do.

V

HELLROT

Had we known we were going to Weg Hellrot, with its bloodcurdling and challenging overtones, we would have been delighted in our present mood of flinging down the gauntlet; the name would also have served well for after-dinner songs and for throwing away to the uninitiated and impressionable. But we knew nothing about the enemy's system of swept channels around the Frisian Islands, or that they were named after colors, this one meaning merely "Bright Red Route." The map on page 75 shows that there were many such channels, presumably to cater for ships of different draughts and to allow flexibility should any be mined. Buoys marked the channels as they did with ours, and here that was even more necessary for the Low Countries are not idly named; the sand dunes rise but a few feet above the sea, and since they are indistinguishable from the horizon on a dark night, to sight them was likely to be synonymous with being aground.

The nightly mean that Alan Jensen had to strike was therefore between the extremes of stranding and patrolling so far to seaward that we might as well not have come for all the chance there would be of sighting an enemy. His was not one problem but many, but he welcomed the challenge to which his faculties were perfectly adapted and from now on his experience really started to build up.

Around one hundred miles separated the easternmost British buoy from our selected arrival point between Vlieland and Texel, so Alan had to draw a line on the chart, mark it off in four hourly steps of 25 miles and there we should be; but what line? Every twelve hours great masses of water funnel down into the southern North Sea, and are met there by a jet through the Dover Strait so that it becomes a constantly moving maelstrom. The depth is shallow and swirling mud or sand discolor the surface on even the finest day; rare indeed is it to be able to see a foot into it, and a glimpse Alan once had of a sunken Thames barge sitting upright on the bottom, with her sails set and drawing fully with the tide, was probably unique. Another characteristic is the short, steep chop that varies in frequency and amplitude depending on whether the wind is with, across, or against the tide.

The whirlpool is slow-moving and will not suck the reckless mariner into some cosmic plug-hole, but rather lure him to his doom insidiously though no less effectively. The stream's direction and rate vary with every ten miles and each half-hour, and although the water moves at an average speed of barely a knot that will produce an error of four miles in four hours, ample for disaster. Alan could spend an hour predicting the tidal streams for a particular night, followed by a close check that he had not, for instance, looked up High Water Dover for the right day in the wrong month. No day passed without a sheaf of chart corrections; new wrecks, new minefields, new lights, new routing instructions, diversions of swept channels; many were not apparently applicable to us, but all demanded detailed examination for fear of missing something momentous, such as the buoy from which we planned to start the long crossing having shifted position.

Having drawn the theoretical line the next problem was to keep to it in practice. Our compasses were the best quality aircraft type, but being magnetic they oscillated with every movement of the boat, always seeking the pole but never settling on it. The rougher the sea the worse the effect, but even in a flat calm an inexperienced helmsman could create it merely by trying to keep his lubber's line constantly on his allotted course. With each use of the rudder the swing increased so that one's wake was serpentine to the discomfiture of following boats, and of Alan who had to try and assess whether the swing was about the mean course or was biased towards one side or the other. A two degree error would put us out by 3½ miles in 100, and that was good steering.

The wind would speed us up, slow us down or push us sideways; but by how much was guesswork, improved upon by gradually increasing flair. Bumping into a head sea would set us back; and a following one wherein the boat first labored foaming in the troughs, then leaped from the crests like fleet-footed Ariel, evoked exhilarated delight in the poet but dark curses from the navigator. And the engines, how fast were they, and consequently the boat, really going? Their revolution-counters were graded in steps of 100 and the needles' wavering had constantly to be watched by Cuthbert and his engine-room team; 50 revolutions wrong and we had gained or lost a knot, yet another four miles at the other side. But to imagine all the engines of a unit purring happily within 50 revolutions of 1,600 for four hours was to dream of a miracle. A dead stop was not too bad for Alan, so long as he remembered to continue plotting for tide and increased wind-drift; but what was he to allow if one engine dropped, say, to 900 revs for 23½ minutes? Soundings were of little help, for the seabed in the area is as featureless as the coast. And so on, and so on; possible causes of inaccuracy were infinite and Alan's concern was endless, unrecompensed by the successful navigator's normal reward of making his desired landfall.

Scott-Paine "Elco" MTB

Alan's chosen course today, September 10, 1942, was North 75° East, which we modified to North 78° East after mentally tossing a coin to allow for the southerly breeze. The time was 1843 when we began the crossing and it was still broad daylight on a warm summer evening;

not that one could ever claim to be really warm on the bridge of an MTB so we wrapped up well. Under their oilskins or waterproof overalls called "goon-suits" the crew worse an imaginative assortment of woollen "comforts" which were sent us in abundance by innumerable Women's Institutes and knitting circles. Never let it be said that such gifts were sentimental or pathetic; they mattered to us in the most intimate, practical way, doubly warmed us in showing that we were supported, needed, indeed loved, and were necessary reminders of that simple goodness for which we were fighting.

Gentleman Jensen appeared from time to time in collar and tie to sniff the breeze and observe passing phenomena, retiring again to record his findings in his navigating officer's notebooks. These scrupulous documents are with me now as foundations of accuracy for all I write; and although I could sometimes wish that Alan had not always been so frankly explicit since what I should like to have

done did not invariably accord with what I did, the record is there and will not be gainsaid. Once he had placed his bet (and the roulette wheel would turn inexorably for four hours before there could be any indication of where the ball might fall), he changed into garments more appropriate to the occasion; but in marked contrast to the majority whose dearest wish was to appear as much like pirates as possible, his appearance was always civilized.

The engines droned, inhibiting speech, and from a state of constant apprehension for the first faltering note I drifted into one of calm assurance when miraculously there was none. The omens were unquestionably good, and my besetting sin of self-doubt gave place to a dominant mood which I now recognized as essential for success in offensive operations.

We had worked out our apprenticeship, the fury generated in the Channel still rumbled, and the gunboat plan seethed in my mind, offering certain success. Added to these we had the assurance of The Nore's support, and the base at Lowestoft, HMS *Mantis*, provided everything spiritual and material that our aggressive purpose needed. Commander Kenneth "One-fixed-one-flashing" Barnard had pierced me with his good eye to determine whether I was the fighting sort; and being responded to in double measure for I feared to find myself in another *Hornet*, we barely allowed ourselves time to exchange pleasantries before plunging into the practical application of The Plan.

There was no problem, for two flotillas of gunboats were based at *Mantis*, one of which was commanded by Lieutenant Bremer Horne. He had already captured an E-boat in fair fight and was enthusiastic to join with us against bigger game, so we devised a series of exercises in working together. His boats were the early Scott-Paine designed, American built "Elcos" which really moved at speeds of well over 40 knots and were reliable too. As armament they only carried one 20mm Oerlikon aft and four 0.5 inch machine-guns in twin turrets either side of the bridge, for the Navy's lack of peacetime prescience had failed to develop a weapon that would overwhelm an E-boat. They were, however, ideal for our purpose; we did not aim to inflict serious damage on the enemy with guns, but merely to rivet his attention so compellingly that he would not notice the infinitely more deadly torpedoes.

There was more difficulty in finding enough MTBs on any one night. I had only been able to bring *234, 233* and *232* north with me as *241* was fitting an experimental type of silencer invented by Mac. Permanently at Lowestoft however were the first three boats of the 22nd Flotilla under the charming and cooperative Dennis Long. He, poor fellow, did not yet have his own boat, and my ruthlessness in seizing *234* now paid off because it was clearly much more practicable for me to borrow his boats than he mine; it really was not fair, but Dennis acceded willingly and has my sincere gratitude.

Another undeserved bonus was that one of the Lowestoft boats, *230*, was commanded by "Polly" Perkins who I had displaced in *234*, and who I had realized in our previous short acquaintance was a born warrior. It was not just that his lower lip projected aggressively over a cleft chin, he subtly but unmistakably conveyed the assurance that he would go for the enemy by his whole manner, though his voice was gentle. I felt in awe of him as I had of Mac, and thought I detected in him too a trace of doubt concerning my own competence; but—and it is typical of human relationships—I was quite mistaken because he had exactly the same feelings towards me as he now tells me, though with the reservation that I was "pretty RN and pusser." He graciously concedes however that I gradually improved; "RN people were all the better for a spell with the RNVR," and with that I heartily concur.

This evening only Polly's and my boats were available out of the total six, a typical proportion, the other flotilla being of the same mark of flying bedpan as ourselves. He was on my port quarter and the starboard barb of the arrowhead comprised three splendid gunboats. Horne himself was away on anti-E-boat patrol, which seemed a pity as we had practiced together and knew each other's mind, but he gave me one of his wingers who, he said, would do the job as well as he if not better. I wondered; Derek Leaf seemed at first sight debonair, gay to the point of exuberance, and totally irresponsible. When I explained my precious Plan he waved airily with a, "Fine, anything you say"; and I could not determine whether he had understood a word. Yet he had an enviable reputation of being quick on the uptake and an aggressive fighter; and now as I watched his team in rock-steady, accurate station, with that general aura of alertness by which one sailor judges another, I thought that perhaps we should be all right. His boat was *MGB 91*, and with him were *82* and *84*.

An hour out into no-man's-land C-in-C Nore made us a signal, which was exciting both for its content and because it showed that we mattered to him. An RAF reconnaissance aircraft had sighted an enemy convoy off the Ems moving westward towards us, and it was planned to bomb it at 0130. That sounded marvellous, and although such a joint operation had never been mooted and far less practiced, I felt we were small enough not to be attacked by mistake and were ideally placed to take advantage of such a vertical diversion for the enemy's eyes. Alan plotted the convoy's position on the chart and guessed where it might be at 0130; there was no reason why we should not be there too.

Astern the sun changed from a white dwarf to a red giant, rested momentarily on the horizon which could not however support his weight. In the North Sea whenever he rose or set we were always scurrying away from him, creatures of the dark as we were, and he usually had something to say.

Now it was, "Good night, you won't be needing me any longer."

"Thanks," I replied, "see you in the morning."

"Well *I'll* be here then."

For a moment he looked like Chad peeping over his wall, "What, no light?" Then he was gone, and slowly our world shrank until it held just ourselves and an area around that was indeterminate, for it is hard to tell how far one can see at night until there is something to see. The water rushed past and under us but the boats themselves stood still, their bows raised like the *Mantis* they came from, and with bridges, masts, guns and hunched figures etched against the faint light of the sky. Dew formed on structure and clothing, everything would be clammy for the rest of the night and I resented that. There are of course worse things than dew, such as responsibility, loneliness and fear; but those are unmentionable even in secret as I had learned from Norway onwards, so I cursed the dew and sure enough the unwanted shadows melted into the tossing wakes. Something was going to happen to-night because I should make sure it did.

At 2230 I reduced speed to 15 knots so as to make slightly less noise, and steered east for our destination six miles off the tip of Texel (see map p. 75). "Action stations!" Torpedoes ready with stop valves open, impulse cartridges inserted and firing mechanisms checked, safety-pins out of the whiskered pistols; guns loaded and cocked; intense look-out; muted voices; "Stop that skylarking then; we're in enemy waters."

At 2315 the momentary stab of a distant searchlight to the southeast, now what could we glean from that? Having grandly promised that we should find an enemy, I be-

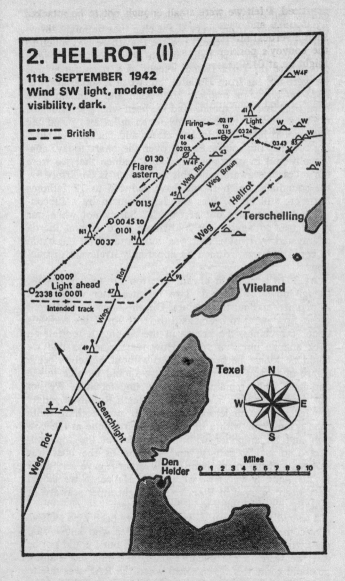

2. HELLROT (I)

11th SEPTEMBER 1942
Wind SW light, moderate
visibility, dark.

━ ━ ━ British

W4F

41
Light

W W
W

.02.17 to
to 0315 0324 0343 85
Firing →

01.45
to
02.03
43
W4F Weg Rot.

Weg Braun

45 Weg Hellrot

0130
Flare
astern

W Terschelling

0115
Weg

N1
0045 to
0101

0037 N

Rot

0009
Light ahead
2338 to 0001 47

91

Vlieland

Intended track

Weg

Weg

49

Texel

N
W — E
S

Searchlight

Weg Rot

Den
Helder

Miles
0 1 2 3 4 5 6 7 8 9 10

gan to realize that success would come from making the
right deduction from every slight clue that he might throw
our way. However I could not see that there was much to
be gained from this light, which was presumably sited
somewhere on Texel Island, except as a reassurance that
we were not far from Holland; but when it shone again at
2328 *on the same bearing,* both Alan and I should have
been triggered to respond. Had we been where we thought,
the land would have been only seven miles away, and the
light would have both looked closer and changed in bearing towards the south. Poring over the chart today, ana-
lytically and in untroubled peace, I deduce that we were
ten miles to seaward, and this conclusion is confirmed by
the soundings which should have reduced to 12 fathoms
but were still at 16. Was this lapse caused by a subcon-
scious urge to keep out of trouble? Surely not when our
mood was so aggressive; I attribute it to mental inertia
aggravated by tension that was concentrated on the battle
to come and was irritated by apparently irrelevant distractions.

At 2336 a gunflash ahead, far; too far to concern us,
though now I wondered. Two minutes later we stopped
as planned and cut the engines. Oh, the blessed relief from
noise; how sweet to hear again the soft lap of the wavelets
under the chines, the breeze in the rigging, a footfall on
deck and an unraised voice. How reassuring too that we
could no longer be heard or seen without ourselves being
aware of it, and better still that we should be able to see
and hear while remaining virtually undetectable. We got
out the hydrophone, a delightfully Heath Robinson gadget
for listening to underwater noises. It was nothing more
than a long pole with a directional microphone at the bottom and an amplifier with headphones at the top connected to a 12v battery; and so long as the boat was
stopped and the microphone in still water it gave very good
results. Since however we were not in Hellrot as we should
have been, or even in Weg Rot but eight miles seaward of
that, there was nothing to be heard, or seen.

I waited for 20 minutes. It would have been nice to have
stayed there all night, secure as a spider who knows that
the fly must eventually come to his web; but I could not be
sure we were in the enemy's path, and nor did I think
he could come this far by 0130 when the RAF was due to
arrive. The renewed noise was horrid even at only 12½

knots, and we became isolated again except through our eyes; I used mine intensively, not forgetting the flanks this time. Our course was North 54° East, parallel to the shore.

Was that a light dead ahead? Yes, there it was again; just a flash but it must surely be a channel buoy, and we were certainly on the enemy's track. At 37 minutes past midnight we came up to the buoy which was black, conical, flashed every seven seconds, and its name was "N." I think now that it must have been "NI."

Popular belief held that both E-boats and MTBs always laid wait near buoys, so I went on for two miles before stopping again to listen. There was not a whisper and at 0100 I pushed on, telling Alan to let me know when it was 0130. He had scarcely done so when, as though at his word, a flare fell out of the sky some distance astern. I awaited whatever might ensue, hopefully but also with doubt, for having just traversed that stretch of water I could not believe that anything could be there. Such was evidently the case for nothing else happened; but it was heartening to know that the RAF had arrived, and now they would presumably search the rest of the area much more quickly than we could.

I stopped for another 15-minute listen at 0145, and just at the end of it came the first real clue; the sound of gun-fire somewhere ahead, perhaps fine on the starboard bow, it was difficult to tell. We pressed on, and at 0207 were rewarded by a beautiful cone of tracer rising from several different sources on the sea.

"Steer for the guns!" I cried; and if I'd had a saber I should have brandished it.

"Steer for the guns, sir," echoed Saunders, unmoved; "course North 74 East."

Now there was some thinking to do. The commander of however insignificant a force is confronted by two distinct but closely related problems. His aim being to fight a successful battle, the tactics he employs will be of the highest importance; and so his task is not merely to make contact, but to do so in such a way that the approach will merge naturally into a favorable tactical situation. With the torpedo as our main weapon we must aim to fire from the target's bow or beam, and that simple need must color all our earlier maneuvering.

I was of course in no doubt that what I saw was the convoy approaching; and my second deduction was that it

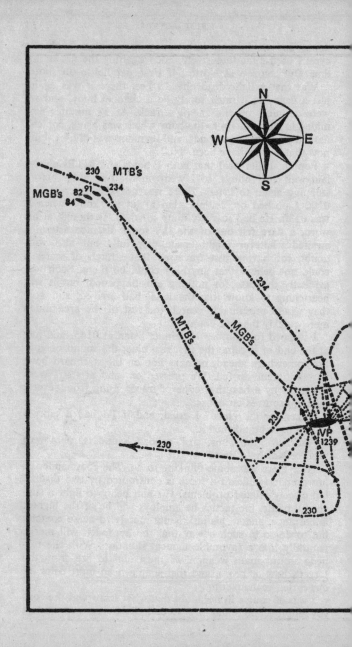

3. HELLROT (II)

-·-·-·-·· British
———— German
======➤ Torpedoes
·········➤ Gunfire

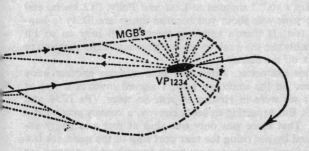

MGB's

VP 1234

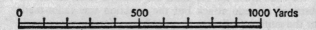

0   500   1000 Yards

was 10 to 15 miles away so that there was no chance of combining our attack with the airmen's. Thirdly, the wind blew from stalker to quarry who would hear our engines' throaty roar much sooner than I would wish. For once none of the premises conflicted, and the simple deduction was that I must wait for the enemy to come to me. I thought it reasonable to close for another ten minutes, and then at 0217 we stopped, looked, and listened.

We continued doing so for 58 minutes and neared the limit of what flesh and blood could stand. The flesh was cold and empty yet no one could be spared from his action station to brew up, and the blood had also cooled markedly from its initial fiery red heat; however fear for my skin was less than fear of looking a consummate chump, having sighted an enemy and then let him get away. The convoy had now had plenty of time to reach us, and I wondered whether what we had seen had been something else. Time also affected our situation for another reason; it was 0315 and only two and a half hours before twilight, so that if we were going to fight a battle we had better do it and be well clear of German fighters by daylight, possibly with damaged boats.

"Let's go," I shouted to Leaf and Polly; "12 knots, and keep your wits about you because things are likely to happen fast. If there's anything there they'll hear us so I'll probably use the gunboats as we planned. Make sure you're quick off the mark."

This felt better. After only nine minutes another buoy flashed on the starboard bow; I altered towards it and at 0343 we were in Hellrot at last. So were VPs *1234* and *1239*. But expecting to see a convoy, a convoy was what I saw. That there was only one ship at first was easily explained by her being the rear port ship of the mass, for her course was easterly and we were overtaking. I guessed her size as 2,000 tons; had the *Bismarck* been reported at sea I should have been in no doubt that I had sighted her, and not poor little *VP 1239*, ex-fishing trawler *Vooraan*, too small even to have an officer in command.

We were much too far abaft the enemy's beam for an unobserved torpedo attack but the situation was tailor-made for the gunboat's diversion; quickly too, for the range could not have been more than 500 yards and we should be seen at any moment. I filled my lungs with as much air as they would hold, raised my voice to its highest pitch, and shrieked across the 30-foot gap of tumbling water and roaring exhausts, "Attack!" and for want of a saber accompanied the command by gesturing with my cap in the appropriate direction.

Leaf, good man, was quicker off the mark than even I, obsessed with urgency myself, thought possible. Those three gunboats leaped forward as one boat like ocean greyhounds, and although the simile is customarily applied to destroyers it fitted the Scott-Paine MGB far better, for the curve of the deck resembled the dog's back when its legs are crossed under it before a great surge of power. No one in the MTBs who watched them go will ever forget the sight.

Obersteuermann Helms of *1239* could not now fail to be alerted, and his immediate reaction was to challenge, which was reasonable; he could not know as we did that everything sighted would be the enemy, and the British had never before penetrated so far to the east. But had he opened fire he would have given himself the advantage of the law which postulates that no one likes being shot at and does not shoot so well when he is. The gunboats got in first, again as one, and their 35 knots very soon brought the range down to what Helms estimated as 100 yards. *1239* was hit as she could not fail to be, and the gunboats were not; but just before the latter's fire became fully effective, Obersteuermann Geerk commanding *1234* in the van saw the point and engaged.

There was a full 1,000 yards between the two Germans which allowed them no mutual support, and Leaf swept on to engage the leading one. He judged her to be an R-boat (See Appendix III) and may therefore have thought himself justified in closing to the killing range of 100 yards, though for myself I suspect he had quite forgotten that his aim was merely to cause a diversion.

As soon as the third gunboat had cleared my bow I turned to starboard to attack from the other side as the plan demanded; Polly followed and almost at once, as the blackness to port was ripped and sliced by stabbing tracer, we two found ourselves in an oasis of perfect peace. It seemed miraculous, as it always does with me when a carefully matured plan actually comes off, but then a snag appeared; just as I thought we were crossing under the merchant ship's stern I saw a trawler escort occupying the very water I should have to traverse to put myself into a

torpedo firing position on her starboard beam. That must
have been *1239* herself, there was no one else it could
have been and now I was seeing her as she really was. But
I continued to imagine the merchant ship somewhere in
the affray to port, and at once decided to return whence
we had come and make my attack from there, the gunboats
having moved well ahead and out of the way.

As I turned, the spell seemed to be broken when the
trawler fired her stern gun at me; but she stopped almost at
once, probably because the gunner became blinded by his
own tracer and I was by no means disposed to fire back
and give him a point of aim. Peace again, and I looked
round for Polly. He had vanished and I said to myself,
biting my lip, "He thinks I'm windy and he's going on by
himself to find his own opening." Polly swears he never
thought any such thing, and my guilt-ridden inference was
thoroughly unworthy. His move was tactically sound, and
indeed I had stressed to him that his job was to do anything, including breaking away from me, that might lead to
a torpedo in an enemy bottom; almost at once I realized
that we were both less likely to be spotted maneuvering on
our own. I brought *234* back under *1239*'s stern and waved
a wand to turn her into a merchant ship again; I may perhaps plead that our eyes' dark adaptation had been shat-
tered by the tracer and there was a good deal of gunsmoke
about. I maneuvered as though we had been in Felixstowe
Dock and half my mind was playing Grandmother's Foot-
steps all over again. But the other half was not fooled;
"This is real," it insisted; "what's that you're holding?" It
was death, in the shape of torpedo triggers.

Leaf circled *1234* at close range, delivering a prolonged
and concentrated burst of fire which struck sparks off the
German as well as penetrating her side and upperworks,
destroying her degaussing installation and badly wounding
one man. Her firing was silenced except for one machine
gun which sprayed wildly, and above all she was given no
chance of interfering with the MTBs. Leaf, his job mag-
nificently begun, slowed down to reorient himself and
search for a new enemy.

Polly gained bearing on *1239*'s starboard beam. He had
not seen the merchant ship, naturally enough because there
wasn't one, and had no fixed ideas about what enemy to
expect; nor had I put him in my mind for I assumed he
had seen everything I had, failing to understand that his

attention before sighting had necessarily been concentrated
on station-keeping. Polly decided to torpedo the trawler;
but since we were urged not to waste those expensive
weapons and *VP 1239* was unimportant he resolved to use
only one. As I observed earlier this, though logical, was a
mistake because the smaller the target the less chance of
hitting without a spread of torpedoes. Polly turned in to
attack, Helms saw him and engaged, seriously wounding
Able Seaman Robinson, and the torpedo was fired. After
the appropriate interval a shout of triumph was raised in
MTB 230; but alas such shouts were almost standard, ex-
pressing everybody's dearest wish, and the Germans were
unaware of a torpedo.

MGB

As I slowly drew up on *1239*'s port beam it really did
seem as though the gods were determined that I should
succeed whether I deserved to or not, for Helms's attention was all on Polly. Now Leaf spotted *1239*, recognized
her as an escort, and came hurtling in from her starboard
bow with fearful momentum. At first his boat, *91*, was
exposed to all the German guns and began to suffer, Able
Seaman Laurie Wade being killed and two men wounded;
but then Leaf led round to starboard so that all three gunboats' weapons bore, and *1239* was severely hit. A long
burst of Oerlikon from *MGB 84* tore up the German's
bridge and wounded the coxswain; another destroyed the
15mm gun and wounded the crew; and finally Leaf came
so close that Helms thought he was going to ram or board.

I was conscious of none of this, partly because of the
smoke but mostly because I was concentrating on what I

was doing with total intensity. At last we were on the target's beam and I turned towards, going astern on the starboard engine to save time, still unobserved. She lives in my mind to this day as a 2,000-ton merchantman with raised forecastle, well-deck with the foremast, bridge, midship superstructure and funnel, another well and mainmast, and poop. I guessed the range as 500 yards but that was subjective and derived from the original fixed idea. If you know what you are looking at on a dark night you can guess the range; or if you know the range you can estimate the size of what you are looking at; but if you know neither and guess one wrongly, the other will be wrong too.

When Helms saw 234 at last he put the range at 150 yards, which must have been about right for at that distance the trawler would have seemed no bigger than she was. Our bows swung slowly towards her, and the moment was at hand when we must justify ourselves and everything that had gone into our boat. There was no hot blood, no lust to kill, no hate; just a sweaty professionalism as though one was lining up for the winning putt.

"Fire starboard!" I had to shout it lest the bridge firing cable failed in which case Jolly had to clout the striker with a mallet; but the fish lumbered out at my pull, its propellers turning as they should. Letting the boat swing a degree or two further—"Fire port!"

The starboard torpedo was the one: 50 yards from the tube it nosed the surface as a swimmer raises his head to see where he is heading, and then settled to its set depth of six feet, leaving a straight, wide track that we watched in awful stillness for it was going to hit. The column of dirty water and smoke was so huge that it hid 1239 from end to end and we never saw her again.

Relief from extreme tension was so sudden and unexpected that I found myself shouting, laughing, and hitting Saunders over the shoulders with such unbridled force that his chin struck the compass sharply. But he did not notice in his own excitement and the rest of the crew went wild too, vying with each other to find an appropriately superlative descriptive phrase and then wrenching open the engine room hatch to try it out on Cuthbert, Clarke and Gilbert.

Even as we congratulated each other a small craft appeared out of the smoke ahead and opened fire at us. It was Leaf, though I did not realize that until afterwards, but the right reaction was the same whoever it was; full ahead and away to the northwest. Lightened by both torpedoes and half her fuel the boat seemed barely to skim the water and our exuberance was if anything increased, the tracer lobbing after us being merely something new to laugh at. Poor Jolly was hurt though, which I did not yet know; not badly, but he had to leave *234*. I wish I could record that I was soberly conscious of having condemned fellow humans to death, mutilation or torture; but I cannot. The thought obtruded later but was firmly suppressed as it played no part in winning the war; we had done our duty and so we laughed, but wars are a pity.

Helms saw the torpedo coming and went hard-a-port to try and comb the track, and although time and distance did not allow him to succeed, his turn did mean that the explosion occurred right forward in the least vulnerable part of the ship. It was shattering, the forecastle was blown clean off, the forward gun went over the side and its crew of five with it; one of them, Mohr, swam aft and climbed on board again but the rest were lost. Helms and his coxswain were thrown off the bridge but scrambled back, hurt, to continue at their posts; the ship flooded rapidly taking a heavy list, and as though that were not enough one of the gunboats approached slowly, apparently threatening to board. Every gun was out of action but the Germans fought back with all they had, hand-grenades; the act was brave and did not recognize defeat.

Of the 27-man German crew only nine were unwounded, but they toiled mightily. The engine still worked, and although steering was impossible owing to the mass of twisted metal trailing from the bow, electricity and pumps were available so that, as the major leaks were sealed off one by one, ultimate disaster was gradually averted. When Geerk could no longer hear our engines he brought *1234* alongside, took off the wounded and prepared to tow; other ships were sent to help, but it was not until 1850 that evening that what remained of *1239* had been moved the 13 miles to Terschelling. It was a gallant achievement, and also a useful illustration of the fortunes of war and weapon effectiveness. HMS *Ark Royal* of 20,000 tons was sunk by one torpedo; *VP 1239* of 173 tons was not.

Home we came in high delight, blurting out a triumphant signal, "Have attacked east-bound convoy, one torpedo hit on 2,000 ton merchant ship." This the Germans intercepted, which does not speak well for our codes, and commented as well they might, "This report is quite remarkable." How can one explain the fog of war convincingly? To distort the facts so drastically one must surely be either a knave or a fool.

I was not a knave as I sincerely believed we had attacked a merchant ship escorted by an armed trawler and an R-boat; therefore I was a fool and am quite content to be so called. But may I plead that in the dark when decisions must be instantaneous, the right answer will derive only from wisdom which is elusive, or luck which is hardly a planning factor? It thus behooves the simple sailor to attempt a grading not too far down the scale of folly. To acknowledge that he is certainly going to be wrong to some extent may well clear his mind sufficiently to make it, for instance, unnecessary to decide what he will see before he sees it, and could prove the best justification for the humble boast, "I may be a fool but I'm not a bloody fool." That kind of fool is surely he who waits to find out all the facts before attacking, because he probably never will.

Even so we won, and the Germans were gratifyingly upset about it. Their Admiral ordered the Terschelling patrol to be increased to four ships, and instituted energetic measures to exchange the Vorpostenboote's 20mm guns for 37mm, to fit armor plating round guns and bridges, and to arm them with flame-throwers and sub-machine guns to repel boarders. But he acknowledged that even these small improvements were difficult because of the overriding need to control sea communications in the Baltic which were vital to the Army's massive drive into Russia, a noteworthy example of narrow waters at the core of a strategic situation.

Back on the jetty at *Mantis,* Leaf and I discussed the night's work; I sat on a bollard but he stood for some reason, though certainly not in deference. We watched his dead man being taken away and that was a good corrective to cockiness; his life was on my hands was the thought that struck deep home—thank God the torpedo hit. Then the wounded were loaded into ambulances which, strangely, did not move off. I asked Leaf whether there were any more, whereupon he smirked apologetically and climbed in himself. He had been hit by a splinter in the groin and at once created a Coastal Force legend by crying in high falsetto, "That was a near one, coxswain!" He was no quivering aspen, this Leaf; and when he was later killed in action a sense of loss was palpable far beyond Lowestoft. My gratitude to him has not faded in thirty years and never will. That this, the Battle of Hellrot, was pathetically insignificant is only too clear from the narrative; yet it could hardly have been more important to us for it proved that success was possible. We were in business, and Derek Leaf had put us in the way of it.

VI

IRON ORE

As we pulled ourselves and the boats together after the action there was no question of anyone thinking himself a fool, or being thought one; that only happened thirty years later when I saw the enemy's records, so that I did not learn the valuable lesson of the *idée fixe* in time to profit from it. We spun our yarn and everyone believed it; as the report which "I had the honor to submit" passed up the line of command, it was embellished by each senior officer in turn. "Lieutenant Dickens fought a successful action," wrote Barnard of *Mantis*. Flag Officer Great Yarmouth called it "a pretty piece of work." "A very good effort by all concerned; cooperation between MGBs and MTBs was excellent," judged the Commander-in-Chief, Admiral D'Oyly Lyon; and even the Admiralty noticed us, "A good example of combined MTB and MGB tactics against a comparatively lightly armed single ship convoy."

Of more immediate impact was the fact that we were news, for the effects of which I was innocently unprepared. Of course we switched on the radio in case we were mentioned, and thoroughly enjoyed what we heard:

"One of our offensive patrols intercepted and attacked an enemy convoy off the Texel. An enemy tanker of medium size was seen to disintegrate after being hit by a torpedo. A large flak-ship forming part of the escort was also probably hit by a torpedo. There followed a brisk action at close range between our craft and the enemy escorts, during which an armed trawler and an R-boat were very severely damaged."

Poor little VPs *1234* and *1239* had multiplied exceedingly after our and the progagandists' imaginative efforts.

Then came a flood of congratulatory letters and telegrams. I replied in the vein that it really wasn't all that marvellous, that it was wrong that my name alone should be mentioned when the credit truly belonged to everyone in the team, and that there were many thousands in the forces all over the world who were doing far more than us. But I lapped it up just the same and it was very bad for me; it would have been worse without the niggling awareness that we must now gird ourselves to doing it all over again, and then again. . . .

Kenneth Barnard and his Base Staff were all over us, his beloved *Mantis* having been placed two clear notches above *Beehive* (Felixstowe) and *Midge* (Great Yarmouth); for while we were busy, Bremer Horne and his gunboats, to their great credit, had harried a force of E-boats, inflicting very considerable damage and casualties. In the natural order of things a rivalry grew up between the bases which was healthy up to a point, but went too far at times, as such rivalries usually do; we all need to feel part of a tightly-knit unit and the spur of competition is essential for high efficiency, but very nice judgment and mature tolerance is needed to know when to stop.

Alan Jensen recorded no operation for three weeks but gave no reason for why we were so idle. Engine trouble certainly played a part and *230* had some action damage to repair, but I suspect that the equinoctial gales were mainly responsible, for we had to admit to being fair weather sailors in the sense that we were out of the fight long before a destroyer. It was not that we could not keep the sea in just about any weather the North Sea could offer, and its more unpleasant moods were vicious indeed; but to give battle, even to seek the enemy, when a boat's speed was limited to 12 knots for the real fear of breaking her back; when driving spray lashed the whole of her, reducing visibility at the same time as making her more conspicuous; when eyeballs were battered, binoculars rendered opaque, weapons inhibited, and electrical circuits shorted; why, there was little future in it and valor suggested a discretionary wait. Tomorrow might be calm, boats and men would still be fit, and the enemy would not have gone away.

For whatever reason it was always tomorrow and tomorrow and tomorrow, and Jamie Fraser's itchy sea-legs gave him increasing trouble. He had welcomed us home last time with full-hearted generosity but his anguish at not having been with us was painful to see. Now his all-consuming urge to succeed in battle seemed ever to be thwarted, and lacking patience to the extent that I wondered if he even knew the meaning of the word, he became rather too taut for comfort, even with me. For his crew, life might well have been really trying had it not been for Arthur (General) Lee, his First Lieutenant, who was mature, sympathetic and equable beyond his years, so that 233 stayed on the rails, albeit tensely.

At last, on the evening of September 30, 1942, I led a great armada of eight boats to sea, and was so proud as I watched them fan out into their arrowhead that I persuaded myself that they must also be invincible. 234 was behaving herself, and we had a new Seaman Torpedoman, Neal ("Great big fellow from Dorset, good type, couldn't fluster him," says Saunders); Jamie and Polly were there, and the fourth MTB was 87 of Long's Flotilla, whose captain's name I cannot remember because he was with us such a very short time before turning home with engine trouble. On my starboard quarter were four gunboats, 21, 18, 82 and 86, and although 82 was the only one to have been with us before we had had plenty of time to discuss and practice together.

The plan having worked well was unchanged; though I emphasized the need for gunboats to keep well clear of torpedo-boats once they had parted company. That would not necessarily be easy, because until we saw the enemy I could not say which side of him the two types should go respectively; they might even have to stay on the same side at opposite ends. So the only golden rules I could lay down for the gunboats were that they must only engage small craft which they *knew* were not MTBs, and must try not to go anywhere near an MTB either as that would spoil her attack. I was a little apprehensive but felt that if the thought was uppermost in everybody's mind the risk could be accepted; I hoped too that the torpedo attack would be delivered so soon after the gunboats' furor had started that both groups would be clear where the other was.

Another point I stressed was that if circumstances were to invite an unobserved attack by the MTBs the gunboats would be told to get lost; and if their martial pride was thereby mortified, they were to nurse their resentment in complete silence. It may have been that these exhortations had an effect on the battle, though not the one I intended.

Tragedy struck. 233's distilled-water tank blew up and

there was no alternative to her turning for home. Jamie's distress was excruciating and his crew had much to endure.

Twin Lewis Guns

The sun descended into a smooth, gentle swell, and night rose from it to encompass us while the heavens remained bright. As colors faded and edges blurred each man used the last of the light to check his gear and weapons. I noticed a strange face whose owner was busy with a stripped Lewis gun, and remembered that this was Petty Officer Douglas Ross who had accosted me on the jetty and asked if he might come for the ride; I had hesitated, admiring his enterprise but wondering whether the risk to a valuable senior rating was really justified.

"I'll bring my own gun, sir," he had pleaded, and of course I yielded. I naturally assumed that his claimed ownership of the weapon was *de facto* rather than *de jure*, "won" perhaps—"Somebody must have lost it; so I won it"—but that was no concern of mine.

There came another most welcome signal from The Nore, and again I felt that we should have a fight. Coastal Command had sighted and attacked a north-bound convoy and would continue to shadow it while the light held. Alan calculated that we could intercept off the Frisian Islands, but that there was no question of making a wide sweep to seaward and coming in ahead of the enemy because we should be nearly at our limit of endurance merely by steering a straight course, and a margin of fuel must be allowed for wide-open throttles in battle. That meant we must chase and overtake from astern, heralded by full-throated exhausts; but having the gunboats with us we could still impose our will on the enemy as we had done before. Since there was no alternative I was pleased to be able to take the decision in plenty of time and get it understood by all the captains.

On the bridge in the darkness I felt, despite the compass, that we might have been rushing in any direction or round in circles; and periodical visits to the wheelhouse to look at Alan's neat lines on the chart were reassuring, for the illusion was strong that one had only to draw such a line to pin-point oneself upon it. All seemed well, no more engines failed, and although fear was ever present there was also room for a rather pleasant sensation of being in command of events, clearly a beneficial result of the last battle. So once I stayed below much longer than was necessary to look at the chart and tucked myself into a corner, thought how delightful it was to command such splendid officers and men who would do their duty whether I was there or not, borrowed a leaf from Drake's book and told the enemy that I should get around to dealing with him in my own good time, and took a dreamless "stretch off the land."

Having previously discovered "N" Buoy, or as I now think "NI," which had guided us to the enemy, we naturally aimed to find it again and, blow me down, we did.

Alan's pride burgeoned and neither of us thought it odd
that astonishment should be our reaction at achieving our
precise intention. Today however amazement is justified,
for the point at which we aimed was some eight miles
inshore of the buoy and five miles south of it; yet on
two nights in different weathers and tides we made exactly
the same error. We closed the buoy and then steered northeast parallel to the coast at 23 knots, sure now that we
should overtake the convoy from astern. After 40 minutes
we altered to eastnortheast as the islands curved, and five
minutes later things started to happen exactly as expected.

A starshell blossomed in the sky on the port bow; or was
it an aircraft flare for there was no noise? We could not
even be sure we were the target but that seemed likely,
it fitted so well with tonight's *idée fixe*. Since the enemy
was going away and we should have to overtake him,
there seemed no point in stopping to assess the situation
as that would give him time to collect himself. Three minutes elapsed before the next starshell or flare but I felt no
temptation to fuss, rather my mind was at peak intensity
and ready for the key decision whenever sufficient data
should be presented. The enemy had at last become a
normal environment.

The second burst was over us and the eerie, pale green
light picked us out in all our nakedness, but still there was
no indication where the perishing thing had come from.
Ha! A gun barked on the port bow and simultaneously
another new planet swam into our ken. The next followed
quickly and from then on the succession was maintained
until the end of the action. Now we could see the guns'
flashes as well as hear their noise and there seemed to be
two sources, ahead and well round to port, surely the rear-
most escorts of the convoy. I was almost ready to let the
gunboats go, and when I sighted a number of ships between
the two bearings I did so.

This time there was no question of shouting as we were
making far too much noise, but Signalman Haynes was
already primed with the message which was very short,
"8A," meaning "Attack before MTBs." Its significance
had been much discussed, even for this particular situation
of the enemy being sighted on the MTBs' side when the
gunboats were to increase speed, cross our bows, and engage the nearest escort while we faded temporarily into

obscurity. There was the appropriate escort right ahead
of us and I still felt that things were going my way.

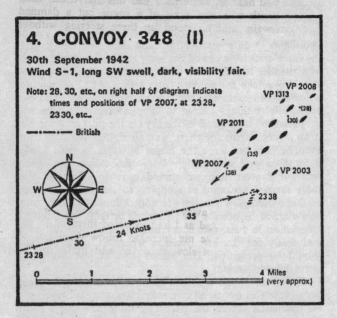

4. CONVOY 348 (I)

30th September 1942
Wind S-1, long SW swell, dark, visibility fair.

Note: 28, 30, etc., on right half of diagram indicate
times and positions of VP 2007, at 23 28,
23 30, etc..

——·—·—·— British

They were doing the exact reverse; particularly German
North Sea Convoy No. 348 which was bound from the
Elbe to The Hook, steering southwest down *Weg Rot* and
straight towards us. The range shortened rapidly, but I
had no idea of the truth.

VPs *2007* and *2003* started firing for effect and succeeded; it was like Barfleur all over again with the rip-
roaring, streaking tracer and the crack of 20mm shells
hitting *234*'s port bow and forecastle. To Polly Perkins
and the crew of *230* it seemed worse, for although they
had been baptized with fire by *VP 1239* three weeks before,
that may be likened to a few drops from a font whereas
this was total immersion. The trauma was accentuated by
Polly's attention having been mostly on station-keeping
and not, like mine, on what was likely to happen next.

"For the first time in my life," Polly related, "I was
being shot at *personally*. Tracer was richocheting over the

boat, streaming through the rigging and making the sort of noise you hear on westerns. I had this marvellous chap "Tiger" Smith who was a bit of a rogue but a damned good coxswain, and he stood up there steering without ducking whereas I had my head only just over the armor plating saying, 'Christ! What's all this? Never seen anything like it.' And then I got the hell of a bang on the head and thought, this is it; but it turned out to be the recognition lights which had been shot off and came down and hit me on the tin hat."

Polly and I were exposed and there was nothing we could do to extricate ourselves; there was no purpose in turning towards the enemy and we could not turn away while the gunboats were still there. What was the matter with them? I swore with all my lung power but the shout just mingled with the din and was lost before it started. When I looked again the gunboats were all jumbled up together but moving away to starboard, except for one which was racing ahead as I had expected them all to do. Well at least that gave me space to follow them out of trouble and I was not slow to do so and make smoke. Glancing astern at Polly I saw that he had been even quicker and had already vanished; that was all right and I commended him, for I now knew that nothing would stop him getting to a torpedo-firing position if it was humanly possible. But as our smoke developed and the enemy's fire wavered, then ceased, I was plunged into near despair at what seemed to be the ruin of my cherished plan, and of any hope of success; for what chance had just two single MTBs of first overtaking and then attacking a heavily defended convoy that was fully alert?

Fury with the gunboats was uppermost in my seething brain, though now I see that, as usual, there were two sides to the case. Had I released them a minute or two earlier when it had become clear that that would have to be done anyway, their leader would have had time to settle his mind and his team into fighting trim, and could then have probed the enemy, chosen the best target and gone for it. I could have followed, keeping him in sight from a distance to establish where he was going, and then broken away for the torpedo attack. I had no right to assume that the situation and right course of action would seem the same to him as it did to me, without telling him; but we had no

form of communication for a message of such subtlety
short of stopping, cutting engines and talking.

As it was, three of the gunboats were as confounded by
the sudden flare-up as was Polly in *230* (Map below).
Only after the attack signal did *VP 2003* become evident,

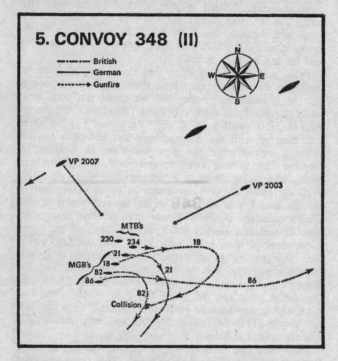

5. CONVOY 348 (II)

- -·-·- British
- ——— German
- ·······→ Gunfire

VP 2007

VP 2003

MTB's

230   234   18

21

MGB's   18   21

82

86   86

82

Collision

and then she seemed so very close that *MGB 21* altered
course to starboard across the bows of her following boats
which were still in quarterline. The second boat, *18,* was
commanded by Ted Smyth and he, being both Irish and an
experienced warrior, had already leaned on his throttles
and kept on towards the enemy, being in no doubt that
that was what was required and that his leader would do
the same. By a miracle of instant thought and action Ted
hurled *18* to port, her lifted bow seeming to pass over *21*'s
stern, and was at once out on his own, drawing the enemy's
fire but also returning it at a range, he estimated, of 150

yards. Four men were wounded in *2003,* but *18* was hit in her turret and Oerlikon, her coxswain, Clark, was slightly wounded in the face, and one sailor was pricked in a rather unfortunate place considering that he was to be married in a fortnight. "Nothing serious," said Ted, though his viewpoint may be thought somewhat detached.

Ted then saw *MGB 21* heading south and knew he must rejoin. The third gunboat, *82,* had managed to claw herself round after *21* and was now on the latter's beam. That would have allowed Ted to slide in astern of his leader, but just as he did so *21* again altered to starboard and Clark, wounded and not being able to see *82* from his position on the wheel, steered straight into her; Ted had no time even to shout, so high was the relative speed. *18's* bow smashed into *82's* side, the double-skinned mahogany ripped and splintered, and a potentially fatal hole gaped in the very forefoot. It was a cruel reward for gallant initiative.

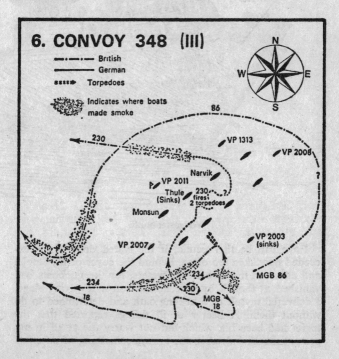

Tragedy also struck the fourth gunboat, *86;* for in spite of being farthest from the enemy her Captain was hit and died instantly. He was Tom Sadleir, son of Michael Sadleir, the writer, and his loss was mourned in *Mantis* with deep and evident sincerity. His coxswain, William Utting, had no idea where to go and who can blame him in that ghastly confusion? Being unable to call Alun Phillips the First Lieutenant, who was aft with the Oerlikon, for the ear-splitting din, he steered east thinking that was the best way out of trouble; the 20mm gun continued to engage *2003* and probably rendered me a signal service.

Vorpostenboote

Rage can be therapeutic, if the stated dose is not exceeded nor taken too often. Behind the cover of my smoke and alone on the face of the waters, for the gunboats had vanished as though by a scene-shift on a revolving stage, I delivered myself of a healing oath and determined to do without them. A bearer of ill tidings reported that the turret had been hit, which did not worry me at all in my present mood; indeed it was always something of an effort

to remember the guns when concentrating on torpedoes. In fact I do not think the trouble was caused by gunfire but by the hydraulic pressure failing owing to the center engine having stopped. That was far more serious but Cuthbert's message had not yet reached me, and although I might have noted the fact from the bridge revolution-counter I continued in purposeful ignorance. It was just as well; issues are so easily confused by facts.

I continued to turn to starboard at slow speed so as to give the enemy time to forget 234; then I gave a burst on the port engine to help her round, reducing again to 12 knots on a course of northeast in which direction I guessed the convoy would reappear. I passed the word round the crew that our golden moment was at hand and they reacted silently, scarcely moving but conveying unmistakably that they were with me. As *234* nosed through the last wisps of acid-tasting though friendly smoke I unaccountably fell in love with her.

The convoy comprised eight ships, and only one, the German *Monsun,* was defensively armed. All the rest were Swedish which may be regarded as bad luck, either on the Swedes for having to submit to their ships being pressed into dangerous waters as the price of a precarious neutrality, or on the Germans for not having enough ships for their essential cargoes, depending on the viewpoint. Curiously, six of the ships were in ballast which may have indicated that they would load coal, the Swedes' price for their ore, at Rotterdam; only *Elizabeth Maersk* and *Thule* had cargoes, and since the latter's port of lading was Lulea, the iron ore port at the head of the Baltic, it is reasonable to conclude that she at least carried that war-winning treasure.

Five Vorpostenboote formed the distinctly weak escort, a measure perhaps of the slight British activity off the Dutch coast up to this time; they were however considerably larger and more heavily armed than our previous opponents, carrying guns up to 88mm whence came the starshell. The Senior Officer was in *VP 2011* on the convoy's starboard, seaward bow, where he clearly thought a threat was most likely for he stationed *1313* further aft on the same side, with only one escort to port, *2003*. An understanding of our torpedo control problem would have indicated the importance of protecting the flanks; but as I had learned in the *Cotswold,* merchant ships needed a ship to follow or they would often stray from the channel, and without another astern to urge them along they would straggle. The guide was *2007* and the corgi* snapping at the heels *2008;* they were doing a good job and the convoy was well closed up, though its formation was not perhaps quite so impeccable as diagram III implies, judging by what I saw.

For there they were, black and lumbering, on our port bow. The change of scene in so short a time was scarcely

---

*Welsh Corgi, a small, short-legged, long-backed dog with a fox-like head, bred to herd cattle.

believable; noise, light and confusion had become quiet, dark and clarity, five merchant ships were within my orbit of vision and, yes, there was the escort, *2003*, where I expected her on our starboard beam. Our way was clear but the range must be closed; what was it? 1,500 yards? How hard it was to judge.

Whether there was any shooting going on I cannot remember, concentrating as I was on my own task, though I think it likely that *2003* was distracted by *MGB 86*, and *2007* by Polly and *MGB 18*, to my great benefit. My target was obvious, two merchant ships overlapping, one in each column, which ought to be hard to miss. We thought we already knew their course, northeast, so there was no need to check that, and the immediate problem was to guess their speed which proved difficult for I could see no bow waves. To be sure I was looking at the wrong ends of the ships for these; had they appeared at the other I might have awakened from my fantasy, but there were in fact none at all because the enemy had reduced to bare steerage way as an antitorpedo dodge.

These technical considerations detracted from the tension as we rumbled ever closer, indeed I discovered that slow speed suited my rate of thinking and felt almost at home. Having decided that the enemy was not going very fast I took a quick look round—"My God!" *2003* was not retreating but coming towards us, and her range was half what it had been before.

My first thought was that she had turned round in order to deal with us; but in that case why had she not opened fire because we were well within range? Could it possibly be that the whole outfit was steering the other way? I looked hard at the merchant ships again but they offered few clues; in those days the "three island" tramp steamer with vertical masts and funnel might have been going either way when viewed as a black silhouette against a scarcely paler background. But now I thought I could see a slightly higher lump of a bridge at the *left* end of an island, and a counter stern at the *right*. Another glance at *2003;* 400 yards if that, well within hitting range and closing fast; we were living on borrowed time. Breaking an *idée fixe* is excruciating, like forswearing a sacred promise, but I did it. Twirling the sight round to southwest and telling Saunders to adjust the course to port, I resolved to continue closing until *2003* engaged and then fired torpedoes;

we were surely within 1,000 yards now, and that was not too far against the wide, double target. *2003* steered to pass astern and cut us off from the world at large, but the longer she delayed engaging the nearer would her line of fire approach her own merchant ships. "Watch her," I told Haynes.

"Here it comes!"

It was almost a relief. "Swing her a fraction to port," I said to Saunders; mustn't save the ship for a ha'porth of care—"That's it, steady . . . fire both!"

"Full ahead! Hard-a-port! Make smoke!" We were just permitted a glimpse of the torpedo tracks running correctly before we became a target for every gun in the North Sea and all was blotted out behind the fireworks. And for the second time in five minutes utter depression succeeded supreme confidence, for I now persuaded myself that I had been weak, vacillating and wrong to change my mind about the enemy's course at the last minute. What a criminal, profitless risk to my crew and boat! Hadn't I always been taught to make up my mind and stick to it? Perhaps I was catching a psychological cold through overexposure to sudden changes of mental temperature; at any rate I was in the right mood for the next message from below, "Center engine out of action, sir."

"Oh, bother!"

The *Thule* was hit by a torpedo on the port side and sank instantly.

The torpedo however was by no means necessarily *234*'s, for *230* was also on the job. But it is at this point that the fog of war descends and refuses to clear; even with both German and British reports spread out on the desk and several personal recollections to help build the jigsaw, the pieces just will not fit and it is none of my business to force them in for the sake of a good story.

The question is, what happened to *230*? The battle's opening holocaust had decided Polly to make his attack from some other direction; and having seen the convoy by the light of a starshell, and being as convinced as I that it was steering northeast—silly fellow!—what better than to cross under its stern and approach from the seaward side. So he did a quick 270 degree turn to starboard to get out of trouble and steered northwest at 23 knots, soon altering to northeast along what he thought was the portside of the convoy. But of course he was in reality trying to cross its front which would have meant a much more prolonged maneuver to allow for relative velocity, not to speak of having to pass close to *VP 2007* who would have been right in his track.

I can only guess that when Polly turned northeast he went between the two columns of merchant ships. He says he was fired on by two escorts to the north of him, but VPs *2011* and *1313* were not in action at this time and I suspect his adversaries to have been *2007* and the merchant ship *Monsun;* he was surprised not to be engaged by the main body but of course they were unarmed. *230's* situation was thoroughly unhealthy, wherever she was, but Polly had no thought but to find a torpedo target; though quite apart from the uncertain prospects of surviving long enough to do so, that was not at all easy. In his own words:

To start with I was concerned that I wasn't going to be able to find a target. It was a worrying thought going back without having fired, especially with Barnard waiting on the jetty; it wasn't that I was scared to face him, nor did I wish to ingratiate myself with him, I just didn't *want* to face him. He exerted just the right sort of pressure that we all needed.

Then the whole thing got a bit disorganized. I thought I was going along the north side between the escorts and the convoy, but I could only see the latter whenever a starshell was fired; I got the impression they were zigzagging. Then I saw this ship, I can still see her, and worked my way towards her by the light of starshell. As usually happened I fired when I wasn't brave enough to close any more and thought, that's my contribution. There was this great column of smoke and I presumed I had got a hit. Then the Motor Mechanic came up and said, "Look! The gear lever's come away in my hand." So I told him, "Go and bloody well stick it back."

Then I lined up on the next ship astern, fired the other fish, and tried to push off. The crew thought it hit but I wasn't looking because shells from this trawler were splashing on either side of us like those pictures of the Battle of Trafalgar. (Almost certainly *VP 1313* who reported a boat bursting out of the convoy at her—she claimed it as sunk.) So I ordered, "Make smoke," but just then my third officer, Basil Gerrard,

yelled, "They've got me!" And they had too, he said
it felt like a damned great welt with a hammer on the
side of his knee; but I said "Never mind about that,
get aft and make smoke," which he did. I can see him
hobbling away holding on to tubes and things; good
chap, County Court Judge now.

Thus did John Perkins exert pressure of just the right
sort. *MTB 230* came out of the jaws of death at 18 knots
on one engine without a single serious hit. But we are
left with the same question with which we started; where
had she been and whom had she torpedoed? It was not to
be expected in the circumstances that Polly's record should
contain courses, speeds and times; and when he says that
things got a bit disorganized that is the honest truth which
nobody, and certainly not I in his position, need be
ashamed to confess. So that whereas he thought he fired
torpedoes on a southeasterly course he might well have
been aiming to the northwest at the *Thule*. Or he might
have been to the north of the convoy as he thought and
hit her from the starboard side, the Germans being mistaken in thinking the torpedo came from port; but then
who was shooting at him if it was not VPs *2011* and *1313*,
and they say they were silent?

The issue is further confused by Polly's action report
stating that his targets were going from right to left, and
his torpedo analysis from left to right. That may have
been a typing error, but I hope I have explained clearly
enough that hitting with torpedoes, especially with only
one, depended on guessing the enemy's movement with
some accuracy. The last undoubted fact to be taken into
account is like a piece from another jigsaw, of an entirely
different pattern and with no slivers of color along the
edges to betray where it might fit: *VP 2003* on the port
beam of the convoy was hit by a torpedo and sank at once.

When I last saw *2003*, after firing my torpedoes in another direction, she was engaging me healthily so it must
have been one of Polly's which got her. If so the explanation might be that he missed his second merchant ship as
the result of setting his aim-off the wrong way, and the
torpedo ran on to hit *2003*. There I shall leave the enigma;
however he did it I think Polly also sank the *Thule* because
of the clearly visible explosion, and he deserved to for
refusing to be deterred by the initial ghastly and vulnerable

confusion and then taking the battle into the heart of the enemy force.

Leading Seaman Utting had steered *MGB 86* first east, then north and then northwest, completely encircling the convoy and never getting out of gun range from it. Phillips at the Oerlikon saw a big flash on *VP 2003* which must have been the torpedo hitting. *86* was hit, not seriously, but Able Seaman Gerard Murray received a nasty wound in the head; in return it was probably she who inflicted five casualties in *VP 1313*, and although Polly and I may not have been conscious of her diversion I have no doubt we benefited from it. At last Phillips arrived on the bridge and very properly made smoke and took *86* out of the action to the west. He thought he was pursued by three R-boats, though there were none such as we now know; whether what he saw were shadows cast by the starshell, or the images of merchant ships and escorts projected forward in his mind's eye cannot be established; but they were real enough to him, and it was a relief when the smoke developed and *86* was behind it.

There were thus two smoke screens fogging visibility to the west of the convoy and that, said Ted Smyth of *MGB 18*, was "providential." The crunch as *18* hit *82* was sickening to him, for he well knew that as water poured into the bow the stern would rise, lifting propellers and rudders clear of the sea to render the boat uncontrollable. But he also knew that if he could just get her to plane, the bow and the hole would hover above the water and she might be allowed perhaps ten minutes grace.

Ted leaned on his throttles accordingly and steered the only course open to him away from the confusion, southeast. At once *18* was alone, planing at full speed by courtesy of her Stoker who was grimly holding a severed petrol pipe with every muscle in his two hands; but brilliantly and constantly lit by starshell she was heading in precisely the wrong direction, for Ted suddenly realized that her salvation lay five miles to *seaward* of the enemy, the standard rendezvous for detached boats after an engagement. He turned west; but appalled at the time it was taking to circumnavigate the convoy he resolved on the last-ditch throw of bursting through; but there was no road that way, and when *2007* saw him coming under the starshell she gave him everything she had. Ted prudently turned back to the west; after all it would be better to abondon the boat, if it came to that, quietly in the dark than at the center of a ring of enemy guns.

Ted probed again a minute or two later but with the same result, and he resigned himself to steering west where at least the sea was clear of the enemy. He took a deep breath but it was not justified for he then saw himself to be closely followed by what must have been another three ghostly R-boats; as with 86 they seemed frighteningly substantial and 18's Gunner used five drums of Oerlikon to exorcise them.

The center engine failed, the bow drooped, the hole sipped water at every swell, and 18 entered the smoke screen—providentially. Two minutes later and in clear visibility again the bow plunged finally to gulp in the sea, and the propellers threshed impotently in air; MGB 18 was a wreck.

Not that Ted was the sort to fold his hands and invite the Lord to have mercy on their souls. Tall, dark and if not exactly handsome, vital with youth, and with Irish understanding and acceptance of conflict and challenge—a leader withal—who although he knew the situation to be without hope gave his men no chance to think so, but busied them cutting away the anchor and shifting every moveable object from forward to aft. Then—providentially —I turned up; and it is pleasant to know for certain that at least once in one's life one has been truly welcome.

234 was quite all right; 25 knots on two engines was fast enough to make her a difficult target and to place her quickly behind her own smoke, although we must have passed quite close to VP 2007. But I was so unhappy at having supposedly fired torpedoes to miss that instant death, if not welcome, could scarcely have felt worse. Now the scene had changed again and demanded fresh decisions; but having identified 18 and established her distressing circumstances these were not difficult. In my experience the nadirs of life derive not so much from a situation's intrinsic awfulness as the dilemma which tears one in deciding what to do about it; once that is settled the mind clears and is more at ease, however strenuous the resultant exertions. 18 could either be towed, in which case we would tow her; or not, when we should take off the crew and sink her. The choices were straightforward, and there was no need to rush the decision for were we not safely astern of the enemy who was plodding his way to

Germany and leaving us farther behind with every minute that passed?

No, we were not. I am conscious, in so often referring to what may be thought the minor technical question of whether the convoy was steering this way or that, of introducing a note of tedium into what should be a fast-moving narrative; but I cannot avoid calling attention to our misapprehension just once more. For several minutes that should have been accounted precious, but slipped by without concern, Ted tried to make *18* go. The propeller tips were in water some of the time and pushed her along at about five knots; but with the rudders mostly in air and every wave slopping over the forecastle she made fierce lunges in every direction between north and south, while trying to steer west. Clearly there was no future that way, and the next thing to try was a stern-first tow.

Convoy *348* resumed its normal speed and pressed on southwestwards, leaving the rear escort, *2008*, to search for survivors from the *Thule* and *2003;* 31 men were lost from the two ships. That would have left me unmoved at the time had I known it but now concerns me, quite illogically; and yet not entirely so for in naval warfare the aim was to sink ships, and if the crews survived, good luck to them. *2003* had been a Belgian steam Pilot Vessel of 320 tons and carried the Flotilla Medical Officer. As one has come from those of his calling, the doctor carefully tended two men previously wounded by our gunboats, ensured they were looked after when the ship sank, and was then lost himself. Less gallant but just as tragic, the cook of the SS *Narvik* "jumped overboard in a fit of sudden madness when he saw the *Thule* sink." But we could not imagine such humanity by the enemy, who remained for us an unreal mixture of formidable menace and the object of scorn; nor would there have been much profit in doing so, for human and indeed honorable as he was, he was fighting for an evil cause and had to be beaten. To me as leader however an awareness of the enemy's humanity was essential, so that I could exploit it.

While preparing to tow *18* I was only concerned with the enemy to the extent of routine sweeps of the horizon against the unexpected; but the German Senior Officer in *VP 2011*, who of course endowed us with the same sinister attributes, was still apprehensive. He had no means of knowing that the attack was over and was therefore not sur-

prised to hear engine noises right ahead of him; he ordered
a group of starshell to be fired and waited tensely for what
they would reveal. It was artificial smoke; what should
he do? It is rarely wise for an escort to leave her convoy
unguarded to chase an ephemeral enemy; but to let the
merchant ships plunge through the smoke might well be
to deliver them into a carefully prepared ambush. He
decided to be first through himself and increased to the
full speed of his 250-ton steam trawler.

Starshell bursting overhead triggered an instant change
in the nature of our activities and their tempo; *18* must be
abandoned and destroyed without a moment's delay. Ted
stopped and I ran alongside; but the swell which had
been no handicap to boats on their own would have
crashed them against each other without very careful han-
dling, and serious damage to *234* was grim to contemplate.
I therefore just allowed the hulls to touch, in the expectation that 12 fit young sailors would leap as one and then
we should be away. Not so; they were surprisingly reluctant to leave their stricken ship, perhaps fulfilling a contemporary misquote, "If you can keep your head when all
about you are losing theirs, perhaps you just don't understand the situation." We had only a few men when the
boats drifted apart for the first time; so half astern, more
starshell, and alongside again with a nasty sounding
crunch which splintered the rubbing strake. Still not every-

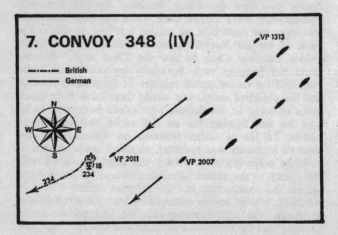

7. CONVOY 348 (IV)

VP 1313

—·—·— British
———— German

N
W ✦ E
S

18
234

234

VP 2011   VP 2007

one jumped however and Saunders reminds me that I became, not to put too fine a point on it, a little testy both at their slowness and my own inadequacy in not being able to hold *234* in position as I was desperately trying to do; a constant jangle of telegraph orders was manfully responded to by Clarke and Gilbert on the wing engines but she would not hold still.

Yet a third run and still the job was not complete; furthermore there was no sign of Ted Smyth, though that should not have been surprising as he would certainly be the last to leave and then only when he had ensured his boat's destruction. It is curious to have to record that no seacocks large enough to sink the boat were fitted, perhaps because such a need for a ship of the Royal Navy was unthinkable and had in consequence not been thought of. *18* had to be set on fire, and that was done by first driving a short length of pipe with a chisel edge through the engine room bulkhead and into the petrol tank beyond. The Motor Mechanic hammered away with what Ted thought was singularly inappropriate verve and cheerfulness, and fuel for the pyre duly gushed; then he was dismissed and made the jump to *234* safely.

Ted did a quick mental check; confidential books mustered and handed across. IFF (a new electronic gadget which did not work but was nevertheless highly secret) destroyed; right! He took his Verey pistol, cocked it, and without giving himself a moment to think better of his resolution, fired the blazing firework into the fuming, volatile mass below.

I suppose that was the most gallant act I have ever witnessed at close quarters for Ted knew, as we all did, how Chris Dreyer had lifted off after doing precisely the same thing. So gallant was it that the first thought to flit through both Alan's and my minds was, why does he have to do it with us so close? to be stifled instantly as scurvily unworthy. The vapor burned with a windy roar and a column of flame and sparks from the hatch, but it did not explode. Ted shook himself, decided he was still in one piece and on deck, and dashed for the side; but *234* had been tossed away.

Why we had no line across I cannot remember, probably because each time we ran in I expected it to be the last; but I should have passed one. However desperate the need, one cannot make a boat go sideways. While I was backing away, Cuthbert of all people, the Motor Mechanic who had no center engine to control, came on deck to see what all the goings-on were about; what he saw were four craft approaching, and delivered himself of the comfortable words,

"Ah, here come the gunboats to give us a hand."

"Good," I grunted, and looked. There were indeed four small shapes. Four? But there were only four gunboats in all and one was already with us. Oh no!

No niceties of ship-handling now as I thrust *234* into *18*'s side for the last time. Ted helped the last young seaman across and then jumped himself; he doubtless thought his troubles were over, but they were just beginning. The smoke had drifted away, and the illusion of four small craft approaching was created by the merchant ships in the middle distance together with *VP 2011* very close indeed, so that all appeared to be the same size. However the difference between illusion and reality was immaterial for *2011* alone had enough guns for four, ranging from 88mm, through 37mm, 20mm and innumerable machine guns, and she gave us the lot. We had none, and only two engines; moreover we were brilliantly lit both by *18*'s fire which leaped and flared, and by a succession of starshell overhead. Moreover again we were heading with the enemy fine on our port bow, our course being dictated by the direction *18* was lying.

Both *2011* and I assessed the range as 100 yards, closing, and although her opening rounds were high I saw no hope. At first that realization was somewhat academic because I still had a decision to make. The turn away must be achieved by using one engine astern, because to go full ahead and hard over would take us right up to the enemy, our turning circle being so wide; for technical reasons the boat would turn more quickly to port than to starboard, and although there was farther to go that way I decided instinctively to do it.

There was nothing more to do than be afraid, and I was. The noise was deafening and cacophonous, numbing but not anaesthetizing me. Infinitely slowly *234* slewed and moved into the direct line between *2011* and the blazing *18*, the point of greatest vulnerability, and her deck was black with the prone forms of both crews pressing them-

selves downward like thwarted burrowing animals. No
one moved but Jim Saunders, and he barely for he had
only to hold the wheel to port and watch the compass
card's leisurely swing from east through eastnortheast,
northeast, nor'nor'east. Floating placidly in its bath of
alcohol it sneered pitilessly, "I can't go any faster and
you won't make it, you won't, you won't. . . ." Jim was
steady as a rock and I clasped his shoulder, as much to
gain comfort as to bestow it.

That moment of certain death was real, logical, ordinary. The boat looked the same as ever, so did the sea;
so even did the tracer which as I had intended we had
learned to live with, and to such an extent that I now
had to recollect that we could also die with it. There was
no exaltation, no philosophical acceptance, no urge to
pray, no sense of occasion; on the contrary I, the great
ego and center of the universe, had become crushingly
immaterial; so long as I could do nothing to save the other
wretches, and I could not, I just did not matter a damn.
Being able to think, and urged perhaps by upbringing,
I at least resolved not to let it be said that I had yelped
or tried to run away on the off-chance that someone would
be left to say it, particularly as neither would make the
least difference; but internally, gripping animal terror
mastered me.

We had not yet been hit, I suspect because *2011*'s gunners had overestimated the range and were blinded by
their own tracer of which they used too much for accurate
shooting; but I could tell we soon should be from the
myriad lines of colored light which formed a painted
ceiling just above our heads, for it was descending. Then
there was a new noise, a gun of course because guns were
our world, but different, sharper and nearer. It was our
own, by God! Pop—pop—pop—pop, a feeble contribution
to the din indeed but the stream of tracer going away from
us, that was marvellous. For the second time I had forgotten Petty Officer Ross but never, never will I do so
again for he was a man among men who gave us back our
lives. His point of aim was marked precisely by half a
dozen gunflashes and he made the most of it, shooting to
hit with concentrated, unflurried skill. At once; at once,
I say, the ceiling of light rose and we were no longer the
apex of a cone, for the gunners were momentarily shocked

and their hands wavered. Ross wounded three of her men
with that one little weapon.

"Full ahead port"; we still had farther to turn but would
no longer close the enemy by getting the boat moving.
Resurgence of hope was like blood to a frozen limb—hell,
for to be hit now would be far worse than it would have
been ten seconds earlier; but there were things to do as
the propellers bit, the bow rose, and cheeks were fanned
with a breath of life.

"Make smoke," I ordered for the third time, and Ted
Smyth, the nearest and most alert, dashed aft to do it.
But the canister was empty, and I knew I must get behind
18 who was better than a smoke screen and a blinding
distraction too. That would not take too long, but even
now I realized that the enemy's guns were shifting one by
one to her; incredulous belief replaced agonized hope; I
told Saunders, "I think we'll make it," and drew a gulp
of free, fresh air. "Cease firing," I passed the word to
Ross. There was no more need to draw attention to ourselves; far better to withdraw in the shadow and let the
moth fly into the candle flame.

18 took a terrible pounding, and her flames soared and
twisted ever higher so that Ted and I had no qualms about
leaving her. Bodies stirred and rose creaking from our
deck—all of them, every single one.

"Carry on living—I mean smoking."

Commander Barnard wrote, pleased with the conceit,
" '*Labore est Orare*'* is the motto of HMS *Mantis*, and
I have established that Lieutenant Dickens did both." He
was wrong though, for real praying was not my line; but
when I rang my mother she answered the phone before
I spoke, with:

"It was frightful, wasn't it?"

"Well yes, it was a bit dicey," I agreed, "but how did
you guess?"

"It happened at ten past twelve, didn't it?"

"I really don't know, I'll have to ask Alan."

"And five minutes later all was peace?"

"Mmm."

"Do you know what happened during those five minutes?"

---

*To work is to pray.

"What are you getting at, Ma? I don't suppose I'll ever forget."

"I prayed as I've never prayed before, and I *knew* my prayer was answered."

Is that extrasensory perception and theological meat a bit too strong perhaps? Well, take it or leave it; but it did happen at ten past twelve.

VII

SOFTLY CATCH MONKEY

"Little ship saves crew under Nazis' nose," ran the head-lines; and it seemed that the public appeal rating of a rescue under fire was greater than a sinking, so that what I knew to have been a thoroughly ill-managed fiasco was presented as an heroic triumph; and Polly Perkins, whose purposeful gallantry had been the only real redeeming feature, received no mention. Publicity is a light so bright that it will always distort to some extent and we were very young and artless to be exposed to its glare; but the con-gratulations which followed were worse for the soul, since they were often overdone so as to express the deep grati-tude of the noncombatant to the fighting man on whom he or she absolutely depended.

Vanity was not wholly to be resisted, but I tried feebly to do so and felt uncomfortable in consequence. One of my most moving letters was from the father of one of *18*'s young sailors who sent me a smoker's knife which he said was a small token of his appreciation, but which to me was a huge one, and then went on, "God chose you as an instrument through which our son might be saved." An unbidden flash of undisciplined thought floored me with a vivid glimpse of my own elemental nastiness, for it said, "God forsooth! *I* did it." I bit my lip, but the mov-ing finger had writ and the blasphemy was on the record. A little good was done however; for while not being greatly impressed with the conventional idea of God I was forced to acknowledge the vital involvement of every-one else in the team, not to speak of the real heroes, Ross and Ted Smyth; and there was also a niggling suspicion that what I had taken for an astonishing run of luck in our activities so far might well demand a more complex expla-nation than that, and involve factors not all of which were readily comprehensible.

Authority was not so easily impressed by glamor and Polly was accorded due acknowledgment for his great effort. *230*'s arrival in harbor was something of a triumph, verisimilitude being added to her story after a quick aside by Polly to Basil Gerrard, whose wounded knee was not troubling him excessively, "You might as well look as though you're hurt." Even so Polly was gently chided for firing single torpedoes, which was fair to some extent for it was obviously better to make sure of one target than miss two. The standard doctrine was "Never fire torpedoes in penny numbers," yet we were torn just the same, being constantly told that torpedoes were in short supply and must on no account be wasted.

Ted Smyth was made to undergo the indignity and implied criticism of a Board of Enquiry into the loss of *MGB 18* by collision; and such was the pomposity and inexperience of the officers concerned that a serious view was almost taken. C-in-C Nore to his credit however quashed such nonsense, perceiving that Ted was a magnificent fighting sailor who should be given another boat and sent straight back into the fray.

Seeking to turn away wrath with a soft answer I said I was very sorry to have aimed my torpedoes the wrong way, and Authority replied coolly that it was sorry too. It also questioned my five minutes delay in breaking up the formation and was right to do so; but I thought it was off the beam in suggesting that there was plenty of time to withdraw and reorganize after being surprised, during which the enemy's course might have been discovered for certain. I could not believe that an enemy who was both alert and composed would be more vulnerable than one in the early stages of bewilderment, however well-organized we too might have become; and I comforted myself that Nelson did not either, for he had said, "Delay favors the defense more than the offense. Time is precious and every hour makes more resistance; strike quick and home." Being a well-disciplined officer however, I determined to bear the idea in mind.

In trying to decide what we ought to do next I was clear enough that we must never lose sight of the ideal of firing torpedoes without the enemy even knowing we were there. Was the gunboat tactic played out perhaps? It was hard to determine, for our recent failure to make it work could be ascribed mainly to our own incompetence, though our lack

of voice-radio for use when boats were separated was a
serious handicap. I could not see how two MTBs alone
could have overtaken the enemy on noisy main engines
and then attacked him with the least hope of success. Perhaps something could be worked out if more MTBs were to
be included in the force, but I was realistic enough to know
that any scheme conditional on that would be doomed, for
the simple reason that half the boats must be expected to
break down before reaching the enemy coast. Appalling
as was the admission, I derived if not comfort, an easement
from bitter frustration and humiliation by treating it as
a planning assumption and tactical factor.

The most important consideration however was the unknown one of what the enemy was thinking, and my
Captains and I discussed this a great deal. How had these
two battles appeared to him and had he realized we were
using gunboats? All we had to go on were Lord Haw-Haw's
news bulletins, which we discounted as blatant propaganda
for had he not claimed four of our boats as certainly sunk
and two more probably, while admitting only the loss of a
patrol boat whereas Polly knew he had hit a merchant
ship? We should have been astonished to learn that the
German Senior Officer really did think his team had sunk
four of us, and that his claim was confirmed by 5th Sicherungsdivision, the shore authority responsible for our section of the Dutch coast. Another of his misapprehensions
was the supposed sighting of at least fifteen torpedo tracks,
but it is clear now, as it could not be then, that although
the enemy was just as confused by our activities as we had
been about his, he did suspect that we were using gunboats
and guessed the reason for doing so.

On the other hand an assessment by the German Head-
quarters of the state of affairs off the coast and what ought
to be done about it was realistic and logical. We should
have been flattered to know that our attacks had caused
grave concern, to the extent that consideration was even
given to sailing the convoys by day and risking air attack
as a lesser evil. Failing that it was absolutely necessary to
strengthen escorts with craft more effective in combating
us than armed trawlers, and a passionate plea was made
for the 9th R-boat Flotilla to be brought up to strength
and stationed permanently in the area. R-boats could not
be built by pleas however; but what could be done was to
reorganize the 1st Minesweeping Flotilla and employ it

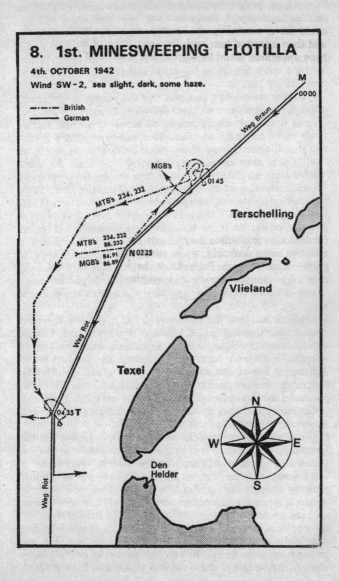

8. 1st. MINESWEEPING FLOTILLA

4th. OCTOBER 1942

Wind SW - 2, sea slight, dark, some haze.

-·-·- British
——— German

M
00 00

Weg Braun

MGB's

01 45

MTB's 234, 232

Terschelling

MTB's 234, 232
       88, 233

MGB's 84, 91
       86, 89

N 0225

Vlieland

Weg Rot

Texel

04 35 T

Weg Rot

Den Helder

N
W   E
S

against us, both on patrol and as convoy escorts. That, in
my present view, was likely to be more effective still for
the "M" Class Minesweeper was a formidable warship. Of
600 tons but shallow draft, she had a top speed of 16 knots
and mounted two 105mm, two 37mm and eight 20mm
guns; I already had an uneasy question mark in my mind
concerning her.

All that we could guess was that the enemy might react,
though not how, and we must therefore be alert for change.
While it was obviously wrong to repeat the same tactics
over and over again, our last effort had been such a botch-
up that it cannot have given much away and we might as
well try it once more, only properly this time. So three
nights later we did, and ran slap into the 1st Minesweeping
Flotilla who saw us off, because they played the game more
properly than we did. Moreover their leader Korvettenkapitän Bergelt not only had us by the short hairs, but being a
regular officer of some seniority he also wrote his report
graphically and accurately, so that for once I can tell a
story in which each side's actions accord with the other's. It
will not be long, for indecisive battles make dull reading,
but important lessons were learned which helped to shape
more effective tactics and signalled the end of the gunboat
era.

Failure was not the gunboats' fault, they were splendid
under their dashing leader Lindsay Thompson, and neither
could breakdowns be used as an excuse, for Commander
Barnard's dynamic team of engineers really seemed to be
getting on top of our reluctant machinery, and eight boats,
including Jamie's thank heavens, ran faultlessly all night.
Indeed I am bold enough to say it was nobody's fault, not
even mine, and that it was the 1st Flotilla's alertness and
efficiency which kept them out of trouble.

Bergelt's orders were to sail from Den Helder in the
evening and sweep Weg Rot and Weg Braun as far as
Point "M" against MTBs; then he was to return, but it
also seems that he was to join a late arriving westbound
convoy though how and when is not clear. We were to
begin a strange relationship with his flotilla, whose nature
is hard to define; it was not love/hate for neither emotion
was present, and it is more than reasonable to ask how one
can have a relationship at all without knowing that the
other party even exists. But though we could only describe
him as "the enemy" the tie was real; we acted, he reacted,

we tried a double bluff and so on. Competition between us was vigorous and grim; and now, long afterwards, when I discover that "the enemy" usually meant the 1st Mine-sweeping Flotilla or a couple of other constantly recurring units I find myself dearly wanting to meet those men and relive with them an intense and intimate relationship which I share with no others.

Bergelt's leader was *M 8* and with him in a diamond formation—clever because three ships' guns would bear against an attack from any quarter—*M 4* (Franz), *M 7* (von Treufels) and *M 20* (Hardamm). The unit reached Point "M" at midnight, turned, and steered southwest down Weg Braun at nine knots with ships' companies at action stations and ready to fire starshell the instant anything was heard or seen. We left harbor with orders to attack a westbound convoy spotted earlier by the Air Force, and aimed as usual for "N" Buoy. This time we must have sighted the right one, or we should not have met Bergelt, and having moved ten miles northeast to what seemed for some reason I cannot remember a likely spot, stopped, alert. The Germans described the place accurately as "British Ambush Position RB 10," and my suspicion grows that they knew considerably more about our organization than we did of theirs. An hour and a half later, at 0142, there they were; four large shapes two miles to landward and we were already on their beam.

The sea was slight and the sky clear, but visibility at sea level was hazy and, although the half-moon was an hour old beyond the enemy, we only saw him indistinctly; it was reasonable to assure him to be part of a convoy. But oh what gall to realize that we could not hope to close silently on auxiliaries without falling so far astern in the process that our torpedoes would be impotent. There was nothing for it but to use the gunboats and I told Lindsay Thompson to go for the enemy's van initially, intending myself to gain bearing behind his cover and turn in to attack from the present, seaward side when the moment should seem propitious.

There was muddle to start with as the boats were lying higgledy-piggledy having been stopped for a considerable time. That was not quite so inefficient as it sounds, at least for the gunboats who would have to use unsilenced main engines to point themselves, but afterwards I made it doctrine that my boats were always to remain in perfect station

when stopped. But whatever we did would really have made
no difference, for the moment our engines started the first
starshell barked and we were all, torpedo-boats and gunboats alike, in a perpetual limelight which had indeed a
tinge of that color. From then on Bergelt saw us clearly
whatever we did, and never again did I see him.

We saw his shell splashes though, and I knew 4-inch
when I saw it for we had had them in the *Cotswold;* but
while taking some comfort from my failure to hit E-boats
in those days it was pointless now to stay there offering
a target, and I led the MTBs away in a circle to starboard.
The gunboats were engaging fiercely on the enemy's seaward bow, so I crossed under his stern to try an approach
from inshore. Jamie thought he saw an opening and went
for it, and then John Weeden in *88* did the same; but
neither they nor I, nor *232* (Charley Chaffey) who had
stayed with me, were allowed any chance of success, or
even a glimpse of what we were up against, for starshell and
gunnery met us everywhere. I had no doubt that the enemy
was a convoy, heavily escorted by major warships, and
decided quite coolly if I may be believed, and truly I was
no more frightened than usual, that to press a torpedo attack home against this scale of opposition from an enemy
I could not even see would not only be foolhardy but
wrong.

We went on probing for half an hour and then, suddenly, the battle ceased and darkness was upon the face of
the deep. Good, I thought, I know where the enemy is
because he's only just stopped his firework display, in we
go! But he just was not there; the frustration was terrible,
but screw my eyes into the void as I would not a clue was
vouchsafed. My night vision had of course been thoroughly destroyed and no doubt I had lost more bearing than I
thought. All right then; at least I knew the enemy to be
steering southwest so why don't we do as the C-in-C advocated and withdraw, reorganize and try again much later
when the enemy might think all was over and we should
know precisely what we were about? The time was only
0230 and four hours remained until twilight, the first port
for which the enemy might be bound was Den Helder 20
miles on, so let's use our speed and wait for him there.

"Course west, 28 knots." It was of course necessary to
make an offing to seaward before turning south, and I can
only presume I did not go faster for fear of upsetting our

delicate engines. On the way I tried some W/T signalling
and that revealed a weakness, certainly of our equipment
but also, I strongly suspected, of our telegraphists' training too. Not that my Churcher was at fault; he was an extremely competent Leading Telegraphist and had no trouble clearing my first message to the C-in-C who would, I
hoped, be concerned to learn how we had fared after our
initial enemy report: "Convoy heavily escorted, attack not
yet completed."

But when Churcher tried to raise MTBs 233, 88 and the
gunboats in order to whip them on to the new line, he was
met by an impermeable wall of silence. I was greatly dis-
pleased, in two stages as had become the usual sequence;
that is, beginning with everybody else and ending with myself; for if they were inefficient it was my fault for not having trained them better, and I realized that I had not given
as much attention to this matter as clearly I should have
done. Life as Senior Officer was often rather disappoint-
ing; as a junior I had envied the captain who could apparently do no wrong, while being free to urge others to the
highest endeavor with singular lack of inhibition; but now
every mistake that anyone made was evidently my fault
which seemed unfair, though it was not. If in consequence
of that disturbing truth a captain's tongue seems sometimes
to have a cutting edge, it may—perhaps—be ascribed to
self-criticism and is therefore—conceivably—morally all
right. Regular and frequent exercises would be instituted
tomorrow, but tonight 234 and 232 pressed on alone.

My heart was not really in the project which seemed too
long a shot with too many unknowns. Navigationally, our
constantly varying courses and speeds in action having
been quite unrecordable our point of departure was uncertain, as was our destination for we could only guess
where the enemy's swept channel might run. It occurs to
me now that our Intelligence might with advantage have
pin-pointed these channels for us, for we know that the
E-boats were supplied with comprehensive charts of the
British network; but I have to admit yet again, with a
sigh, that it is not for me to blame them unless I, as a
potential beneficiary of the information, had stated the
need and I cannot remember having done so.

In reconstructing our detour from Alan's notebook I am
surprised to find that after making some miles of southing I
reapproached the enemy's track slantwise at 12 knots, in-

stead of going boldly the whole distance to seaward and
then coming in at right angles on auxiliaries. No doubt I
had a reason which might have been that I was scared of
miscalculating the enemy's movement and of again finding myself abeam or astern of him; the gradual approach
was more likely to result in an interception but would not
offer so good an ambush. But what chance was there of
Bergelt allowing himself to be ambushed knowing us to
be about? To my mind at the time very little, but I had not
yet begun to think of my enemy as a man with weaknesses
just as I had. What more likely after a thoroughly successful defense in which the cowardly British had been routed,
than to call for a nice hot cup of ersatz coffee and a glow
of self-congratulatory euphoria to allow eyelids to droop
ever so slightly at the time of night when life is anyway at
its lowest ebb?

The lesson to be learned from my half-hearted effort is
that it is always worth having a go, for it very nearly came
off. Through no fault of Alan's we crossed the enemy's bow
and stopped a mile or so inshore of his track, which would
have been fine had it not been for the moon, higher now
and in a dead-straight line from him to us. He could not
but see us before we saw him and the accustomed assault
and battery began again; largely for form's sake I spent
20 minutes poking my nose in from various angles to absolutely no purpose and then, since daylight approached with
all its terrors for us marauders of stealth and darkness,
pushed off disconsolately for home. The 1st Flotilla were
already at their own front door and stepped inside for a
cozy breakfast, more than satisfied with the night's work
although the gunboats had, very creditably, wounded two
men. But wait, Herrn Bergelt, Franz, von Treufels and
Hardamm, we shall meet again.

The main result of this skirmish was to purge our minds
of misconceptions, and we saw clearly a step into the future.
Our three recent encounters had been, as Macbeth had it,
"full of sound and fury," the last certainly signifying nothing; and it now occurred to us to question Isaiah's dictum
that "every battle of the warrior is with confused noise."
Since it was we who made the noise it might be open to
us not to do so; surprise was of the essence as we had always known in theory, and had now proved in practice. We
had known too how desirable, not to say marvellous, it
would be for the main engines to be silenced, but we

NIGHT ACTION 123

needed this last battle to show us precisely why. We could not have expected a better initial interception, yet the torpedo's limitations demanded that we achieve a firing position near the enemy's beam, and being initially astern of that we had to make a noise in order to overtake because at six knots on auxiliaries we might have been standing still. With a flash of revelation I realized that to be silent at even moderate speed would improve our chances enormously by offering scope for variety in tactics. The gunboats' noisy diversions would surely become less important and might even prove dispensable.

I pressed the need to Barnard, and he nobly pitched into the crusade with inspired zeal and a complete absence of hierarchical humility. Experiments were in train with several forms of silencer, though hardly with that crash, drop-everything-else urgency which our need now demanded. The most promising seemed to be a sort of dustbin affair called a "Dumbflow." Without wishing to be too technical, without indeed wishing to be technical at all, it seemed that exhaust noise was caused by the hot, high-pressure gases expanding into the atmosphere, which they did like balloons bursting at the rate of 600 a second. Well now, I have already explained how the cylinders were cooled with distilled water when there was any, and of course that became very hot too and had to be cooled in its turn, in a typically complicated cycle beloved of engineers, by a constant flow of sea water. What more logical then than to whirl both water and hot gases round and round the dust-bin until the gases, being cooled, contracted to near atmospheric pressure and emerged with but a sibilant murmur?

The engineers however having thus brilliantly conceived, forebore to give birth because they had fearful misgivings that back-pressure might at best reduce the engines' performance and at worst do serious damage. That was where the non-technical user had a key role to play, for I knew we needed the thing so badly that it was well worth blowing up an engine to prove it would not work, if there was the slightest hope that it would; and as for a reduction in performance, surely that could be simply overcome by fitting a means of bypassing the dumbflows in emergency? We said so, Barnard and I, importunately and forcefully; the work went forward amain and eventually succeeded beyond our softest, whispering dreams; though not of course before the

next battle, even though I passed some of the interval enjoying my first leave since we became operational.

All of us from *234* found that leave to be extremely
pleasant. Fêted and pampered we revelled in what we took
for our just deserts, not considering that the homage stem-
med much more from the Navy's Public Relations organization than from what little we had actually done. "Everyone wanted to buy me a beer," Saunders told me; "and
when we got into the papers my Mum would say, 'Oh dear
my boy's been in action again with that Peter Dickens.'"
It was certainly delightful to have a Mum to fuss over
one for she gave one reassurance, security and a sense of
purpose; so long as she did not become weepy and sentimental for that would make one guiltily uneasy if one
could not respond with the same intensity of emotion. But
mine only did that once or twice when a saint would have
cried out, and since I followed suit spontaneously all was
well; how she managed to discipline herself the rest of the
time beats me.

Meeting one's friends and relations was a surprisingly
good correction to cockiness, for eulogies could not be
stretched beyond the first five minutes and then everyone
else's lives had to have a look in. All were hard, with
shortages and restrictions and no glamor to compensate,
some were downright dangerous and not a soul but worked
overtime and then a bit longer to keep the nation alive and
fighting. I soon realized how lucky I was to have my job,
and was humbled to feel that I and my like were the spear-
point towards which countless, trusting millions thrust their
immense efforts. We could fail, and must not.

I peered out of the overcrowded train in order to gauge
the wind strength and determine whether we need go to sea
that night, and remarkably difficult it was to catch a bare
twig's movement through the smoky windows. Screwed-
up tension returned with the diminishing distance to
Lowestoft, yet I wanted to get moving again; we had been
granted all the training it was reasonable to expect and
must now use it to pull off a real success and contribute
something positive to the war effort. But it was hard facing
the grim music again. The cause was not simply fear, but
apprehension of the total effort needed to combat an enemy
just as strong, just as brave and just as intelligent as oneself; an effort which, far from being merely concentrated
at the moment of battle, demanded constant concern for

training, morale, material efficiency, and peering anxiously into the unknown in the field of tactics. Still, one must make the effort or die unhappy.

Not that I was prepared for death or reconciled to it, and I saw no merit in myself or anyone dying in this minor campaign of attrition. Indeed I had emphasized in my report of the last action that it was fruitless and suicidal to press home a torpedo attack against such opposition, and was most relieved when both Barnard and the C-in-C ungrudgingly endorsed my view and lack of action. Satisfactory as it was to have got the point accepted I then saw that it would add to my responsibility, for the different degree of acceptable risk in each situation would now have to be assessed, and the danger of letting caution slide into cowardice was almost more terrifying than the enemy's guns.

Go to! Without main engine silencers it might not seem that we had much scope for a change in tactics, but all of us, my captains, Barnard and I, were clear that a change there must be for its own sake; noise was anathema, silence golden. Furthermore we thought we knew two things about the enemy; one was that he had reinforced his convoy escorts so that once alerted there would be less chance of our penetrating his screen; and secondly that in each of our three encounters he had heard us before seeing us and would expect to do so again.

Both these assumptions were right, even though the first was based on the false premise that last time we had been up against a convoy. Fifth Sicherungsdivision had also changed the 1st Minesweeping Flotilla's orders from joining convoys as they entered the area, to doing so at latest before dark, and only to patrol independently on nights when there was no convoy. So it came about that Convoy 1974 of about eight merchant ships sailed from The Hook for Germany at 0900 on November 9, 1942 with a through escort of VPs 1109, 806, 808 and 2008, augmented by M 8 with Bergelt embarked, M 4 and M 7, and also an escort destroyer (Flottenbegleiter), F 4, of comparable fighting effectiveness with one of our Hunt Class. That was a formidable change from our last convoy.

Our start was depressing for the boats were up to their old tricks again; 234 did not leave harbor at all and 232 and 88 broke down on the way, leaving me with only Jamie Fraser in 233 and David Felce's 83. I was not too

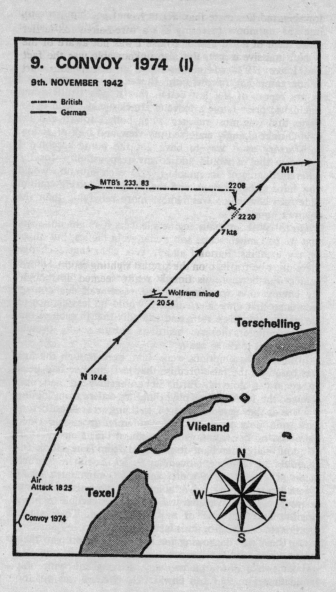

9. CONVOY 1974 (I)

9th. NOVEMBER 1942

‑‑‑‑‑ British
——— German

MTB's 233, 83

2208

2220

7 kts

M1

Wolfram mined
2054

Terschelling

N 1944

Vlieland

Air
Attack 1825

Texel

Convoy 1974

N
W   E
S

downhearted however; that would have been difficult with Jamie at my elbow quivering like a wire-haired fox-terrier at the scent of a rat, and of course I was not aware of the enemy's massive escort. But also unknowable was the fact that Convoy 1974 was getting off to an inauspicious start and Bergelt too had every reason not to feel altogether happy.

A Coastal Command patrol had spotted the convoy at two in the afternoon and at 1825 there had been a bombing attack by four aircraft, though no hits resulted. At 2054 however all the ships were jolted by a heavy explosion as the steamer *Wolfram* hit a mine; she was well inside the swept channel, as Bergelt was careful to point out to his potentially critical superiors, but her degaussing equipment had recently failed. Her engines stopped instantly and Bergelt reduced the convoy's speed to five knots while the situation cleared, but the *Wolfram* was in no state to continue and *VP 806* was left behind to look after her. Later she sank.

We had been briefed on the aircraft sighting report before leaving harbor, and this time it really seemed as though we should be able to bypass the convoy well to seaward and come in quietly ahead of it. *233*'s First Lieutenant and Navigator being General Lee I had thought it unnecessary to take Alan as I usually did when riding in someone else's boat, and I was justified as General did the job superbly.

I should dearly like to know whether Bergelt was apprehensive about MTB attack that night; knowing the convoy to have been reported he might well have been, and if he had tried to put himself in my mind and doodled on the chart with a few rough calculations derived from such data as the time of evening twilight, our cruising speed and radius of action, and of course his own intended movement, he should have been able to deduce that his time of greatest danger was quite a short period between about 2200 and midnight. Whether he thought on these lines I shall probably never know because, sadly, he died after the war; but I rather doubt it as I cannot honestly give his escorts credit for being keenly alert, and also because he placed them in a curiously ineffective formation, the reason for which he did not record.

Having discarded our lame ducks we bumbled over without incident and, as I can now assure General, almost exactly along his intended track. Arriving at the point where silence was to begin we cut main engines, but bless my soul the noise continued. Uncertain of myself I naturally swore at someone else, David Felce of *83*, but unfairly as his boat was as quiet as a mouse. Then I thought, crikey we're being chased by E-boats; but the quality of sound was not quite right for that, and there was nothing to be seen although the night was fine, calm and clear. When in doubt look upwards however, and there was the explanation; 213 beautiful Lancasters droned overhead in an unbroken stream on their way to bomb Hamburg, and now looking more intently in the right direction we could see the occasional spark from an exhaust. Bless the dear brave boys! and if ever a hint of criticism of Bomber Command's strategic policy had escaped me, which it had, I took it all back that night; though in all honesty I must admit that it still returns to bother me sometimes.

Lancaster Mk. I

Only seven minutes after turning south, and having made good less than a mile (because one of *83*'s auxiliaries did in fact make a clattering noise in its silencer so that I could now swear at David justly and tell him to switch it off), there was the enemy. The bombers were *deus ex machina* in very sooth, for without them we must certainly have been heard; we had not gone far enough to seaward through ignorance of where the enemy channels lay, better intelligence would have helped us to plan our approach more expediently. As it was the blurred outlines ahead sharpened until the whole concourse stood out like do-it-yourself models, seeing no evil, speaking no evil and thanks to divine intervention hearing no evil; and best of all we were on their bow. The appropriate word was "classic" and everybody, in voices hushed with awe, used it.

We pointed straight at the leading ship, offering our narrowest silhouettes; by doing so we should lose bearing, but that was all right because I could soon see clearly that the convoy was spearheaded by a solid phalanx of warships which we should have to let pass anyway. *F 4* led; on her quarters were at least two "M" Class minesweepers which there was no difficulty identifying this time, and only then came the leading pair of merchant ships. These would have to be our targets if we were seen early; but sweeping aft with my glasses along the not very tidy lines I saw a couple of gaps followed by three ships huddled together, overlapping and asking for it; they had no escorts anywhere near them; "We'll go for them," I said.

There was however no going for any ship that was not directly in our path. Although both we and the enemy were crawling, the combined speed of approach was higher than that of either and we should soon be so close to the leading escorts, if indeed we were not already, that any alteration of course would expose our beams and give us away. The next logical step in this train of thought was uncomfortable; if we did not approach quite close to those bristling batteries we should not later be able to reach effective torpedo range of the merchant ships, so in order to attack at all I must put us in a posture with absolutely no options. We should be stopped within hitting range of the guns and pointing toward them, our auxiliaries would be clutched in, and even if our main engines were substituted in the shortest possible time our wide turning circle of 600 yards would take us even closer.

I could easily have thought of that point when deciding on the silent, unobserved attack, and perhaps I did to some extent but the visual presentation now made a considerably more vivid impact. We drew ever nearer and I watched those ships for signs of excitement, putting myself behind their Zeiss binoculars and trying to forecast the moment when they must see us. Before it came I waved to David and we stopped, using an occasional touch on the engines to keep our bows pointing at the enemy. We could no longer move in any direction, the die was cast, the boats burned. For heaven's sake think of a better metaphor than that, I thought.

"Note the time, General."

"2200, sir."

The range I guessed at between 1,000 and 1,500 yards,

and having ceased closing except for the small rate created
by the enemy's movement, for we were still before his
beam, I began to feel more hopeful because human nature
is assiduous in looking out ahead and has to be forced to
glance in other directions. Whether Jamie could contain
himself however was another matter. "He was jumping
around a good deal," recalls General, and that was right;
his character was built for lightning decision, instant action
and full speed, and now his duty was to do nothing, nothing at all and for an interminable period. Was that possible? I sincerely hoped so but eyed him warily for signs of
imminent explosion.

For myself I was all right; that is to say my heart was
pounding like a run V-Drive and I was scared stiff, but
that is much better than being scared into a jelly which had
happened at *18*'s rescue and I could now appreciate the
difference. Besides, inactivity suited my ponderous thought
processes, for there would be things to do in due course and
time was available to mull them over, plenty of time. The
enemy advanced agonizingly slowly, and although eons
seemed to have elapsed since we had stopped, the destroyer
in the van was only now drawing abreast of us. Perhaps
my racing pulse had somehow put the time scale into
slow motion.

"Time, General?"

"2222." It had; those three merchant ships were still
infinitely far away while we remained in the position of
greatest danger, facing three big guns in the destroyer and
two in each of the minesweepers, not to speak of countless
37mm and 20mm automatics. Nevertheless it was all
bearable because the prize was great.

I felt we ought to be plotting the enemy to determine
his speed, but without knowing the range and guessing it
wrongly the answer would be no more accurate than
observation. I knew that submariners used a method they
called a "bearings only plot," but that was clever stuff
which had to be learned and practiced at leisure; perhaps
I should do so, but now I could no more have reasoned
academically than I could calm Jamie down. We had a
radar set, or R.D.F. as it was still called, and credit is due
to whoever had the imagination to fit us with it; but it has
not seemed worth mentioning so far because, alas, it could
hardly ever be made to work, and when it did its performance was markedly inferior to the human eye except

perhaps on the darkest night in a thick fog. It would have been useful to check the target's range before firing torpedoes but here again it failed because the ground-wave, an area of electronic clutter around the transmitter in which no echoes were detectable, was so huge. At our present range there would probably have been a reading, but if the set was working, which I cannot remember, I certainly should not have switched it on any more than I should have made a W/T signal, operated the echo-sounder, or lit a cigarette, for my whole being was concentrated on giving the enemy no means of detecting us by any means whatever.

"Er—General?"

"2223½."

" 'Time ambles withal.' Jamie, take it easy. Why on earth d'you suppose the Hun has put no escorts on the flanks; what's the catch?"

"Perhaps he has to keep them all in the swept channel"; and that certainly seemed likely for the whole enemy force was strung out in two closely spaced lines. I could not know that it was even more likely after one ship had been lost to a mine.

"All right; but then why not put a couple of escorts in the middle of the convoy, he seems to have got plenty?"

That seemed such an obvious precaution that we peered for the hundredth time, but the merchant ships were unguarded. Right astern of them I could see another minesweeper and some smaller craft, no doubt the three VPs.

"Let's start closing, it's money for old rope," urged Jamie eagerly.

"(a) No"; (it was true that we were now just abaft the nearest minesweeper's beam but it was far too early to move). "And (b), don't tempt providence." (I remembered taking a shot at a sitting pigeon at 20 yards—sporting or not, wartime larders needed filling—and missing.)" "Check your gear again," I told him. "Your time will come and then I'll want everything you've got."

2225; the longest five minutes of my life had dragged by, and now as we fell astern of the warships the sensation was not unpleasant, and the picture I had formed of the whole line erupting into a blazing, spitting dragon of German hate and frightfulness receded. Every child delights in the sense of power to be derived from seeing without being seen, and we had been in company with this convoy

10. CONVOY 1974 (III)

The picture as we saw it – German records are not precise.

Wind NW-2, sea slight, dark, visibility good.

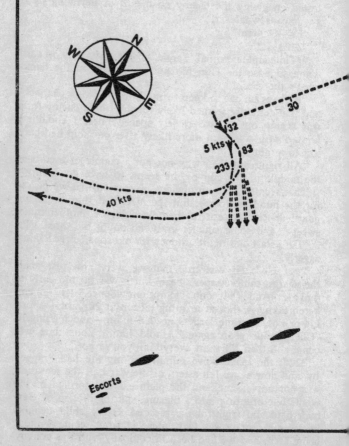

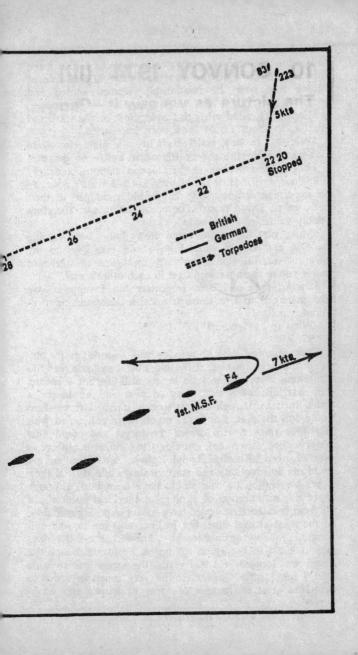

831
223

5kts

22 20
Stopped

22

24

26

28

- - - British
——— German
▭▭▸ Torpedoes

7 kts.

F4

1st. M.S.F.

for so long that we seemed part of it. True, we aimed to do it a mischief and the party would have to end in tears; but that would be so far into the future at this rate of ticking that now the relationship seemed settled and cozy.

"Happy?" I called softly to David, close on the starboard quarter; to shout would have been impossible.

"Yes, sir," he lied, and I explained the plan. Having to look away from the enemy I became aware of the men in both boats crouched at their action stations, and very still. Poor devils! How could they know I wasn't going to do something damned silly that would endanger all their lives, unless I told them? The conversation was therefore doubly valuable, and I added;

"Make sure the engine room crews know what's going on. Oh, and David; when I go ahead ease over to my port quarter, I'll almost certainly disengage to starboard and if you're there we won't get in each other's way."

Strange, time had been forgotten; but I supposed we had managed to live through another interminable two-minute spell.

"What is it, General?"

"2229."

Four minutes! The knowledge was disturbing, for my mind had been running at the old slow speed whereas the panorama before us was no longer still-life but a movie. The warships were well away to port and no longer a lethal menace, though of course one starshell from them could foil the plot. But I was much more concerned with the three ships which formed the target and could now observe their movement, noticing their different aspects as bow changed to beam. Should I shake myself out of my comfortable immunity and start closing while still on their bow? Navigationally that would have been best, although there was no question of aiming for the ideal point ahead of them because that would have meant exposing our sides at the most crucial time; but instinct told me to wait still longer, probably again because I knew that a sailor does not look out so keenly on the beam. Besides although the range was long, over 1,000 yards, the target was so wide that I felt justified in not closing very much in order to reap the great advantages of firing at leisure and unobserved.

"What's his speed, Jamie?" We had of course been trying to assess that for the last ten minutes, but now we must decide. It was certainly under ten knots, but after my convoy experience in the *Cotswold* that did not surprise me, having ceased wondering how ships could go so slowly and actually get anywhere.

"Six," he said authoritatively; he was a Scot, remember.

I guessed eight and we compromised, which turns out to have been correct; but since any avoiding action the enemy might take, such as slowing or turning, would lessen the hitting aim-off, I settled on 6½. I wondered how to coordinate *83*'s torpedoes, and kicked myself for not having spent all that waiting time devising a scheme to produce a fan of torpedoes with just the right angle between them. In fact I doubt whether it would have made any difference; such plans are best contrived and practiced while undistracted, and I thought it important to let the captains aim and fire with complete freedom and uninhibited by some new method which they may have only partially understood. What I did tell them was to fire their torpedoes individually, taking for each a separate target out of the bunch of three ships; that, together with personal and material errors, should form a spread zone of some sort and avoid all the torpedoes following each other along the same line.

"Right?" I alerted Jamie and David.

"Right," they acknowledged.

"Right!"

I did not ask the time but it was 2232; we had lain stopped for 12 minutes during which the enemy might have seen and thwarted us. Now the initiative was ours, and with the soft hiss of black water as the boats came back to life there came also a mood of determined aggression that was really quite grim; it was not hate but cold and steely professionalism, and if Bergelt had met us face to face at that moment he might almost have trembled. We had to succeed, and for the first time I allowed myself to believe that we were going to; and then I was struck by the thought that the enemy would quite probably fail to see us even after we had fired, so why not just stop and watch what happened? Then whatever claims we made would be fully justified, and it could even happen that we should be allowed to creep away as silently as we had come, leaving the enemy wondering what had hit him and probably concluding that it was a mine or, preferably, mines.

This I kept to myself, wanting neither to count chickens before they hatched nor to distract the captains; time enough in the event.

David came neatly across to the port quarter and we closed for exactly two minutes, shortening the range by about 300 yards to what I estimated as 800, though David thought it was 1,000 or more. But the three target ships still overlapped and looked huge, the nearest having the aspect of a 5,000 ton tanker which was quite big by coastal standards; we were perfectly placed ten degrees before her beam.

"Right."

Telling Jamie to take whatever time he needed for perfect accuracy I took a step back to give him and his redoubtable Coxswain Bob Henry all the room they needed. Did I say Jamie had no patience? He slowed so much that night that I should have screamed out loud had I not thrust my gloved hand into my mouth to plug it. Steering with precision on auxiliaries was not easy because very little water flowed past the rudders which therefore took a noticeable time to have effect, both in starting a swing and stopping it. Henry, taut as a bowstring, was putting everything he had into the job and it was too much; never could he steady *233* on the right course but swung to and fro across it, putting on large amounts of wheel and instantly taking it off again, his body twisting and his knees bending and stretching. And Jamie was going to wait until his sight was on and steady however long that might take; four times we swung before at last with a rumble and splash the first fish went, aimed at the tanker, and then the second at the right hand of the three ships. David got rid of his at just about the same time, taking the tanker and left-hand ship as his targets and using an enemy speed setting of five knots.

The Germans really ought to have seen those splashes and heard the impulse cartridges and torpedo engines, for the visibility was perfect under the stars and a breeze wafted from us to them. So still was the night that the slightest break should have disturbed the senses of all those officers and lookouts who had the strongest possible vested interest in keeping alert, their own lives; but after the torpedoes had plunged, nosed and plunged again the stillness remained, and in my own heart it was absolute. 800 yards at 35 knots—oh about 40 seconds I supposed but could not possibly bring myself to do the mental arithmetic—a very long wait anyway; but I was inured to waiting, my whole life seemed to have been one long wait and I had just a little more wait left in me.

Not so Jamie. "Crash start!" he yelled, and jangled his engine telegraphs with hideous energy and discordant bell-ringing, slamming them finally to full ahead with a snort that was like a safety valve lifting.

"No!" I cried. "For God's sake no!" and yanked the telegraphs back to stop, but I was far too late; the engine room crew had had the signal they were expecting and punched their starter-buttons as they had been eager to do for many a long minute. The racket was deafening, and instantaneously I was wholly deflated with postexcitement reaction and impotent rage; where had all that adrenalin gone so quickly? It was worse because Jamie's deviation was a minor one; if the torpedoes were to hit, the enemy would probably see us anyway and the only thing that really mattered was whether they did or not, and that he could no longer influence. But I dearly wanted to see them hit, to savor what might be accounted a triumph and to report it with authenticated accuracy, collecting whatever glory might come our way. Seeing myself thus shamefully unworthy as I hoped others could not, I was further depressed.

"All right then," I shouted as I now had to do; "full speed, come round to northwest." And then, with redoubled ire as I became aware of our own bullets whistling past my ear, "who told you to open fire? What d'you want to do, give them an aiming point? Stop it!"

Bergelt was undisturbed by any shadow of suspicion of the lurking menace eyeing him greedily from the shadows, until:

Loud sound of engines astern followed by light flak on the port side of the convoy. *M 8* fired starshell by the light of which two S-boats were seen. Immediately afterwards two heavy explosions in the convoy. Fire opened with 105mm weapons; enemy moves rapidly astern and out of range.

We had time to see one torpedo hit the tanker before the tracer became too blinding. "Cor!" ejaculated everyone, and I was mollified because the vast spout of black water up her side to above mast-height was incontestable evidence. "There's another!" they cried, but I was not sure. There was a flash certainly but it could have been a gun firing, and the crump of a heavy explosion which reached us might have come from the hit we had seen, taking the slow speed of sound into account. I therefore claimed only one hit, having grown up with a horror of boasting; but in fact the German *Rotersand* was hit twice, and the Swedish *Abisko*, 3,085 tons with a cargo of coal, once.

Tracer arched like broom in blossom but did not distract us from appreciating the wild, barbaric beauty of the scene as the two boats, each three tons lighter without her torpedoes, flew out of danger at over 40 knots. Nothing came our way, and when *233*'s aerial fell down just as my deliberately delayed enemy report was being transmitted I was of the opinion that that was exactly what it had done, fallen down; unless perhaps we had shot it away ourselves in that burst of misplaced enthusiasm.

Then we came home. But the Germans, perhaps feeling that they had been robbed of their share of the battle, decided to have one all to themselves and it is only fair to record it. *F 4*, the destroyer, did what we had done in the *Cotswold* and pursued, knowing she would not be leaving the convoy unguarded; but as with the *Cotswold* her 27 knots were quite useless against our 40. I remember Jamie nudging me and saying, "Don't look round now, I think we're being followed"; and perhaps I did not because no impression of *F 4* remains. She however reports hitting us for six and thus forestalling further attacks for the time being; but before she could close in for the kill the stars were blotted out, a crescendo of noise rose shrieking in pitch then sharply fell, and a widely spaced stick of bombs straddled her. Having performed her immediate task *F 4* prudently reversed course for the convoy.

Imagination plays many tricks; but that aircraft called for investigation and sure enough 22 Stirlings and 8 Wellingtons of Bomber Command were out that night off the Frisian Islands. They were not bombing but laying mines, which they called "gardening," and it is most unlikely that the pilot in question even saw the *F 4*, his whole effort being concentrated on panting his "veg" in the waiting drill.

"Incidentally," I asked my informant, "how did you know where the channels were?"

"Oh," he replied; "we had detailed charts of the German routes, navigational aids and everything else."

"Well I never!" I murmured, deeply moved.

While the *F 4* was still away, a renewed attack was thought by the Germans to have occurred from the starboard side at 2304; *M 8* fired starshell and *M 4* and *M 7* engaged two imaginary targets hotly until 2318. *Rotersand* and *Abisko* had of course stopped and poor little *VP 808* was left alone to look after them. She had a rotten time; surrounded by ghostly S-boats who attacked again and again she fought like Wolff at Narvik and reported destroying one enemy with a clearly visible hit from her 88mm, but not before the *Rotersand* had been hit by another torpedo. Then a slightly garbled passage in the German report refers to a distinctly garbled operation which took place at 2342 when the Senior Officer, expecting the enemy to be still in contact, decided to cover the convoy from astern; but not having signalled his intention a near-collision between *M 8* and a Vorpostenboot resulted. Lastly, at 0006, one and a half hours after we had left the scene, the *F 4* came hastening back with starshell and all guns blazing towards the south; everyone else joined in.

Five minutes after leaving the enemy I stopped and cut engines so as to collect David's impressions while they were still fresh and unembellished; and I also took the opportunity of inviting Jamie, I fear with some emphasis, to consider seeking approval for any drastic action he might contemplate in the future, especially when the ear of constituted authority was within two feet of his mouth. Starting up again our engine noise acted as a bellows to the enemy's fire astern, sending the sparks leaping and spitting with rekindled though aimless fury.

As may be imagined we gloated in the visual evidence of the enemy's confusion, but at the same time learned the serious lesson that he was not necessarily being stupid. After all, when a German lookout reports excitedly, "Schnellboote!" and you cannot yourself see it, are you going to assume it is not there, or do you touch off a starshell quickly to make sure? Or even if you rather think that an oil-slick, a catspaw of wind or a stray moonbeam has caused that line on the water, are you going to shut your mind to the possibility of its being a torpedo track? Not unless you are very stolid. That being so it became

open to us to engender chaos of a most profitable kind if
we were to apply our minds to it, especially after this
example of how brilliantly we could succeed without even
trying. At 0015, when 40 miles on and afar and asunder on
that lovely night, starshell still lobbed over the horizon,
lazily, gracefully, soundlessly.

The confusion round the convoy spread inevitably to 5th
Sicherungsdivision, though slowly and in small doses. Only
at 0043 was a report received that could be called comprehensive, and it was that to a fault. It was a *cri de coeur**
from *VP 808* saying she was standing by the two torpedoed
steamers and, for God's sake, help! That was bad enough,
but the signal received at Cuxhaven read as though *all*
the steamers in the convoy had been torpedoed and that
VP 808 alone had lived to tell the tale. "It seemed to be,"
they reported, "a convoy catastrophe of major proportions;
all salvaged measures were taken and large numbers of
ships and craft sent." They ruefully confessed that only
a few of those were needed, though they did a good job
in keeping both the *Rotersand* and the *Abisko* afloat to
reach Borkum and later Emden, the latter after jettisoning
800 tons of coal. Since however it is not in the nature
of senior officers to stay rueful for long, the rue was passed
down the line and Senior Officers of Flotillas and Commanding Officers admonished to be more prompt and explicit in reporting contacts with the enemy.

Convoy 1974 had had a rough ride, but even as the
survivors plodded wearily along the last stretch to the
Elbe another ship fell victim to a mine. Although she too
limped home it was an unhappy voyage with disturbing
overtones to those responsible for maintaining the vital
coastal traffic. It may be remarked that two of the four
casualties were caused by mines, which in the course of the
war took a far higher toll than either aircraft or MTBs. In
these narrow, shallow waters where the enemy was severely
limited in his choice of routes, mines could be laid continuously and with far less risk than shooting affrays, and
would operate in weather when no other activities were
possible. Minelaying was one of Bomber Command's major
contributions to the war effort, though they thought it un-
glamorous and a sideline.

The final German assessment of our efforts was, first,

---
*Cry from the heart.

that at least eight S-boats were present of which two were destroyed; wrong! And that our allowing the leading escorts to pass before attacking the convoy's soft flank was "to some extent clever"; wrong again! Although it is ungracious to disclaim such a rare tribute from critics who were hardly sympathetically predisposed, we were prisoners of circumstance and could do nothing but what we did, that is to say nothing. There is no mention of the unguarded flanks, whether explanatory or censorious, which would have been interesting. Lord Haw-Haw did not expound on our virtues needless to say, but Their Lordships sent a charming little note which went to show that results are what matter in this world, irrespective of the effort involved. I basked in the benevolent though undeserved smiles on those august faces which had so recently scowled with displeasure over that little matter of the trawler I sank with the *Cotswold*, and I hoped they would allow that the score was now settled.

VIII

"EXPECT UNSUCCESSFUL ATTACK"

OR

"OH, THE SHAME OF IT"

The running time of this harrowing tragedy in one short act was about five minutes and there is no reason why it should take much longer in the telling; but first to set the scene. Five evenings after the silent battle, four boats had left harbor, and as usual only two reached enemy waters; so far so bad, and impotently angry I only half accepted the inevitability of these constant breakdowns, beginning to wonder whether factors other than rushed design might be found to play a part. I knew only too well the semitorpor I always had to fight down when action promised; a state of mind that said in effect, "Get me to the church on time and I'll go through with the business, but don't expect me to make any of the preparations because I'm just not up to it." Having passed the stage when I imagined myself to be unique in having weaknesses I wonder how a motor mechanic, thus languid as well as being permanently numbed by head-splitting noise, would tackle a complicated repair job with the hot engine room heaving and pounding, and every taut nerve ending crying out that if the damned thing won't work we can all go home.

Experimenting with this theory I stopped taking reports of breakdowns at their face value and made it clear that only one outcome was acceptable, to mend it and press on. Sometimes I would give helpful advice from my fund of engineering experience such as, "Have you tried the salt-water pump?" and the chap would dash off. He only

needed a little encouragment and as often as not would
come back flushed with pride, to report that all was well.
Needless to say the trouble had rarely anything to do with
what I had suggested, but that was not the point.

I knew of course that men existed who would deliberately
throw wrenches in the works to avoid action, though the
awareness had to be most carefully concealed lest an honest
man should suspect that disloyalty or cowardice was even
being considered. Thank goodness none ever came my way,
and as for my Cuthbert falling even momentarily from the
highest standard of duty, the idea was wonderfully, reassuringly laughable. Admirably stolid, and I hope he will forgive
me for using the word which is intended as wholly lauda-
tory, he became ever more alert and competent as tension
mounted until, when the rest of us wondered whether we
could take much more, he rode easily on the crest of the
wave at the peak of his powers.

Tonight however it was 234 who fell out first, and I had
to call 233 alongside and step over to her with my "staff."
That comprised Douglas Gill, still with the Flotilla as Spare
Officer and living up to his reputation of being present in
every action, and Haynes, the Signalman; Alan Jensen had
of course to take our boat home. I was not then too unhappy, for the two reasons that I felt at home with Jamie
and General Lee, and was absurdly relieved at missing an
assignment tentatively fixed for the following day.

As was the excellent wartime custom, 234 had been
adopted by Hunstanton in Norfolk and the whole crew was
invited there to be fêted and assured of constant interest
and support, probably of the most acceptable and practical
kind. One might think that the reverse of dismaying, but
the prospect of making a speech to the Mayor and Cor-
poration was enough to send me scurrying for shelter on
the enemy coast. I told Alan to confirm the visit first thing
in the morning, to be well away from Lowestoft by the
time I got back, and to take my truly sincere thanks and
good wishes to Hunstanton.

The change in 233 after her first success was remarkable
and pleasing; Jamie was relaxed and confident, and the
crew had an indefinable air of having been initiated, of
belonging as of right in the front line. But confidence was
misplaced because one engine ground to a halt and would
not respond to any treatment. Jamie was beside himself

with rage and grief, but he had to go, for there was no
question of continuing with two engines on such a long
trip. Douglas, Haynes and I humped our gear and ourselves into *83*, her captain David Felce being less experienced than Polly Perkins who, with his crew from *230*,
was for some reason manning *88* that night, although
she properly belonged to John Weeden. My force thus
comprised two boats neither of which was in my Flotilla
and in whose training I had had no say, and one of them
was strange to her crew. It was a thoroughly messy arange-
ment, though typical of war when tidiness must often be
sacrificed to ensure that the war goes on.

It was cold, wet, rough and utterly depressing. I missed
Alan the Navigator too; though I did not realize by how
much until I studied the German report which showed that
the measure of his absence was no less than 19 miles between our estimated and true positions. More shameful
still we were 22 miles from the Terschelling coast, instead
of 10, where I should have said we had not the least chance
of sighting anything. It was my fault of course; knowing
83 to be new to the game there was nothing to stop me
checking every detail of the working myself, but with a
combination of idleness and not wishing to hurt anyone's
feelings I let it go. I did however realize that our position
was bound to be uncertain to some extent, and since the
visibility was low I patrolled on auxiliaries northwest and
southeast across the enemy's track to improve our chances
of seeing something. At 0150 we were on a northwesterly
leg, miserable, far from home, hunched in vain attempts
to stop water going down our necks, and yearning for the
time when we could turn west. The possibility of seeing
an enemy hardly crossed our minds.

Kapitänleutnant Friedrich Paul had commissioned the
brand new Elbing Class torpedo-boat *T 23* at Danzig in
July, and had spent the intervening period testing, tuning
and working up. They were fine little ships; we should
have called them destroyers for they were nearly the same
size as our "A" to "I" Classes, displacing 1,300 tons with
a speed of 33 knots, and mounting four 105mm, four
37mm, nine 20mm guns and six torpedoes. *T 23*'s war
station was to be at Brest and now she was ready to go;
after a final run over the degaussing range in the Elbe
she sailed at 1830 on this her first operational sortie in

company with the *Kondor*, one of the old Möwe Class
of 900 tons and three main armament guns whose captain
was Peter Pirkham.

Paul was expecting trouble sometime, somewhere, for a
strange reason. In the torpedo-boat *Jaguar* he had, very
properly, engaged and captured our *ML 306* during the
St. Nazaire raid in March, and afterwards he was told
he had been threatened by the BBC on the lines of, "We'll
get you when you next go back to sea!" One used to
hear tell of this sort of thing the other way round from
Lord Haw-Haw, though I never met anyone who had
actually listened to such a broadcast. It is a surprise to
learn that the same thing was also assumed to happen on
the German side, but there remains something of a mys-
tery about the business. Certainly the BBC had not told
me to, "Get Friedrich Paul!" I wish it had, and also told
me where he was to be found, for the possibility of an
encounter at that moment was as remote from his mind
as it was from mine; to see an MTB in that visibility would
be next to impossible and in any case the wind and sea
were marginal for their operation. His crews were in two
watches so that only half the armament was manned, but
all boilers were connected so that full speed was instantly
available, and watertight doors and hatches were shut
as would be expected in dangerous and mineable waters.

The two ships steamed in line ahead at 19 knots along
the outermost route, which kept them clear of other traffic
and allowed high speed in low visibility. When five miles
short of "M2" Buoy where course would be altered to the
southwest, Paul entered the charthouse to check his position, putting on his dark glasses as he did so to preserve his
night vision.

Curtain up!

"What's that?" I asked suddenly. It was a whitish blur
on the starboard quarter which was odd; normally anything one saw looked black. I had been looking in that
direction because Polly was astern of station and I cursed
him silently, then retracted for as usual it was my fault;
auxiliaries had no margin of speed for station-keeping
and it was up to me to reduce. But now there was this
thing . . .

"It's a bow-wave, by God. Enemy in sight!"

It was a perfect ram's horn, and I know I used the word to myself at the time, because I remember recalling Chief Petty Officer Michelmore in the Seamanship Room at Dartmouth saying, "Now this 'ere's your ram's 'orn 'ook," and wasting valuable seconds doing it. We were dead ahead of whatever it was but our speed, though slow, would take us clear of its track, and anyway I could always crash start and get out of the way. So I was more concerned for Polly, who if he did not do something soon might well find himself in trouble; I yelled at him with all my power, there was no question of flashing with the enemy in the same direction, but the sound was tossed away on the wind. Poor old Polly!

I thought at first I was looking at a trawler pushing the sea ahead of it; but decided to attack if that could be managed since we were unlikely to find anything more worthwhile on a night like this, and there was obviously no chance whatever of slipping away unnoticed. The problem was to point the boat towards the enemy and at least 100 yards from his track, for that was the range below which the torpedoes would not be triggered even if they hit. These conditions were almost a contradiction in terms, particularly because the firing position would have to be achieved on auxiliaries to avoid alerting the enemy; could it be done in time, so painfully slowly? We should have to try and see, but I thought so. Had I been collected enough to do a very simple piece of mental arithmetic I should have been surprised to find that at six knots we covered 200 yards in a minute, and the enemy would take much longer than that to come up with us; the operation was perfectly feasible, especially as we must be virtually invisible to him.

I therefore did nothing but continue at full speed on auxiliaries, and when I looked again at Polly he was doing the same; ow! Then back at the enemy—

"Trawler my foot! It's a bloody great destroyer—and there's another astern. All right then, we'll get him." "Or," I added to myself, "he'll probably get us"; because I could foresee even then that to be stopped and pointing towards those two juggernauts at 100 yards range did not bear thinking about. I therefore did not think about it; there wasn't time anyway and whatever was to happen would be over so quickly that fear would not be able to squeeze itself in. Gosh they were big! They couldn't be cruisers

could they? Probably not but nothing smaller than the
2,500-ton Narvik Class. What a prize! What a glorious
moment! What a privilege to be here!

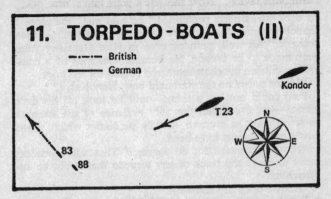

11. TORPEDO-BOATS (II)

—·—·— British
————— German

Kondor

T 23

83

88

N
W · E
S

All that or something like it seethed in my brain, but I
gave not one thought to the crew of *83* around me. That
was the moment to brandish the old saber and fire them
all with my *élan*. Not that they failed; far from it, everything in the boat worked and each man did his job to
perfection, but they did not enjoy themselves as I did. Why
should they? They did not know what was happening nor
what they were to be called upon to do, and neither did
they know me. A very few words would have sufficed but
I kept it all to myself, even from David; and when I
snapped at him, "set 20 knots on the sight," I did so in such
a way that he had no idea what I meant.

How many minutes or seconds we have been steering
away from the enemy's track I cannot possibly say, but
now we were well on the leading ship's bow and would
soon have made all the offing time would permit. But what
of Polly? His Welsh Torpedoman Davies made the sighting at last, and it is interesting that Polly too thought he
was up against a trawler patrol. Worse, he thought his
trawler was steering northwest and he altered course 90
degrees to starboard to lie in wait for it. In that he succeeded; "when I next looked round," he reported; and his
choice of words shows that he had, like me on so many
occasions, decided what the enemy was doing and then
assumed with complete confidence that he would do it;
"there was this damned thing almost alongside, 40 yards

if that, and so close I could see rust marks on the side
and a chap smoking a cigarette. He shouldn't be doing
that, I thought."

Friedrich Paul agrees with that last sentiment. "Smoking
on deck was strictly prohibited," he told me; "therefore I
cannot imagine that a crew member would have been
doing it." Ah well, perhaps even in Nazi Germany rules
were made to be broken. He became conscious of a com-
motion outside the charthouse and rushed for the door.

"Motor noises on the starboard bow, Herr Kaleu."*

Paul could not see a thing—until he took off his dark
glasses—but even then the only evidence of the enemy's
presence was the murmur of 88's auxiliaries which shows
how close she must have been.

"Hard-a-starboard for 40 degrees!" That was a prudent
move to comb the track of any torpedo that might be approaching.

"Alarm; open fire starshell!"

Bells clanged and Polly heard them, for they were designed to be audible in adjacent ships and 88 was indeed
adjacent; men rushed up from below, shouting was universal and guns leaped into movement, probing for him.
Polly heard and saw it all, and in less time than it takes to
tell ordered, "crash start, full ahead, hard-a-port, steer
north!" As the T 23 flashed past, Polly saw the Kondor
coming straight for him and realized he was hopelessly
placed for a torpedo attack on either ship. There was
nothing for it but to get clear and try again later; so he
made his exit, pursued eventually by just one stream of
tracer from the first German gunner to collect himself.

Paul's 40-degree turn to starboard both handicapped
and saved 83. Had she kept her wheel on, T 23 would have
come straight at us and might even have brought off a
successful ram. As it was she would pass at a bare 100
yards and forced us to turn and fire very quickly or not at
all, even though the torpedoes might not explode at that
range. I wondered whether to start main engines for more
power, but we were still unseen and any hold-up in the
engine room would make the boat uncontrollable. Putting
the port engine to half astern therefore, and with the starboard still at full ahead we turned desperately slowly
towards our massive enemy. On she came with boiler fans

*Short for Kapitänleutnant.

roaring and wake rushing; would we get round before she was past? Yes, just; but there would be no question of steadying the boat for firing, the moment of which must be timed to the split second because our rate of turning must be added to hers of crossing and she would appear to flash across our bows. The torpedo sight was entirely unsophisticated and had never been designed for such a combina-

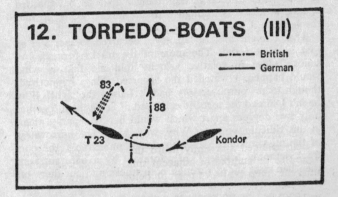

12. TORPEDO-BOATS (III)

-----·--- British
————— German

tion of circumstances, so that I decided it would be more of a hindrance than a help; why, the second or so the torpedoes remained in the tubes after the triggers were pulled could add a ten-degree error; and frankly I wonder whether my fingers, or David's either and I am sure he won't mind my saying so, would have proved steady enough to twiddle the gadget with anything approaching precision.

"We'll fire by eye," I told him; "I'll tell you when, stand by!"

Only our and the *T 23*'s ship noises disturbed the silence and no light or flash punctured her silhouette. I jacked myself up behind David and his Coxswain, William Murray, with a foot either side of the bridge so that my eye was on the centerline and I could use the bow as a foresight. Moods are strange things and even as I measured the narrowing angle between our stem and *T 23*'s I gloried again in the breathless excitement of the moment which I knew even then would be unique in my life. It was straight out of the *Boys' Own Paper;* we were soldiers of the King facing fearful odds, or Tom Thumb against the wicked giant. Poets and intellectuals din into us that there is no glamor or romance in war; but for good or ill—and if the cause is good, for good—there is, there just is.

I was hopeless with a shotgun, but at least I knew that the right drill is to swing steadily from behind the bird and squeeze the trigger without checking. When I missed which was normal, it was always behind the target through failure to follow through; now when the swing had to be in the wrong direction that danger had to be guarded against at all costs, though with the target taking up half the horizon it should not be possible to miss at all.

That I might miss ahead never occurred to me, and so that is what I did. The moment the tracks formed, my sailor's sense of relative velocity told me that is what would happen. I watched the accursed things hypnotized, though to no purpose; *why* hadn't I used the sight? *Why* hadn't I spread the torpedoes instead of firing them together only two degrees apart which would hardly separate them at this ridiculous range? Why, why, why? The narrowness of the miss made the anguish almost unbearable, the port track scraping across *T 23*'s forefoot by a bare six feet; then her mass sliced through both tracks and cut them off short.

There can be no romance without the risk of mortification and I felt so flat that I had to jolt myself to get on with the next essential of removing ourselves from the scene without unnecessary delay. I had in fact considered this matter. It is remarkable how many different things one can think of in a short time if one has to, and the answer was given by a mental arithmetic calculation so simple that even I could solve it; the enemy was 100 yards dead ahead, our turning circle at speed was 600 yards, and 600 into 100 would not go. But there was plenty of room between *T 23* and the *Kondor* astern of her, and the circumstances seemed appropriate to another of Nelson's maxims, "The measure may be thought bold, but I am of opinion that the boldest measures are the safest." So, since safety was what we needed, off we went.

There was only a moment's anxiety lest the main engines should fail to start, but they roared reassuringly into life and then we had only five seconds to run before we were between the ships, when neither would be able to fire for fear of hitting the other. In fact Paul, alert though he now was, had no idea where we were until we started up. His attention was wholly concentrated on watching for torpedo

tracks and these he saw, but only after they had crossed
his bow. He would have had no hope of avoiding them
had they—ah, woe is me!—been aimed to hit, and would
have been wiser to act as had Knowling of the *Cotswold* in comparable circumstances and hurled his ship
about, violently and unpredictably, ignoring possible minefields. Now he saw us, "but only for a few seconds like a
shadow" before we were in line with the *Kondor* and fire
had to be checked before it was opened.

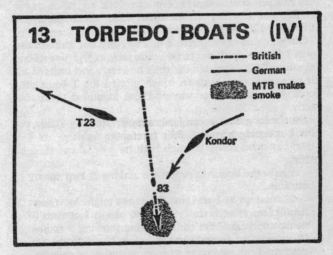

Pirkham, in the second ship, appreciated our intention
clearly, and as we raced across his bows put his wheel over
to port to have a try at ramming. I saw him do it but
could not make out what he was up to for he had no
chance of catching us, light as we were and at full throttle.
If he had been able to hit us and reduce our speed that
would have been different, but still not a gun spoke; then
we were through and vanishing behind our own smoke.

Curtain.

Weighed down as we were by sorrow, it was doubly sad
not to have enjoyed that big dipper ride to the full for it
was not the sort of thing one did every day; still it was fun
in retrospect, especially Murray's steering which was con-
fidently accurate and instantly responsive to every order.
But the moment we were safe, guilt rose up again to hit me

between the eyes; why, for crying out loud, had I not thought of dropping our two depth charges set shallow under the *Kondor*'s bows as we crossed them? I think that words failed me; I hope so for they would not have been elegant. Nothing else happened, for although Polly and I both tried desperately to find the enemy again so that he could use his torpedoes we were frustrated; first by not being able to communicate because of all the other traffic on the W/T net—presumably there was some excitement off the English coast—and I felt our lack of voice radio keenly; and secondly the Germans soon turned southwest at Point "M2" and that we could not predict.

Our signaled report arrived at The Nore not quite in the form I intended: "Two large destroyers, expect unsuccessful attack." The staff got the drift however, and ordered an air reconnaissance at dawn which spotted the T-boats proceeding on their serene way and also identified them correctly.

On the long haul home I mentally drafted my action report, but could somehow never get it quite right:

Sir,

I have the honor to report the sinking of two enemy cruisers . . .

2. Anxious as I was that the range might have been insufficient to activate the torpedo pistols I confess to being unprepared for the somewhat startling outcome. The starboard torpedo struck below No. 1 turret and detonated the magazine with an explosion of cataclysmic proportions which rendered us totally blind and perforated several eardrums. In consequence the impact of the port torpedo was not observed but is thought to have been in the vicinity of the engine room. *MTB 83*'s situation then gave rise to some concern as fragments of the target ship descended around her; one particularly large object which I gained the impression might have been a complete gun-turret fell close alongside, rocking the boat and drenching her from end to end.

3. We were now engaged by the second enemy ship which must have sighted us in the flash; she illuminated us with a well-directed searchlight and the best way out of the difficulty was not immediately obvious. The torpedoed ship's engines had clearly

stopped, but we could now see dimly that her way had carried her far enough across our bows to make it impossible to disengage ahead of her, observing that this class of MTB is handicapped by an uncomfortably wide turning circle. It was similarly impracticable to turn to port without colliding with the second ship, and the only avenue (if the word is permissible) offering marginal hope of escape was straight ahead. I therefore ordered the Commanding Officer to crash start his main engines and steer at full speed for the rapidly diminishing gap between the ships, at the same time bringing his depth charges to the ready, set to 50 feet.

4. As we gathered way the searchlight drew aft only slowly, indicating that our course was taking us barely ahead of the second ship, if at all. We therefore kept as close as possible to the leading ship, a matter of yards, and on coming abreast of her she was of course illuminated by the searchlight and we could see that she was already low in the water, and turmoil reigned on deck with men running in all directions. It was also seen that in stopping she had slewed through a right angle and now lay directly athwart the hawse of the second ship.

5. The sequence of events at this moment was rapid. The searchlight was suddenly obscured and a black triangle appeared in the sky to port, which it took me an appreciable time to realize was the enemy's bow at a distance of about 20 yards. Our speed was however adequate to scrape clear and I ordered depth charges to be released. The steadiness of the ratings concerned is to be commended, for the great bulk of the enemy towered over them and they were less well-placed than I to appreciate that she would pass just astern. She did so and embedded her stem in the flank of her consort, striking a cascade of sparks and heeling her on to her beam ends; then the depth charges exploded, all sources of light were extinguished, and we had to imagine the terrible scenes of carnage and destruction which we had brought about. This we did without pleasure.

6. It then became my disagreeable duty to ensure the destruction of the second ship which I could see to be stationary, the leading ship having evidently

sunk. *MTB 88* had initially disengaged to the north having been too close to the enemy's track to fire torpedoes, and I now fired bursts of tracer into the air to guide her back. Lieutenant Perkins appreciated the situation perfectly, and approaching quietly on auxiliary engines hit the target with both torpedoes. She sank in five minutes, watched by both MTBs who then closed and recovered as many survivors as could be accommodated and guarded. When clear of the scene of action a signal was sent in plain language which it was hoped would be intercepted by the enemy so that he could rescue the large number of men remaining in the water.

I have the honor to be, Sir,
Your vainglorious and boastful servant,

I liked it, especially the crocodile tears and magnanimity to a fallen foe which Nelson would certainly have approved, and could only tear it up with a bitter wrench:

Sir,
I regret to report . . . I missed.
Your wicked and slothful servant,

The nightmare returned regularly to plague Polly, David and me, causing us to writhe in impotent anguish like Marley's Ghost over his own misdeeds. As the years passed these visitations became less frequent, though at any time it could happen that those torpedo-boats flashed across the retina and one's whole frame would shudder involuntarily. Now at last I believe the specter to have been laid, through being in contact with Friedrich Paul; a man—no longer "the enemy"—whose heart yearned for his wife and two young children as he headed into the darkness towards a station he knew would offer little but hardship and danger. I am very glad indeed the war was won without the *T 23* having to be sunk. She became known as a lucky ship with good reason, and not just on account of her brush with us; that bewildering experience helped however in setting her young crew on its toes and beginning the process of turning her into a happy and efficient one as well.

"I don't know if you remember," Christopher Dreyer was yarning over old times many years later; "in the early days we only had two rudders which gave us rather a wide turning circle?"

"Well yes," I was able to reply; "it so happens I do remember that, quite well."

IX

BACK TO BEEHIVE

"I am to inform you that, in a recent Coastal Force action, an MTB unexpectedly passed close ahead of an enemy destroyer and did not drop the depth charges with which she was equipped. Their Lordships wish to emphasize the necessity for Commanding Officers and personnel to be always alive to this method of inflicting serious damage on the enemy."

We were in closer contact with My Lords of the Admiralty in those junior days than I ever was again; and since their glory as an independent board has now departed and with it (perhaps coincidentally, perhaps not) our country's greatness and indeed security, their pronouncements should be recorded as history. The language was that of Pepys; but what matter, for was it not the instrument of enormous power which had ordained the peace of the world for a century and the integrity of our land for many more? I resolved, first to do as Their Lordships directed should a depth charging situation recur, and secondly to try and ensure by all honorable means that it would not.

Our stay at Lowestoft now ended because new MTBs were coming into service and *Midge* (Great Yarmouth) and *Mantis* (Lowestoft) were building up their flotillas, whereas at *Behive* (Felixstowe) there was only the old 4th, still gallant indeed but running out of Isotta engines. We owed much to *Mantis* for its dynamic support; acceptance by Kenneth Barnard was the key, and that was achieved by willingness both to seek action with the enemy and to sit up half the night being instructed how to make money in the City. His skill and influence were reputedly considerable and had even been used to further his present task, by such methods as demanding a badly needed spare part direct from the manufacturers whose controlling interests he had already contacted.

Yet *Mantis* was a prickly place, for not all the junior officers were as pampered as I and internal stresses were evident. Tommy Kerr at *Beehive* shared only one characteristic with Barnard; as "dugouts" with no career prospects they were unbowed before authority, incurring its displeasure with composure if thereby their young men were sent to sea with all they needed. Kerr's mien was gentle, smiling, even fatherly which he was well qualified to be by age and experience; but his paternalism was without patronage which is ineffective with grown-up children, especially those who go out to war and leave Dad behind. Rather he took the line that senior officers of flotillas and captains of boats who could be trusted to take their own decisions in action must be allowed and encouraged to do so in harbor—even thought some of the results made me wonder if he was right. Rules and restrictions were kept to a minimum and he had his own unobtrusive methods of checking inefficiencies and of easing square pegs out of round holes. Trust developed, and I spent many hours in his room at the Pier Hotel (now The Little Ships) discussing just about anything; he was always available, and no one can remember his not being on the jetty when boats were entering or leaving harbor. He rarely criticized, yet the atmosphere was charged with high endeavor; his task was not easy but he achieved it with distinction.

If we were to get to sea in the best possible shape the base had to hum and it did, the *Beehive* staff working all the hours there were. There was Percy Odell and his team who gave us our torpedoes. Those were then the only weapons which propelled themselves without manual control, clever boxes of tricks which demanded great skill and meticulous attention to detail if no component was to fail at the moment of moments.

Musson and Woods looked after the guns; automatics all of them, with many moving parts which were unlikely to click, clank, clunk over each other after several hours dousing with salt water unless maintenance was perfect, and the long snakes of belted ammunition had to be uncipped and each individual round cleaned, lightly oiled and replaced every time they got wet. Woods's enterprise and initiative were in the best naval tradition; with Hichens as Senior Officer MGBs, demands for improvisation were incessant, whether to modify existing weapons or fit new ones, and Woods always found a way. I wanted 20mm Oerlikons on the wide open spaces of our foredecks, and was at first put in my place by Authority on the grounds that the necessary strengthening would weigh several tons and reduce our performance. I was persistent however, thinking how reassuring it would have been at *18*'s rescue to spray *VP 2011* with explosive shells from such a weapon, which being hand operated would fire without hydraulic pressure from our uncertain engines. Woods fixed it, aided by the Shipwrights who evolved entirely adequate support weighing only a few hundredweight, and by Tommy Kerr "winning" an unauthorized gun and mounting.

Old Lillicrap reigned over the Shipwrights in the great hangar along the hard, and in him past and present met. Our boats could hardly be more up to date, yet they were built of wood as Nelson's had been, and strangely satisfying were the sounds of plane, saw and mallet on chisel, the feel of ankle-deep shavings and sawdust, and the sweet smell of newly worked " 'onduras me'ogany." Lillicrap's standards were so high that it was hard to prise a job away from him until it had reached perfection whatever the urgency, and his decision on what should or should not be done was adamantine. His weakness was the Battle of Jutland as Henry Franklin, having frequent occasions to be in his office, discovered.

"What's that you were telling us about the *Queen Mary* blowing up, Mr. Lillicrap?"

Ten minutes later the Master Carpenter would shake himself back into the present and ask, "Was there something you wanted?"

"Well I just thought it might improve our fighting efficiency if we had a shelf in the wardroom with holes shaped for Gordon's Gin bottles."

Henry married Lillicrap's Wren Writer in due course, but that had nothing to do with fighting efficiency.

The Engineers' dedication could not have been higher than the rest's, but it was tested more sorely and had therefore to be more resolute. Coatalen, Perry, Pickard, Osborne and their Engine room Artificers worked unceasingly, only to have the results of their labor thrown back at them whenever boats returned from sea and sometimes even before they went. They won through in the end and the story of operational availability in 1943 was one of slow, grinding improvement, but the goal was so far away that it must have daunted any but our engineers.

Ian Trelawny was Staff Officer Operations. He was still far from fit after Barfleur, his Achilles tendon healing only slowly and with considerable pain; but it was grand to be with him again, and absolutely confident that we should be sent to sea imaginatively and fully briefed.

There were many other departments, electrical, stores and victuals, signals, administration, medical, which more than pulled their weight, and through them all forming the great majority was a comely regiment of women. The Wrens, with great hearts though somber plumage, had a hand in everything. They cleaned the ammunition with infinite patience and were fully aware of the significance of that irksome task, as they often showed by being on the jetty when we returned after an action, asking anxiously, "Did it work all right?"

They ran the harbor craft. One day Kerr was being ferried across to Harwich when a tearful coxswain put her head into the cabin, gulping, "Please sir, I don't know where we are." It was just in time for they were nearly at sea en route for occupied Europe; but, determined to succeed, she could eventually go alongside ships under way, and rebuke the sailors for dilatoriness with heaving lines in language as basic as theirs. The Wrens coded, sorted and distributed the signals; they cooked and catered, and Chief Wren Maud Robinson's massive two-egg breakfasts beckoned enticingly from across the sea, but did far more to stiffen morale than seduce from duty. Particularly emancipated was Joan Baker who drove one of the tractors which towed the 50-ton boats on cradles between slipway, crane and hangar. In the torpedo shop Wrens checked pressures and carried out maintenance schedules, and were often partly covered by a viscous black mess called heavy torpoyl which might have been thought unfeminine until they explained that the stuff was simply wonderful for the skin, like olive oil to sardine canners.

The task of exercising command and control over this bevy would have daunted most men, but not Tommy Kerr. Unmoved by winning smiles or melting tears, he would admonish, "Don't you cry at me; seven days' leave stopped." He understood too the tensions which can build up in a community of women and deflated them deftly.

Naturally enough the girls' services to the war effort continued after working hours, and their association with the men was thoroughly healthy. "There were five or six of them in a cabin," Coxswain White of *241* told me. "They'd do anything we wanted like sewing, and every time we came back from sea we'd get a phone call to see if we were all right. We had some good parties with them and they'd always chip in and pay their share; two of our crew married them, but mostly the lads liked going on the town by themselves." The relationship of fighting men being wholeheartedly supported by women brought out the best in both, and few were the cases of real impropriety or of men becoming so love-lorn that they lost their will to fight. I formed the view that the standard war story in which the men were all hopelessly entangled in love affairs at the same time as behaving like heroes was rarely true to life. For myself I was very dull; feeling that unconditional love, and I saw little point in any other sort, would take most of my time; I decided quite consciously that it would have to wait until more became available.

Hichens's gunboats were cock-o'-the-walk at *Beehive*, and rightly so for their battle honors were impressive. As with Jews and Arabs, Greeks and Turks, Irishmen and Irishmen; MGBs and MTBs were virtually indistinguishable to the outsider and were consequently rivals. Yet they were not deadly ones and for that Hichens' maturity and forbearance, astonishing in a man so singleminded and decisive, must take the credit. His magnetism and reputation were such that his officers and men gave him everything they had. Though putting tremendous effort into all he did he was unconcerned with smartness as an aid to morale, for that was as high as it could be; he preferred his boats to be clean because they worked better that way, but the men could look and behave more or less as they liked which was not at all the way an RN officer thought proper. I hope I can fairly claim not to have been an exponent of "bull," both Saunders and White reassure me that I was not, but I knew very well that my Flotilla needed all the boost to morale it could get and that smartness would help.

It was irksome at first to have to court unpopularity by constant bullying: "Put your cap on straight; salute smartly; clean out of dirty overalls as soon as the dirty job is finished; square off those ropes; train your turret fore

and aft; haircut!" There was no doubt that the 21st Flotilla
found it irksome too and I began to wonder whether I
was destroying morale rather than strengthening it. But it
worked, and the secret was to introduce a positive element;
I had a pair of beautiful little brass dolphins which had
been in my father's old ship, the *Repulse,* and mounted
them on the wings of *234's* bridge, demanding that they
should always be brilliantly polished. The idea caught on
and each boat blossomed with something attractive and
individual; old Harry of *241* revived his peacetime skill
and "tiddleyed-up" the splinter matting round her wheelhouse until it was a joy to see; boathooks sprouted blue
and white "Turks heads" and painted valve handles were
found to be brass and polished. Brightwork might just conceivably flash in the moonlight and give us away; but its
value as a vehicle for pride in self and boat was great, the
effort involved being mostly spontaneous rather than imposed, and I took the risk. The brightest and best ornament
had to be earned, a brass swastika for every torpedo hit;
so far *233* and *234* had one each.

The boats being thus lovely and the men smartly dressed,
the desirability of showing them off to best advantage
naturally followed. Station-keeping continued to be my
fetish and we were now achieving a high standard; but
nobody else could see that so we worked up a bit of show-
manship in harbor. Whereas before I had waited anxiously
for each boat to be reported ready I now assumed that to
be the case, and as I stepped on board at sailing time
precisely, ordered "start up!" Engines came to life not one
by one but all together, shattering Felixstowe Dock with a
mighty and bellicose roar. The seagoing boats having
previously been mooored in the right sequence with mine
on the outside I would slip, followed by the rest at exactly
two lengths intervals. A bare 30 yards separated the berth
from the point where Tommy Kerr and Ian Trelawny
stood to receive our salute, and it was just possible in that
space for the crew to get the fenders in, coil down the
ropes and fall in smartly on the forecastle.

Then the pipe would trill, the men sprang to attention
and the Captain saluted, pride burgeoning as with the
gladiator's farewell, "Ave Caesar, morituri te salutant!"
(Hail Caesar, those about to die salute thee). Tommy's
return salute always ended with a circular wave of bene-
diction and he wore a cheerful smile, but his Adam's apple

jerked noticeably and Ian's exceptionally warm heart never failed to be meted. Jingoism? No! Mock heroics? No! Brutal militarism? No! No! No! You who live in freedom remember that that was how you got it because there was no other way of giving it to you; and stiffen your response to threats of tyranny or you will find yourselves at best doing what we did all over again, and at worst in the Never-never-never Land—the first Britons to become slaves.

Salutes however did nothing for our engines which performed no better at *Beehive* than they had at *Mantis,* and the only boat available for our next operation on December 18 was *241.* How pleasant it was to be back with Mac and Henry, that seemingly ill-assorted pair who in fact complemented each other ideally, especially now that there was no restraint between us. Their coxswain, Petty Officer Edwin "Knocker" White, completed the management team and guided his two young RNVR officers as the Royal Naval senior rating has traditionally done with nicely blended tact and authority. There were no defaulters in *241* because White, a big chap, had his own methods of influencing people which also, human nature being strange and complex, made friends too—in due course. *241* was no use by herself, but the new Senior Officer of the 4th Flotilla, John Weeden whom I had met and liked at Lowestoft, was enthusiastically cooperative and we were usually able to form a quorum by pooling our resources.

We only got halfway to Holland because *MTB 30* hit a mine. I was so taken aback that at first I thought the explosion to have been internal; mines were not our normal concern for we were supposed to float over the top of them and must have done so many times. There was a flash, quite a small one, but the effect was final; horrible too. *30* stopped instantly, and by the time the rest of us had slowed and returned she had no forward half, except for a small piece floating detached with Tony Halstead her Captain sitting on it, hurt. He had swum there, having been blown off his bridge for quite a distance, but was luckier than his companions on the upper deck who had suffered the same fate though with piteously mangled legs from which Able Seaman Finlayson died before reaching harbor. There was none of the purpose or distraction of battle and I cared desperately. Sub-Lieutenant Hudson, Able Seaman Nisbet and Telegraphist Miller were below and died instantly; groping for some shred of comfort I thought that at least their next-of-kin could be assumed that they had known and felt nothing.

All those who could be were quickly picked up, mostly by the other two boats, and because the sea was choppy making it extremely risky to transfer badly wounded men from boat to boat, I called off the operation and sent them home without delay; even so the ride was torture for them. Perhaps I should have continued with two boats, but the astonishing fact was that 30's damage was so localized in the forward half that the rest seemed almost intact, and in it were three priceless Isotta engines.

I decided to try a tow, and Henry jumped on board 30 to work with her Motor Mechanic, "Gentleman Jack" Forsyth. The two of them did wonders in wretched and dangerous conditions; but the forward engine room bulkhead leaked badly and suddenly the wreck sank under them, thank God when neither was below. They were soon on board 241, but while still floundering in the icy slop Henry said something. It was compulsively funny in circumstances where humor seemed inappropriate to the point of indecency; but it was a classic in its way and should be recorded—except that we have both forgotten what it was.

1943, and with it a New Year's Tactical Resolution.

To sum up our experience so far, silent and unobserved attacks were the most effective; if however we were seen and engaged before firing they were likely to be the least so because a mass of tracer concentrated at oneself was totally blinding, as well as dangerous. Since of their nature the boats were small and unsuited for slogging battles on level terms, diversions were indicated to allow the MTBs to attack unobserved and benefit from the illuminating or silhouetting effect of enemy gunfire in other directions. As diversionary agents gunboats were inflexible and wasteful of effort; should they be presented with a torpedo target they could not exploit the opportunity, they could easily cause confusion with the MTBs, they might not be needed at all and would then have been wastefully diverted from their proper task of guarding our own coastal traffic against E-boats.

Light dawned. A force composed entirely of MTBs could split up as early as sighting of the enemy permitted,

and each division would then try for an unobserved attack
from divergent bearings. Both might succeed, but if not
it was likely that the enemy would see one rather than
both, and that one would immediately assume the diversionary role by opening fire and making a noise; it should
not close to hitting range because damage might prejudice
its chances of a torpedo attack later, and I was soft enough
to abhor risking lives unless the returns were commensurate. Should the first group succeed, the roles of the
two divisions would be reversed; indeed that could happen
even if it failed, and the two functions could be tossed
to and fro indefinitely which ought surely to confuse the
enemy so thoroughly that sooner or later he would leave
an opening unguarded. So that we ourselves should not
become equally confused it was important that having
been allotted a sector a division did not stray from it.

Two boats would have been just sufficient to operate
these tactics, though obviously that number in each division
was preferable. However we still had to double the number we first thought of to allow for engine breakdowns,
and even though the 21st Flotilla now comprised five
boats there was not the least chance of four being operational together. Peter Magnus had joined and he was a
stalwart, in direct contradistinction to his boat, 224. She
and her twin from a yard in the north, 223 commanded by
Tom Neill, had scarcely achieved their maiden voyages
when they retired to Poole with innumerable, incessant,
ingrained and ineradicable defects.

Both captains had been eating their hearts out in scarcely
bearable frustration and sad congratulatory telegrams had
reached us at Lowestoft, "Leave some for us." Now 224
had limped to Felixstowe with misaligned propeller shafts,
a condition much dreaded by marine engineers for its
attendant problems are almost insuperable, and with all
the inherent defects of the class as well 224 was pretty
low in the form-book of greyhounds of the sea. A complex
MTB was a formidable challenge to the simple yacht yards
all over the country where they were built, some of which
with the best will in the world just did not possess the skill.

Our first chance came on January 18, 1943 when John
Weeden joined me with 69 (Bob Morgan), 32 (Norrie
Gardner) and 70 (Jack Saunders). I had 241 and, amazingly, 224 in which I embarked; but because her chances
of staying the course seemed slim I took 32 into my di-

vision and left 70 and 69 with John, so that if we were able to use the diversionary plan there would be no doubt how the force would split. This was a buccaneering enterprise in which I was given no intelligence of a particular enemy but had freedom to make my own decisions, and no commander can ask bettter than that. Also encouraging, the first of several improvements had arrived, the Mark VIII torpedo which was the type designed for submarines. It had a speed of 45 knots which reduced the aim-off angle and gave the target less time to evade, it carried an enormous warhead of 750 lbs, and was one of the most reliable weapons ever produced.

The Hook of Holland seemed a likely place to start, but on the way we sighted a buoy marked "K" which flashed every six seconds. It had not been there in peacetime and nor was it British, so it must presumably have been German; but we would have been even more interested had we put two and two together, for its position was close to where 30 had been mined. We did not then attribute her loss to anything but rotten bad luck, a drifting mine probably; and only today do I discover that the Germans had an extensive system of outlying minefields completely covering this section of the Dutch coast, which they periodically "freshened up" with the aid of "K" Buoy to guide them.

Alan Jensen was with me of course, and he was really finding his form as Navigator, delivering us to where he said was five miles short of the harbor entrance but which was actually a mile or so farther in. This was a fault on the right side, because the visibility was good and the moon full so that we should have seen the Dutch coast before hitting it. And there was the enemy, two trawlers, which my orders allowed me to attack. The enemy was always a chilling sight and perhaps more so than usual now for it was a full two months since our last meeting and we perhaps felt a little over-secure. I bolstered myself to doing something, knowing I had the power not to, and to pretending I liked it. My Coxswain Jim Saunders was in 224 for some unremembered reason and his nerves were just as bad as mine, though we both thought the other to be made of unyielding steel.

"I didn't used to get scared in harbor," he told me. "It was when you said 'Nuts starboard!' ['N' for Nuts = signalese for 'Enemy in sight']. O Christ! My heart pounded away and I'd say, 'Our Father which are in heaven' and all that lot. Then I'd write myself off and the fear went; besides there was too much to do in action and I had to do it properly, no question."

I stopped the unit and talked to them, as I had formed the habit of doing whenever time permitted for there was no call to rush in if the enemy was unaware of our presence. The method might seem primitive but the most sophisticated system of telecommunications is a poor substitute for speaking face to face.

"This is what we're going to do," I would say and explain the plan. "Have you got it?"

"Yes."

"Right; now you tell me what you're going to do."

Nothing could be more certain or secure than that. Tonight the plan had to allow for a restraint imposed by our new torpedoes which were so precious that they were not to be used against anything so small as a trawler; on the other hand 69 and 70 were equipped with ancient torpedoes called Mark Xs, and nobody minded what happened to them. There seemed no hope of an unobserved attack on such a bright, clear night, so I told John to wait where he was relative to the enemy and that I would work round to the inshore side and cause a diversion. He would have to be patient because my maneuver would take a long time on auxiliaries, but the enemy's speed was slow and there seemed no reason why I should not get there in the end.

Having cast myself in the role of the troops of Midian, I set off with the 1st Division to prowl and prowl around, keeping the enemy just in sight. "Christian dost thou see them?" No; perhaps he had not understood that survival in this transitory life depends on watching as well as praying. We prowled for 35 minutes, a very long time and easily our record, but I had an indefinable sense of confidence. Another ship, by God! Beyond the first two and bigger, surely she was bigger? I so wanted her to be a target for a Mark VIII that I soon persuaded myself that she was an 800-ton coaster of the same type as my *Doggersbank* at Dunkirk, and decided to attack. The overall plan needed no modification because John would get his diversion whether I attacked or merely made a noise.

We arrived on the enemy's beam unseen, and in order to remain so I took 224 alone to make the kill. Still unduly

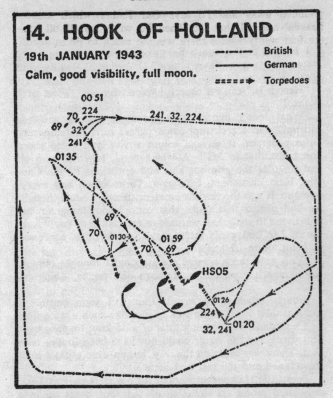

14. HOOK OF HOLLAND

19th JANUARY 1943

Calm, good visibility, full moon.

—·—·— British
———— German
=====➤ Torpedoes

concerned not to waste torpedoes I told Peter Magnus to fire just one, which was silly and I knew it. At a range of what would have been 800 yards from an 800-ton ship the moment had come. We had debated whether the enemy was stopped, perhaps waiting to enter harbor, or even anchored, but decided on a speed setting of three knots, heading south.

"Signal from *70* sir, am attacking with torpedoes." It was nicely timed.

"All yours," I told Peter, and stepped back to await events.

Peter yanked his trigger and nothing happened. I waited further for the torpedoman to hit the striker as taught in the drill, and waited in vain.

"What is the delay?" I thundered in my best gunnery manner.

"Lost me mallet."

I looked at the boat's bow and it was swinging away from the target; "Don't fire!" I ordered, loudly and urgently.

"Here it is," came a cheerful voice from aft. "Fire, sir?" Woosh!

"What does it matter what you do so long as you tear 'em up?" was a recurrent catch phrase in a contemporary radio program. It seemed sound advice and I set about doing just that to *MTB 224* in general, together with all and singular the grievous sins and omissions of the Captain, First Lieutenant, Coxswain, Torpedoman and everyone else. It was the terrible amateurishness, when I thought we had passed that stage, that caused something already taut in me to snap; as I warmed to my task they could hear me in *241* 200 yards astern, and Saunders has confessed to being quite frightened:

"You gave them a good old rucking; I thought blimey, the Skipper's gone barmy, I mean he's raging, doing his nut."

Bitterly ashamed of myself though I soon became I thought then I was doing well in covering such a wide field in 15 seconds, the running time of a 45-knot torpedo over 400 yards, for the range could not have been longer than that. There was more on the way, but an even greater blast supervened and the rest was silence.

Poor little Hafenschutzboote (Harbor Defense Boat) *05*, converted motor trawler *Deli* of 161 tons, went up in a sheet of flame and exploding fireworks that would not have been disproportionate for a battleship. As our eyes followed the fireball ever upwards we gasped with awe and deduced, reasonably, that it could only emanate from a fully laden ammunition ship. *HS 05* had been stopped, and the torpedo would not have hit had it been fired as intended; our luck was fiendish and I felt very humble.

John Weeden approached the other two trawlers as the explosion occurred, and as intended the enemy looked the other way. Both boats fired unobserved, but using speed settings of three and four knots respectively and only one torpedo each they missed ahead. The enemy came to life and John withdrew on main engines for a short distance. Meanwhile I too had started mains, collected *32* and *241*, and dashed up and down on the shoreward side which drew the enemy's attention and enabled John to start creeping back for another try. Having seen the firing occasioned by his first attack I thought he had finished and left too early; but all was well because the enemy probably heard all our engines receding to seaward and turned back to *HS 05*, whose position was pathetically marked by her vertical bow, to look for survivors.

How anyone lived through the holocaust is incomprehensible but three did, and cried out for help to *70* and *69* approaching their firing positions. Simultaneously the boats were seen and engaged, and immediately fired torpedoes; John followed his track all the way and saw it hit without a shadow of doubt, the trawler seeming to disintegrate. Then they disengaged, being fiercely engaged by the last trawler, and Jack Saunders was slighty wounded in the face. It will be a disappointment to those concerned that this hit is not mentioned in the German report; but the latter is not very detailed and I cannot rule out the possibility altogether. Then the survivors from *HS 05* were rescued.

We all met again to seaward of the battlefield, and as *70* and *69* were now disarmed and short of fuel I sent them home. They had not gone very far however when they ran into another trawler patrol which John reported. I did nothing because it was not worthy of my superior torpedoes, but later he said it might be a convoy and I then spent a most frustrating three and a half hours searching for something I knew must be within a few miles but never finding it. There was no convoy; but two trawler patrols code-named *Cairo* and *Duala* were trying to find us as earnestly as we were trying to find them, and if only they had stayed still we might all have been satisfied.

The implications of this maritime blind-man's buff were enigmatic. The patrols were there to intercept and destroy us; but they were most unlikely to get within range unless we first attacked them, because otherwise they could never catch us, let alone see us. We for our part were only encouraged to attack patrols when it seemed there was nothing more important to go for, and then only with old torpedoes. So what was it all about? What strategic principle demanded such confrontations when the main concern of both sides, the convoys, was not involved? Perhaps the answer will become clearer as the future unfolds.

In spite of our one success the night had been very wearisome; and then we ran into thick fog on the English coast and had to make fast to the Cork Light Vessel until the afternoon, Chief Wren Robinson's breakfast remaining a tantalizing mirage. But two advances had been achieved; the diversionary plan had worked without a doubt, ably implemented by John Weeden, and it was clear that intelligence was needed to do it well; and we had exchanged a number of W/T signals all of which had arrived quickly and accurately. A useful precedent was established by Their Lordships who commented, "Although in this case only one torpedo was required to sink the enemy ship, it is considered that both should have been fired." Quite right; it had just been a pity that they were so hesitant earlier as to whether Mark VIIIs were too precious to use or not. Lesson learned? To temper one's discipline with what one's seniors are likely to say after the event, as well as what they have actually said before.

X

THE BARRELS AND
THE BULLFIGHT

1943 was break-even year in the war at sea. New construction slid down the ways in increasing numbers; weapons and equipment shown to be needed in the dark days had been developed; spare parts built up, maintenance facilities improved, and administration progressed from hand-to-mouth expediency to efficient preplanning backed by adequate logistics. In the Atlantic the U-boats were held, then beaten; and even Coastal Forces received their share of the cake.

Alas, there were still too many crumbs in *224* who retired again to Poole, exhausted after her one effort. With her went Peter Magnus, never to return to me which was a sad blow, for despite my despicable ranting I had recognized him as a first-class fighter which he later proved himself to be in command of his own flotilla. Tom Neill arrived in *223* however, and Poole had dealt well with her shortcomings so that she became as good a runner as the rest; or as bad a one, for although hope was in the air no improvement in reliability was apparent in the first quarter of the year. Sudden breakdowns or prolonged unserviceability continued to add frustration to the tension inherent in our way of life, and became no easier to bear. Jamie Fraser took it badly as his nature dictated, until the passion within him burst, most surprisingly, into poetry:

ON RETURNING FROM AN OPERATION
By James L. Fraser (*with apologies to John Masefield*)

Orange-box of Beehive, from distant Hunnish shore,
Rowing home to haven for engine-lifting time,
With a cargo of troubles,

Purolator bubbles,
Overheating thrust-blocks and boost plus nine.

I became ever fonder of Jamie, for his enthusiasm
certainly, for his bubbling sense of fun and his quickness
of thought and action, all of which overlay a surprising
sensitivity. He was desperate to prove himself in action,
but the glory that would bring seemed immaterial to him.
"He *was* a nice feller," says Tommy Kerr, "he really was."
"Smashing bloke," thought Jim Saunders. "His Coxswain
Bob Henry and his crew thought the world of him; always
talking to them and cracking jokes."

Mind you, he was quick on the draw in harbor as well
as at sea. It was not that he did not suffer fools gladly,
he did not suffer them at all; and since Jamie's definition
of a fool was catholic there were times when the restraining hand had necessarily to be laid upon his shoulder.
I certainly came into that category when we first met; his
subtle insubordination may have been unintentional but
it was not to be borne, though try as I might I could not
get the message over. The issue was finally resolved in the
worst possible way though perhaps the only one, in front
of the men. We were lying cut and I said to the captains:

"I'm going to do so and so."

Jamie replied, "I think it'd be better if we . . ."

"You think it'd be better—what?" I demanded icily.

"I think it'd be better if we . . ." he repeated unabashed.

"Go on," I rapped, in what I hoped were accents of unmistakable menace. "Finish what you've got to say."

"I *have* finished." There was a long pause before he
added, "Sir."

"Bearded bastard!" commented one of my own crew
about me; or so I am told by Saunders whose ears must
have been sharper than mine.

I am sure Jamie was astonished to find he had offended;
after all he only wanted to get at the enemy, but now he
saw clearly that the only possible way of doing so was as
part of a team under an acknowledged leader and threw
himself into that.

Dumbflow silencers and triple rudders were approved to
be fitted and available; that was great news and it was no
wrench to withdraw boats from operations for the work
to be done, especially as the vile winter weather precluded
much seagoing anyway. I stepped up the intensity of train-

ing, knowing the standards I wanted, but there was no need to drive for we were now truly of one company; and on a less elevated plane everyone knew for certain that they would soon be in action, and that a boat not at the peak of efficiency would be a dangerous one to ride in. Saunders tried to explain the men's attitude to battle, not altogether successfully. They enjoyed scoring a torpedo hit well enough but their overriding concern, he says, was the probability of survival, and to that end they felt much *safer* in an efficient boat under a captain who habitually went for the enemy than with one who somehow always managed to stay out of range.

With improving smartness came pride and a certain amount of rivalry. My pretty dolphins were evidently a source of temptation, and once Saunders discovered to his horror that one was missing:

I spent all afternoon begging and praying around the boats, because I knew that if you found out there'd be stoppage of leave for the whole Flotilla. I eventually found it with Bob Henry of *233*, and then I got my own back. We had shore electric power and one day he was rigging the leads in his boat; I watched till he touched them and switched it on from the jetty. He screamed and chased me all around the base, and I had to lock myself in Rose Cottage—that was the name of the Coxswains' mess, I don't know why; we had a messman there called Greg and all he had to do was cook roast beef every day of the year, with onions on top—and I reckon he'd have killed me if he'd caught me. Like concrete it was, the roast beef, because the senior Coxswain liked it that way, old Tom "Dollar" Hartland of Hichens's boat. Smashing man but his crew wasn't smart like ours. They were always in action and getting hit and, funny thing, wherever they were hit there was the rum bottle and it had to be written off "lost by enemy action." I said, "What a pity the rum bottle got broken, Tom." And he said, "Yes, but I just managed to save that little bit out of the bottom."

We ran a Rugby team, the leading lights being Henry Franklin, Arthur Lee, Tom Neill and his First Lieutenant, "Fish" Salmon, though most of us joined in to keep fit

and work off some of our surplus energies in harbor. But
a game generated a thirst, and that was a condition needing no stimulation in our community for our young men
were of an age when to drink was manly, and the more
the manlier. Ranting, roaring and pub bashing were apparently necessary to fulfillment; though I found the incessant recounting of Bacchanalian exploits and the planning
of future ones very tedious and wondered where the line
should be drawn.

Firm self-control is the first essential for a successful
fighter; yet taut nerves must be eased, and I know for sure
that wine is the greatest material gift vouchsafed to us by
the Almighty, and am prepared to do battle with anyone
who holds that to be blasphemous.

"Fill ev'ry glass, for wine inspires us, and fires us with
courage, love and joy," as Gay asserts in *The Beggar's
Opera.*

What infinitely satisfying memories I have of mornings
after returning from sea. Peeling off layers of clothes sodden to the innermost; hot bath, luxurious and prolonged;
breakfast to the Wrens' smiles and liberality; a couple of
hours' leisurely administrative work; down to someone's
boat to drink and yarn, drink and discuss, drink and look
forward; lunch; and finally the sleep of the just, in pajamas
between the sheets. But note this: have yourself called at
6:30 even though you think you can sleep the sun round,
wash the gum out of your eyes, dress, do something, join
the rest for dinner, and go back to bed at the usual time.
Otherwise you will wake cold and empty at 2:00 a.m.
and spoil the whole effect.

I tried to tone down the wildest excesses, with little
success as Henry Franklin and others now inform me.
Another new discovery is the considerable proportion of
people who thought as I did but who, feeling themselves
to be isolated in solitary stuffiness, were ashamed to let on;
we were a feeble lot.

We operated regularly during February and March 1943,
becoming very cold and wet but never finding the enemy.
Remembering our mothers' exhortations always to wear
dry socks and underclothes or we should catch our deaths
of cold, we wondered why we were so surprisingly fit after
being soaked to the skin for perhaps eight hours on end;
or as the French say, soaked to the bones, for the body-
heat in one's very core would release itself to atmosphere

in a series of convulsive shudders. A westerly gale would
blow up during our patrol and when we turned for home
—crash! For a minute or two hope persisted that we
could maintain our 25 knots, and not just because that
would take us back in a flat four hours; with our bows high
the mass of white water wrenched from each wave by the
jarring impact of our flat bottoms was flung in wildly
glittering pinnacles and cascades to each side, so that we
in the center were dry and exhilarated, with only the
sledgehammer jolts to our spinal columns to cushion as
best we might.

No good! Even if we could take it, no craft ever built
could stand such battering, though these boats of ours
were wonderfully sturdy and evoked my constant admiration and gratitude. Down to 12 knots. The first wave was
the worst; one should have been ready for it but always
seemed to forget how quickly the boat would decelerate.
The mass of water just kept coming, undeflected by the
bow whose only effect was somehow to give it extra
velocity. One's face and ego smarted as though from a
gratuitous, insulting blow, but there was no one to hit
back; the first icy trickle penetrated one's neck's defenses
of tightly packed mufflers and beard, gloomily presaging
"the main" which would inexorably "come silent, flooding
in"; and as the wave swirled and sloshed inside the bridge
there began an equally remorseless upward soak. Eight
hours to go, but the figure was meaningless except as a
synonym for infinity, and the endurance called for tested
one's will to the limit. Saunders said he would not have
cared if the boat sank, and I half-seriously considered
putting the sea astern and running for Rotterdam.

To look out ahead continuously was more than one's
eyeballs could stand, so one crouched and bobbed up
whenever a sea had gone over; but every seventh wave or
so one got it wrong and took the cataract full in the face,
to stand there bemused and streaming like a slapstick
comedian enveloped in custard pie, except that there was
nothing funny about it.

Came the long-awaited dawn with a sneer, for all it
showed was the great size of the waves, our pathetic speed
through them and our vulnerability to enemy aircraft or
returning E-Boats; the wretched Gunner had to stay in his
turret against such a contingency for one presumed there
was just a chance that the weapons would fire. Apart from

him and a helmsman one allowed everyone to go below if they wanted to, but whether that was any more congenial amid the brutal buffeting of the boat and the fetid stink of salt and vomit may be doubted for many stayed up. Once when the enemy danger had passed, or we were so utterly weary that we no longer cared, I sat on the bridge deck holding the bottom spokes of the wheel and steered by keeping the waves astern rolling in a constant direction. In *241* they found a fish swimming around the bridge and were proud of that.

Navigation? The compass swung in wild gyrations, one could only guess how much speed was being lost to the seas, and if one had been able to get a pencil and ruler near the chart for the motion it would have been impossible to make a mark on the sodden paper, because nothing anywhere inside the boat was dry. But we had only to steer west to hit dear old England somewhere between Kent and Yorkshire, and fill in the time somehow. I would bet with myself how long it would take for my upper and lower wetnesses to meet and at what point they would do so; that was soon over, so I might try half an hour's singing which was not antisocial for the sound was mercifully borne away on the wings of the wind; lighting a cigarette could sometimes be achieved by two or three men together and would take a splendidly long time which was really the object, for the number of puffs possible before the thing became a soaked sponge were hardly satisfying. Reciting half-remembered odes over and over again, trying to recall the words and fix them permanently, was most effective and accounts for my still being pretty well word perfect in "The Bad Child's Book of Beasts." My repertoire was not exclusively Belloc however, and the 107th Psalm struck an apt note:

They are carried up to the heaven, and down again to the deep . . . they reel to and fro, and stagger like a drunken man: and are at their wit's end . . . they cry unto the Lord in their trouble . . . and so he bringeth them unto the haven where they would be.

But we weren't fussy, any haven would do.

One calm evening in March on the way out, the sea was studded with floating mines; at least, what else could those dots be, bobbing in the gentle swell? Moored mines certainly broke adrift from time to time but surely never in such numbers. Better investigate, gingerly; not quite black, brownish; ovoid, not round like mines, more barrel-shaped; great heavens, they *were* barrels! The tension was scarcely bearable, didn't they pack salt pork and things in casks, as well as beer? We nudged alongside the nearest and turned it gently with a boathook, seeking clues. Guinness!

The war was forgotten in an instant, and seamanlike preparations were put in hand for embarking the treasure. But then I sternly intervened; we could not take those things into action, they were huge and would leave no room to move on deck, and I imagine the nut-brown Liffey-water spraying everything through countless bulletholes. It naturally never occurred to me that any of my sailors might be tempted to insert a gimlet and spend the rest of the night prone and open-mouthed beneath the resultant trickle; of course not.

"Overrated stuff," I said; "top bitter. Form arrowhead, 25 knots, course north 73 east." But then sensing growls of incipient mutiny, I added, "We'll pick them up in the morning, if we're spared." "And if," it occurred to me to suggest to Alan, "we can find them again."

Then began the epic voyage of Alan the Navigator which is sung in fable and ballad to this day. For to win our prize we had to sail over the wine-dark sea to Ijmuiden, to do battle with the enemies of freedom who hurled fiery bolts at all who approached their shores; and the south wind blew and the tides swirled and would have swept us from our course, but the sailors prayed to Poseidon to take them back to their golden treasure and the kindly sea god touched Alan with his trident and endowed his hand with infinite cunning so that wherever the ships went there went his pencil on the chart and he never once applied a reciprocal bearing. Then we turned south along the hostile shore past Zandvoort, and Noordwijk of the many wrecks, but with never a sight of the dreaded foe; and Poseidon placed a buoy in our path which we recognized for a favorable portent and pressed forward with renewed zeal.

"I see black ships!" cried one, and fear gripped our hearts. But Alan laughed and said, "That is Scheveningen of the tall palaces, you foolish fellow; a blessing indeed for it gives me a firm fix."

On we sailed to the foemen's very lair at The Hook, but they lurked inside and feared to accept our challenge so now our trial was over and we could steer for our hearts' desire. The helmsman drew furrows in the sea that were true as swordcuts, and the stokers willed their engines not to falter and kept their needles on the line with ne'er a flicker. And the course was Alan's course; and although the casks had never ceased moving as the sea moved with tide and wind-drift, the god told him where they were and there he headed.

Rosy-fingered dawn tipped the sea, and our hearts lifted with the ships' prows as they clove the glittering water into churning foam. But when the prize seemed within our grasp a man smacked his lips and said, "Cor, just wait till I get me chops round that wallop"; and Poseidon heard it and frowned, saying, "These sons of men must learn that the gods' gifts are not to be taken lightly"; and he sent a fog so that we could scarcely see each other and water dripped from our noses, and barrels seemed to be over us and all around but when we looked straight at them they vanished. So we were humbled and carried out a square search, and when we had been tested enough the joyous cry was heard, "Object bearing green 50!"

Mortal men could never have lifted those casks unaided, but strength radiated from the magic liquid and in they rolled as though with a heavenly heave from under. And when we had put the Sunk and the Rough and the Cork behind us and passed the Spit of Landguard, the news swept before us through the land and all the young men and maidens ran to do us homage, and the old men limped behind; and a mighty sound arose which was never heard before nor will be again of the clashing of mess tins, fannies, dustbins, chamber-pots and every type of cauldron. And men became as beasts, contemptuously forebearing to pour a libation to their Olympian benefactor; and Poseidon's wrath was terrible, and changing himself into the guise of a Customs Officer drove raging on to the quay in a mighty chariot, to sweep away every single cask before our fuddled and fearful eyes.

And the casks still at sea bobbed, rolled and drifted for many a long day; and at last the good Poseidon guided them to the far-off country of the gentle Danes, then writhing under the cruel heel of a wicked tyrant, who mixed the elixir with black bread and made Øllebrød as their strange custom was. So they were sustained in their struggle, for never was tasted such Øllebrød before or since.

"What happened the next night was this," White of *241* told me, feeling justified in relaxing the lower-deck security code after 30 years: "we were at sea again, and I said to a lad, 'let's have a cuppa.' But when he came back his face was white and he said, 'look what's come out of the water-tank'; 25-gallon tank it was and there wasn't a drop of water in the boat, only Guinness. But the weather blew up so we had to come home and the Skipper never knew. Right Royal I'd have looked. Never found out who done it."

The Guinness saga was a pleasant introduction to MTB warfare for Ken Hartley and the crew of *244* who had recently arrived as a replacement for *237*. She was a great boat, and never once broke down if Ken is to be believed which he must be, despite the astonishing nature of his claim. He had been with a chemical firm in Rochdale with no experience of the sea; but like all my RNVRs was determined to get there, into Coastal Forces and at the enemy; he had served a thorough apprenticeship since the start of the war and I was delighted to have him.

While *234* was laid up for modifications Alan took the opportunity to join an East Coast destroyer and study our anti-E-boat defenses, which had progressed considerably since my *Cotswold* days. Basil Gerrard was appointed to relieve him and confesses to having thought, "My God, why should this happen to me?" He said, "I'm afraid I'm not as good a navigator as Alan," and I replied, "You will be," which he took for a grim exhortation but was in fact kindly meant for I knew he would be an asset. When Alan returned Basil stayed on in *234*, for although only two officers were allowed by complement our experience had shown that three were essential in the leader's boat; one to command, one to navigate and one to supervise the crew in action.

I got the 'flu, and Robert Hichens came to cheer me up. I asked him what were his plans for after the war and he replied, so casually that I could not at first put a meaning to his words, "I shan't survive the war."

I said something banal like, "Oh, go on!" But he was not fooling, and slightly amplified his point though without particular emphasis or philosophical analysis:

"I'm quite certain of it; but not to worry"; and he smiled. I stared rudely, trying to understand but failing. If I knew anything in that line it was that I *should* survive, not through logic but merely that I could not comprehend not doing so; and as I stared, a conviction which had been growing on me during our months together in *Beehive,* that Robert not only stood head and shoulders above the crowd but possessed the elements of, yes, greatness, became fixed and permanent. Despite our being nominally equal as Senior Officers of MGBs and MTBs respectively I acknowledged his superiority with uncharacteristic disinterest, and still hate it to be thought that he and I were in any way comparable.

At the end of February and all through March our engine reliability became if anything worse than it had been, especially *234*'s; we became half-ashamed to admit belonging to MTBs and the gunboat people were only human in wondering whether our reported successes from Lowestoft had been genuine. More galling still the weather was fair, and MTBs from other bases scored an outstanding run of successes; Gemmell from *Midge,* Wright from *Mantis* and Ward from *Wasp* (Dover). Today, I am proud to be able to tell them the great results of their actions in the words of Konteradmiral Lucht in command of North Sea defense, Befehlshaber der Sicherung der Nordsee: *"On account of increasing S-boat attack in March 1943 we had to go over to a system of sailing the convoys to pass through the danger area by day, despite the risk from air attack which soon developed on a heavy scale."*

I must emphasize that there was no hint of rivalry between us and Coastal Command Strike Wing. We never met yet we were the *Yang* and *Yin,* two complementary halves that together completed the circle of the 24 hours, they by day and we by night, to ensure that the enemy would always be at risk. It must be acknowledged that they made few attacks during the winter, having been withdrawn from operations in November 1942 after severe losses for re-equipping and training. They re-entered the fray in April 1943 in great numbers and with immediate success, far outstripping us in achievement for the rest of the war. But the fact that they were greatly helped to achieve that good start by being presented with daylight targets off the Dutch coast as a result of the MTBs' efforts at night has not, I believe, so far been brought out.*

In April our machinery clicked into gear at last, and stayed there; breakdowns became no more frequent than was reasonable to expect under wartime stress, and engines began to be changed for no other reason than that they had run their statutory 500 hours. No praise can be too high for those who achieved this triumph by their slogging, disheartening, unremitting overwork, from the Engineers and Artificers at the bases back up the line to the spare parts organization and the centers where engines were reconditioned. We had our Dumbflow silencers which really worked and boosted both our morale and operational capability; no longer the pitiful crawl at six knots which got us nowhere, nor the agonizing and dangerous wait while shafts were clutched from auxiliaries to mains. Our triple rudders reduced our turning circles by much more than a third through some freak of hydrodynamics; indeed our first turn at full speed was thrilling, like a Spitfire at full bank; but it put such a strain on the hull that an order had to be issued to take it easy, in Lordly language of course. In 234 Mayers proudly appropriated the Oerlikon, and Able Seaman Jock Craig joined to take over the 0.5s.

There came a new intensity of operations. That month we were out nine times; and though that will not seem much to escort ships who ran virtually nonstop, we spent all night in enemy waters at full alertness and tension, and I began to feel tired. But we were enthusiastically determined to re-establish our reputation as a fighting flotilla, and to ensure that we could never again be thought to be doing less than others to win the war. We sighted the enemy twice in the first half of the month; on the first occasion it was a trawler patrol early in the night which I let go in the hope of finding something bigger, and on the second he vanished and could not be found again. That I did not like at all, for I well knew what people were likely to say about a captain who they think may not have "used his utmost endeavor to close an enemy which it shall be his duty to engage."

On the 12th Hichens was killed, at close range and gallant to the last. Several attempts had been made to relieve him from command for a rest, and to pass on his ex-

---

*See S.W. Roskill, *The War at Sea*, Vol. II, pp. 259, 369.

perience to the young idea; but he had resisted them, being
big enough to defy authority when its decrees conflicted
with what he conceived to be his duty. I cannot define
what I felt as I saluted his body being carried up the steps
at the dock entrance; there was no shock because I knew
what had happened to be inevitable, but sadness at the loss
of someone so outstanding was poignant and very deep, so
deep that I quite forgot the selfish picture I had at first
formed of my own corpse being carried up those same
steps. Remember Hichens: a perfect, gentle, indomitable
knight in very truth.

The *Beehive* became noticeably depressed; and Jamie
Fraser in particular was suddenly very quiet, making oddly
wistful and apparently irrelevant remarks. What with one
thing and another it became really very important to the
21st Flotilla to find an enemy and get its teeth into him.
When we sailed on the 17th for our April sixth operation,
Jamie said to his bosom friend General Lee, "I wish you
were coming with me"; but that was impossible for Arthur
had very rightly been promoted to command one of the
4th Flotilla boats.

Jamie, Mac and I; we were the three founder-members
of the Flotilla and old, old friends of nearly a year's standing; it felt grand to be together, secure and aggressive at
the same time. We were, I thought, as well trained as we
could be, but nothing is ever perfect and I find I told Alan
to remind me to be beastly to Mac in the morning for leaving harbor with fenders over the side. We waited all night
off Ijmuiden for a convoy to turn up but of course none
did; and since we were growing ever chillier, heavier-lidded
and less alert I decided to spend the last hour of operational time in a sweep down the coast to The Hook; that
should wake us up and give more chance of finding an
enemy. The night was beautiful with the moon in the southwest, a slight breeze and perfect visibility, in other words
almost hopeless for reaching torpedo range unless we could
surprise the enemy by our tactics. All our training and experience would be needed for this job.

I held the usual briefing with the boats lying close to
each other, the wavelets gently slapping their chines. To
cover the distance we must sweep at 35 knots, and that
meant stopping as one boat the moment anything was

sighted or we should throw away surprise of any sort. Then Jamie was to create a diversion up moon and to seaward, using all his cheeky gusto to attract the enemy's attention, but without putting himself in real danger if possible. I stationed him on my port quarter so that he would have to cross between me and the enemy; then, when he opened fire or made smoke, I hoped that Mac and I would fade into obscurity.

"2,000 revs!" Mac and Jamie closed in on either quarter of *234* and stayed there, 20 feet away, as though fixed. Every detail of their boats was clear in the bright moonlight and I could even see their concentrated expressions and those of their Coxswains, White and Henry, as they applied their quite exceptional skill. My Saunders's course was rock-steady as it had to be, and with the Dumbflows operating the rush of wind and water were as loud as the engines and enhanced the thrill of speed and proximity. I found myself gasping with unadulterated joy at this scene of transcendent beauty and achievement, and paused to fix it in my memory; how important it is to do that if life is not to be a sad progression of jam yesterday and jam tomorrow, if there is a tomorrow, with a perpetual sense of loss in always failing to recognize the significance of something outstanding while it is actually happening.

Coastal Forces gave me several such indelible images. Only a week or so before, the same three boats were returning in the morning and I was enjoying a well-earned doze in the wheel house, when Alan woke me with, "*233* and *241* are doing something funny." I creaked through the narrow door to the bridge muttering grumpily, "I'll soon see whether it's funny or not." It did not seem to be; the two boats had separated on either side and were now racing back towards *234* at 40 knots on what seemed like collision courses. It was appallingly dangerous but there was nothing I could do but hold steadily on at 25 knots, because whatever relative velocity problem they were trying to solve would be invalidated by my least deviation. One boat swept across the bow with a margin of no more than a rapidly decreasing six feet, and the other simultaneously passed the same distance astern; then *234* became smothered in foam and heaved wildly on the two crossed washes.

Why this shattering of the tranquil dawn? First, fun;

secondly Jamie and Mac were surely trying to take the
mickey* out of me as a pompous, "pusser," over-serious RN
officer, in which they completely succeeded; and thirdly
I think they were proudly showing off their complete
mastery of the skill which I had demanded that they acquire, knowing instinctively that pleasure would outweigh
my fury. It did, and in some indefinable way their hare-
brained escapade bespoke their loyalty and our unity, so
that rightly or wrongly I took it for the greatest compli-
ment, and drenched and dripping, laughed and laughed
again.

Then there were the porpoises which shared with us a
patch of phosphorescence. To our dark-adapted eyes the
brilliance of the great silver-plated bodies, miracles of
streamlined perfection, as they leaped from the black depths
curving and dripping cold fire was dazzling. Then they
were back in their element with never a splash as though
holes had opened to receive them, and down, down, leaving
trails of opalescent light wherever they swam. How many
there were I cannot tell but it seemed like hundreds, at
every depth weaving patterns of silken spaghetti and playing Macs and Jamies across our own brightly foaming
bows. They were breathtakingly lovely and one did not
need to be a poet to appreciate them, nor to realize that
what we were seeing was likely to be unique for most of
us. If appreciation of a present wonder jerks a tear of
joy, or a grunt such as is, I guess, customary at the cli-
max of sexual love, only a fool will suppress them. Poor
fool!

So now to seize the fleeting moment forever took only
as long as the click of a camera's shutter, and then I quickly applied myself to the job. My eyes were those of the
unit, for the other two captains must keep one each of
theirs for station-keeping. No spray reached the bridge and
there was remarkably little vibration, but even so to put my
face into the 40-knot wind invited blurring tears and I had
to strike some ungainly attitudes to give myself a steady
horizon and a chance to see the first break in it. Our high
speed dictated intense concentration, for a minute's delay
in sighting would mean half a mile less range, and that
might make the difference between blundering into action
and using the finesse which was our only chance of success.

---

*Make fun of.

Thirty minutes of this was eye-aching and phantoms began to flit across my vision. I strained to see the real thing, yet feared I should; only another half hour and we could go home.

"Huh? Yes. STOP!"

I whirled round, yelled, threw my arms up like a traffic policeman, and allowing a split second for the message to register yanked the telegraphs. The three flying hulls curtsied in unison to a halt; they were beautiful to the last, but enough of that.

Trawler patrol—three ships—approaching—suitable targets at this time of night, the ban on using Mark VIII torpedoes having been lifted—the plan would do.

"Happy, Jamie?" I asked with fluttering heart and matter-of-fact voice.

"Aye aye, sir." The "sir," once unthinkable now passed unnoticed.

"Right; keep up your diversion long enough for me to get in my attack. After that I'll try and keep them occupied for you; OK?"

"Yes."

"Off you go then, good luck."

At that very moment the enemy challenged and lobbed a few languid and uncertain tracer rounds in our direction, just what I had tried to avoid. But Jamie knew what he must do and left us quite slowly so as not to rivet the enemy's attention too early, heading straight for him. Then he turned to seaward and let fly, knowing that his own tracer would blind the enemy to us. The last I saw of him was as he increased speed and the enemy's guns sprang into action, all satisfactorily directed at "puir wee" Jamie. But he was in his element and I could not bring myself to worry about him; he *must* have enjoyed himself to have acquitted himself so brilliantly. Not for him the slow, patient stalk which suited my ponderous thought processes; his brain was of quicksilver and he played that German bull like a *banderillero* leaping to plant his darts with perfect timing as the vicious horns swept a harmless inch past his lithe belly. In—a burst of fire; out—a puff of smoke; in again twisting and turning at full power, and never retiring for long enough to let the quarry look around him for the matador who shunned the limelight while preparing for the kill.

The enemy was probably so bewildered by Jamie's light-

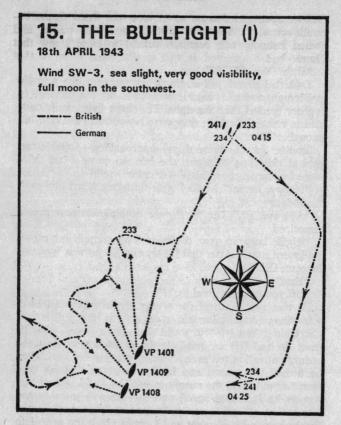

15. THE BULLFIGHT (I)

18th APRIL 1943

**Wind SW-3, sea slight, very good visibility,
full moon in the southwest.**

—·—·— British
——— German

ning darts that he judged *233* to be several boats, for his
final assessment of our complete unit was eight. He may
also have submitted to the natural instinct that expected
attack from the direction of England, moon or no moon.
He was what the Spaniards call a brave bull, meaning a
stolid one who charges the first man to wave a cloak at him,
because VPs *1401, 1409* and *1408* must have seen Mac and
me, beam on to them and bathed in moonlight, had they
even glanced in our direction. At least we were not audible,
downwind and running on our port engines with their
silenced exhausts away from them, and I began to realize
with growing amazement that the plan was going to work.

As we opened our angle on his bow the three shapes became clearly silhouetted against moon and tracer; and when, nearing their beams, I turned to close I saw that Jamie had disoriented as well as distracted them so that their line was in confusion.

Mac had slipped in astern of me for the stalk but now pulled out to port. I told Haynes to flash "Flag 4"—attack with torpedoes—on the dimmest of dim lights and if ever there was an unnecessary signal that was it. The range was down to 600 yards, closing slowly; the center trawler drew ahead of station and would soon overlap the leader, so that if I chose my moment well I could hardly miss one or the other. This was too easy, what had I done wrong or forgotten? Safety latches? OK. The two black shapes drew together; gloves off, clammy.

"Fire both!" And then an endless wait of 20 seconds. I glance at *241* and saw one of her torpedoes launched, and then back to my target as a quickly erupting black cloud obscured both ships. If that was a hit it was most unspectacular; one would have expected a flash from a 750-lb warhead exploding only six feet below the surface. Surely it must be? Yet I was painfully aware that torpedo hits are only too evident to those who want to see them. One of the trawlers appeared from the cloud.

It was time to move. I told Saunders to steer northeast and jangled the telegraphs, leaving them at full ahead; Cuthbert was quick to react having felt the torpedoes go, and the boat, light without them, flew. The enemy could not fail to see us now and as usual our escape dash was spectacular through the gay tracer; but there was little danger for the shooting was panicky and erratic, the Germans having been caught on the wrong foot at every stage, and having covered a bare half mile and feeling master of events, I stopped rather contemptuously to size up the situation. The shooting stopped too as I had arrogantly anticipated; without our stern plums the enemy's gunners were blinded by their own tracer and lost their aiming point.

My view was clear again, the smoke-pall had dispersed, and—oh no!—there were still three trawlers; Mac and I must both have missed. "What's the good of you?" the *Somali*'s Captain had asked, and there was still no answer. Then the center ship sank; she just slipped away without fuss or flamboyance as she had taken the torpedo. She

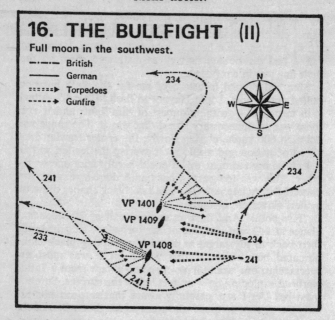

16. THE BULLFIGHT (II)

Full moon in the southwest.

—·—·— British
———— German
======▶ Torpedoes
-----▶ Gunfire

234

234

241

234

VP 1401

VP 1409

233

VP 1408

234

241

241

was the *VP 1409*, ex-steam trawler *Limburgia* of 217 tons, and she took two officers and 11 men down with her.

The Flotilla had thus so far killed 70 to 80 men. That is an uncomfortable thought today but then we hardly considered it, far less worried. Quite the reverse in fact for it was relief that flooded through me; all the effort, money, experience, manpower, training which we represented— that is to say a part of the nation's war effort which might have been used in other spheres—were wasted unless we *sank* the enemy during the fleeting seconds when the opportunity offered; the war would not be won by good intentions, we earned no bonus marks for trying. My satisfaction was therefore sober, but the crew not thus inhibited raised a cheer, and banged on the engine room hatch to tell Cuthbert, Clarke and Gilbert.

I searched in vain for signs of a hit by Mac; pity! But presumably Jamie still had his torpedoes, so clearly I must try to create conditions in which he could fire them with some chance of success. I noticed that the only gunnery

20 mm Oerlikon Gun

in progress was at the southern end of the enemy's line which was obviously occasioned by Mac; Jamie's section was unnaturally quiet. I must therefore attack the van end and, disagreeable realization, do it forcibly because Jamie would be approaching with the moon behind him and the enemy must be made to believe that *234* was a real threat. Certainly our new Oerlikon would help persuade him, and I told the two gunners that our survival depended on straight, steady shooting. I put it in the form, "Here's the chance you've been waiting for, lads," but felt slightly sick myself because this eyeball to eyeball business would be dangerous. Despite our rivalry with the gunboats I gave them best when it came to stand-up courage; not for me the crude bludgeoning of gunnery in-fighting, rather the rapier-thrust of a torpedo—from a safe distance.

We were seen as soon as we started, and although the shooting was not at first accurate there was foreboding in *VP 1401*'s big 88mm splashes and our highly prized Oerlikon was a toy in comparison; never mind though, we were a difficult target and this was the right thing to do. I retained a sense of dominance for it was we who acted while the enemy merely reacted. At about 500 yards I swung the boat to starboard enough to allow Craig to engage with his 0.5's; I liked the steady, unflustered way he did it and the faultless regularity of his weapons—bless those Wrens. I liked too his streams of tracer which filled the view and made the enemy's fire seem less. The machine guns were able to fire more or less continuously, so it seemed right to start them well outside effective range and make it clear to the enemy that he was supposed to look in our direction.

At full speed the range quickly closed and the enemy's accuracy improved; his tracer was flatter in trajectory and the sonic boom of his overs were close and loud. Having told Mayers to delay opening fire so as not to expand his 60-round drum outside hitting range, I now shouted and waved at him to begin; but whether he was aware of me or not was immaterial for he knew this to be his moment.

Oh, very pretty! The enemy's shape was hidden by tracer but his gun-flashes gave Mayers his aiming points and on these he concentrated to the exclusion of noise, light, wind, bumping and every other distraction. At once *1401*'s fire lifted high over our heads and we had imposed our will on her again. I drove on to exploit this and do what damage we could with our tiny shells; we might perhaps detonate an ammunition locker and set the ship on fire, but although nothing like that happened we did hit her and wounded several men. We were untouched. I brought the range down to about 200 yards, twice what Hichens had considered effective but quite close enough for our purpose, and then turned north and away when I thought Mayer's drum must be nearly empty; trust my crew though I did, a bungled re-load in those circumstances was possible and would be embarrassing. We could always come in again.

In my report I noted; "It became evident at this time that *233* was not attacking," though why I thought so I cannot now remember. Mac's engagement was certainly over and all guns on both sides were silent.

"Steer west; carry on smoking—tell the engine room it's all over."

Tension drained away, tongues were loosened, and Saunders's specialty of hot, greasy soup with glutinous lumps in it appeared from nowhere to be savored as nectar. I loved the intimate, generous camaraderie of the cigarette; one man would light another's, a match expertly kept alight in cupped hands, or often with the glowing tip of his own;

those with their hands full would be given one already lit, and there were no barriers of rank. "Here you are, 'Swain," said Mayers to Saunders, his inveterate enemy and firm friend, and even I was included. It was always a good moment, and we of *234* were mightily pleased to belong to her and to each other.

We met Mac, poor Mac, despondent and apologetic. He had been influenced by the order not to waste Mark VIII torpedoes and had fired only one, missing ahead; then, since he had allowed a mere four knots enemy speed, he concluded that his target must be stopped and fired the second torpedo accordingly; but as it left the tube, gouts of smoke issued from *VP 1408*'s funnel and she gathered way, causing that one to miss astern. As Mac spoke I kicked myself hard; I was by now entirely convinced that torpedoes must be fired in pairs or not at all but had not said so, assuming I suppose that my captains would read my mind. When would I ever learn?

"Seen anything of *233?*" I asked.

Yes, she was disengaging to the west so we set off in pursuit. No message came from her but that was only mildly disquieting because of our absurdly outdated W/T sets. It was not until dawn that we sighted her a mile away on a parallel course; she looked in good shape with three engines running well, and I looked forward to hearing Jamie's account of his adventures for it was bound to be colorful.

But there was no Jamie. Instead a white-faced boy revealed clearly that he was at the end of his tether long before he was near enough to tell us why; then, "The Captain's dead! The Captain's dead!" Our eyes moved to the forward petrol hatch for confirmation; what Jamie had left behind was so very small under its canvas shroud. Something quite big had gone.

In the quiet of the *Beehive* office we analyzed what had happened. After missing with his torpedoes Mac, disgusted, had gritted his teeth and determined to do something useful at whatever cost. Knowing the plan was to create a diversion for Jamie he had closed *VP 1408* and opened fire; old Harry was up to form and hit her, causing casualties. But because Mac could not conceive that Jamie would succeed from up-moon, he had crossed under the motor-tug's stern so as to occupy that side himself and allow *233* the shadows to landward. Since such a course had never occurred to me I had not ruled it out as too likely to cause confusion and felt wretched yet again; what on earth was the good of a leader who could not communicate? But voice radio might have helped prevent disaster.

Jamie had continued his diversionary tactics for ten long minutes, as I already knew for they were still in full vigor when I pulled my triggers. He had then disengaged temporarily, but only in order to return for a torpedo attack; encouraged perhaps by Mac's and my gunnery he judged the moment superbly, but as 233 neared firing range undetected by both the enemy and Mac, 241 came roaring across her bows and revealed her in all her vulnerability. VP 1408 saw her chance, shifted her fire from 241, and with no deflection on her gunsights delivered a concentrated, devastating blast at 233. Jamie died instantly, hit in the head; his coxswain, the doughty Bob Henry, was badly wounded and Ordinary Seaman Brown was also hurt. The boat was struck in many places including the port torpedo tube, and all her wounds were in front. Gordon Fish, the First Lieutenant, very young and very new, inherited this blood bath and disengaged, quite rightly.

Mac and I mourned our loss together, mostly in silence as our natures dictated. We were perhaps unduly downcast, Jamie having been rather special because his ebullience perfectly complemented our reserve and we needed him. He was a real friend too, as he was to many, in particular Alan Jensen and General Lee who lived with him in the RAF Mess, and General could not bear to go on board his old boat, 233, for some time. I also felt suddenly weary of the whole messy business of war and wondered whether our hitherto prodigious luck was on the turn.

But Admiral Rogers at Harwich struck the right note in a kind though mathematical signal: "Congratulations on a successful action. I am sorry you have lost a good officer but the account stands well on the credit side."

Jamie's father, an old Chief Pilot on the Irrawaddy, made the same point in reply to my letter of condolence, which had been less difficult to write than some for my praise could be truly unstinting. Utter sincerity infused his formality:

> We are indeed pleased that James was esteemed by his fellow officers; we shall miss him terribly but shall ever be proud to remember that he gave his life in his country's cause.

That his action in which he lost his life was worthy
of mention in your official report is a matter of satisfaction to us, and for his memory's sake we hope it
may be recognized by the Admiralty. (It was, with a
Mention in Despatches.) We pray for the success of
yourself and your brothers-in-arms in your future operations.

Repining was nonsense. Hichens and his gunboats had
had far more men killed every time they fought; and the
exchange of one young man for an enemy ship sunk was
insignificant in comparison to an army battle for a few
miles of desert in which the casualties might be numbered
in tens of thousands. The war remained to be won and won
it must be; morale demanded that we forget quickly and
press on. But—oh Jamie!

XI

THE FOUR HORSEMEN

We learned from the Bullfight that the diversionary plan could be made to work and there seemed every reason to go on using it, especially because it was capable of great variation so that the enemy should not be able to detect too much of a pattern, at least for a time.

There were other interesting things we might have learned had the Germans minuted their action report to us, one being disturbing: "Our radio intercepts service reports that at 0401 *MTB 234* reported three auxiliary vessels in position (such-and-such). The position is slightly too far north."

That was my enemy report, transmitted as soon as Jamie opened fire, and as such was uncoded on grounds of speed as was the rule; there was thus nothing unexpected in the enemy getting the message, but he certainly should not have been able to identify the originating boat with her frequently changed call-sign. As to the position being in error I spring to Alan's defense; the one we gave was ours, we were two or three miles north of the enemy, and I believe that Alan was spot on. But then comes: "At 0530 *MTB 234* sent a message that she was on a course of 260°, 25 knots and requested fighter cover."

The Germans should not have been able to decode that, even though their doing so might have had the beneficial effect of deterring them from sending their own fighters after us. Of course we only carried the simplest coding system for the good reasons that we operated in enemy waters and that it had to be looked after by unpredictable young officers, *vide* this whimsical advertisement in *The Beehive Almanac:*

LOST. Two code-cards between Felix and Orwell Hotels. Finder please communicate with *MGB 79* or direct to Wilhelmstrasse.

* * *

Now it seems that we might just as well have carried no codes at all.

More encouraging to us would have been 1st Sicherungsdivision's conclusions. In paraphrase:

> Of the eight S-boats one was certainly sunk, one probably sunk and two were damaged. On the other hand the loss of a VP Boat is very much to be regretted as we were already short of suitable craft for this work. As a result of this action I consider it absolutely necessary to strengthen the patrols to at least four boats each, which will mean reducing the number of groups at sea.

One would not have thought that the enemy would care very much about the loss of one armed trawler; but since he clearly did so, why did he send them out asking for trouble when there was no convoy to defend? Perhaps because he truly thought they were knocking off one or two MTBs a night, which would certainly have been a useful profit. And for our part, why did we have to attack the patrols at some risk when our main targets were merchant ships; because the enemy did not like it? That was certainly a reason of some sort and a chain of logic builds up, but surely there must have been some more fundamental reason which has not so far emerged.

Three evenings later we were off again, the base having done a wonderful job on *233*. Her crew however were not so easily repaired; having lost their two strong leaders, Jamie and Bob Henry, they were listless and I was worried. The traditional treatment of putting them into action again immediately seemed indicated, and I told Tom Neill to take temporary command and sort them out. Although new to our Flotilla he was an old hand, with a DSC, and did the job wonderfully; he made them double everywhere, was satisfied with nothing but perfection, and found things for them to do the whole way to Holland to take their minds off their troubles. Then they took the battle in their stride and afterwards two of them thanked Tom with visible tears in their eyes for they had been in danger of being lost.

The battle? Oh yes, the battle. Its title is "The Bottom" and it ranks with Barfleur and the T-boats for unrelieved, lip-biting, white-knuckled woe. Four of us went to The

Hook; in my division I had *232*, commanded by a newly promoted young gentleman called Val Ohlenschlager who sounded as though he ought to belong to the other side but was as English as a gaily debonair Regency buck. "O," his full name was altogether too difficult, had a penchant for parties and fast cars, run it was said on 100 octane MTB fuel which was very naughty and blew one sparking plug clean out, with a bit of fighting when his mood served. Tom and Mac formed the other division. We thought the enemy was a convoy leaving harbor, but he was in fact one of 1st Sicerungsdivision's augmented patrol groups of five ships led by *VP 1311* and including *VP 1417*, a Pilot Vessel of 500 tons which was shaped like a merchant ship and looked big, adding verisimilitude to our mistake.

It was another lovely night with the moon now full to the south, and again I had small hope of an unobserved attack; but as we closed I saw that the enemy was very near to the shore indeed, and some ships had their navigation lights on as though they were still in the process of forming up. Let's catch them like that, I thought, and crept inshore with *232* to the north of them and down-moon; but since the move was something of a gamble I left the 2nd Division to seaward so as to have them well separated and ready to begin the diversionary game in the second phase. It would have been wrong to send them to the up-moon side for that would have blown the gaff before I was ready.

As we stealthy predators slithered towards our prey we were not seen as we should have been, and yet I was pleased to find that I was developing a sixth sense which warned me when that would happen. The land showed up clearly now, with buildings and the two great curved moles which marked the river mouth; and the nearer we came the better, for what more natural than a couple of small craft, waiting perhaps to take off pilots? I even told Haynes to keep his finger on the navigation light switch so as to reassure the enemy should he be at all uncertain of our identity. We had Lieutenant Commander Hey on board *234*, the Torpedo Officer from the working-up base at Weymouth, who had come to see how things should be done and now we prepared to show him.

"Always start by having a good all-round look in case you're being jumped from behind," I pontificated. "Nothing there? Right; now what enemy speed shall we set? We've been watching him for some time now and I shouldn't think he's going any more than five knots, would you? Sight

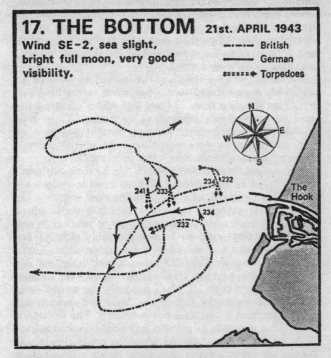

17. THE BOTTOM 21st. APRIL 1943

Wind SE-2, sea slight, bright full moon, very good visibility.

—·—·— British
———— German
======▶ Torpedoes

set. Angle on the bow about 85 degrees, d'you think? Not far off anyway. Range 500 yards? Really we're very nicely placed you know, it doesn't always happen as neatly as this." And truly it was miraculous, with what must have been *VP 417* presenting her full beam sharply silhouetted by the moon's silver backdrop and no more dangerous than the old paddler in Weymouth Bay.

"Ready both—steer two degrees to starboard—stand by! I always used to forget to trip the safety-latches," I smirked to Hey; "nothing can be more infuriating—fire both! Now we have to wait a bit, always rather tiresome."

We waited, and tiresome it was. The two fish leaped over the bow with their propellers whirring correctly, dived as was normal, and stayed down as was not; so far inshore

had we come that there was quite simply insufficient water
for them to recover from their initial dives and they just
stuck in the mud. With less pomposity and more concentration I might have thought to tell Alan to take a sounding,
which he would otherwise not have done for fear of the
noise being detected on the enemy's hydrophones. Saunders
passed the word to the crew, aside: "The skipper's missed;
don't anyone dare say a word."

The enemy saw us then and we turned to seaward at
full speed, edging round to the southwest across his bows
to take his attention from *233* and *241* whom we saw waiting in the wings to starboard as we passed. They were
separated from each other which I thought was wise of
Tom, and when we were well clear, with all the enemy's
gunnery chasing after us, they came in to attack.

Both missed, Mac unaccountably, for he took two overlapping ships as his targets and fired both torpedoes together in accordance with the doctrine now engraven on
his heart. He reported the range as 1,000 yards which
would have been a bit far, though I doubt whether it was
as much as that; even so he was probably right to fire
when completely unobserved as I had often done. Tom's
target was obviously *VP 1417* again, a lucky ship, and his
torpedoes were running true, the starboard one to miss
ahead and the port to hit, when suddenly she turned away
and combed the tracks. If that was deliberate avoiding action the German report does not mention it. The secondary
effect, Tom said, was to provoke her neighbors into engaging her hotly and scoring hits which he could clearly see.
Pained, she fired no fewer than three bursts of recognition
fireworks and when those failed to deter she replied with
her own guns. The German report makes no mention of
that little incident either and I trust I am not maligning
them, but Tom saw it all very clearly; it was only when *233*
and *241* exposed their beams to disengage that they were
recognized as the real enemies.

I made a wide circle round the enemy and stopped to
the south of him, to discover that "O" had not fired when
I had for some doubtlessly good reason, though not because
he was wiser than I and knew the depth to be too shallow.
232 therefore became the last hope of the side, and I
signalled the 2nd Division to continue its diversion to the
north and led her back to the enemy, releasing her to do the
final bit on her own. "O" was seen before he was ready,

pressed on and fired from 700 yards, and missed as seemed
to be foreordained on that inglorious night. *VP 1311* reported the near-miracle of one torpedo passing ahead and
one astern; and they were not imaginary ones either because she heard them coming on her hydrophone.

We had not realized that the enemy was behaving
thoroughly offensively as soon as he woke up to what was
going on, and had actually tried to pursue us on two occasions. That was a good tactic as we were confused by his
frequent changes of course, and because his turns towards
us would automatically comb the tracks of any torpedoes
which happened to be running; so although it might seem
over-sanguine to chase a 40-knot boat in a 12-knot one
there was merit in aggressive tactics as there often is.

It has also become clear that although the Germans
objected to losing VPs they were prepared to risk them in
order to destroy MTBs, and that was the sole object of
these patrols. It is not clear why they reasoned like that
when their overriding aim was the safety of their convoys,
which would probably have been better achieved by cluster-
ing all available escorts round them; and when they knew
that there could be no engagement unless we the enemy,
with our small size and high speed, elected to start one.
We might be minelaying of course but even then we had
the initiative, and if our planned position was occupied by
a patrol we could either wait for it to pass or lay our
mines elsewhere. And we? Were we right to attack and
give the Germans the opportunity of sinking us they
sought? Was the Knight Errant achieving a valuable strategic purpose in having a tilt at any Wicked Knight he
happened to come across in his roamings? Our orders were
still couched in the sense that, "You might as well have a
go at the trawlers at the end of the night if there's nothing
bigger about," which was hardly an inspiring inducement
to risk lives and boats though I felt instinctively that it
was right. But why? I propose to let these questions brew
a little longer still while the evidence accumulates.

241 was tense; two misses in three days were deeply
worrying to Mac and his crew, for if ever a boat was
dedicated to prosecuting the war it was that one. We all
saw their unhappiness but could do nothing to help; in the
wardroom we said nothing, which may have made it worse
for Mac who probably thought quite wrongly that we eyed

him with intolerable patronage. The Lower Deck made it
quite clear that they did:

"Going to sea tonight, Knocker? Well that'll give Jerry
a nice let-up."

Coxswain White would retaliate of course, but without
conviction. It was not to be borne, yet what could be
done? Torpedo aiming was a skill like hitting a ball in the
right direction with bat, club or racket, and everyone knows
how sometimes that will never go right however hard one
practices. Whatever the fault Mac determined to overcome
it in his own way, and that meant inventing a gadget. He
saw clearly that for the captain to set the sight and give
the coxswain constant wheel orders was time-wasting and
unnecessary, so he devised a system of rods which re-
produced his own settings on a fore and back sight in front
of the coxswain who steered so as to keep them in line
with the target. So simple when one thinks of it, but nobody had.

The "Mac Repeater Sight" was ready in *241* by April 28
and the three original musketeers were on the prowl again.
In *234* I was determined to have a "Top" to outweigh "The
Bottom"; in *241* Mac was the same only more so, growling
like a man-eating tiger; and in *233* Peter Standley had
arrived to take Jamie's place and was out to prove he could.
That was not easy, his predecessor was still being actively
mourned, and coming from outside *Beehive* he had to pick
up our ways in a very short time. A greater contrast is
unimaginable; Peter was quiet, courteous, self-effacing, the
scion of a long line of solicitors in a Norfolk country town.
That was fine, for there were many budding lawyers in
Coastal Forces besides Hichens, and all those I knew made
good warriors, perhaps because of their ability to follow a
line of reasoning to its logical conclusion, mistrusting shallow argument and animal instincts. Peter was penetrating
with his questions and I liked his puckish grin; he would
be all right.

We were told to sweep between Ijmuiden and The Hook,
but there were so many lights showing at the former place
that I decided to stay there in case they portended the arrival or departure of shipping. Hoping again to find ships
leaving harbor in a preoccupied frame of mind, we closed
to within a mile of the breakwaters; the lighthouse was lit
which was hopeful, but the other lights which stretched
along the coast in both directions glowed as though their

purpose was illumination. We could not guess why this
should be though the explanation is quite simple, fortifica-
tion of landing beaches against the much discussed Second
Front.

Nothing came our way for hour after hour but I still felt
we were in a good position; although the April moon was
now old and would not rise till dawn, the weather remained fine and the visibility excellent so that I was sure
we should see anything passing to seaward as well as
traffic to and from Ijmuiden. So it happened; the enemy
was a group of the 14th Patrol Flotilla some of whom we
had met in the last two actions, and the time being late in
the night they were our proper targets. Such groups were
familiar sights in Coastal Forces and had been dubbed
"The Four Horsemen of the Apocalypse" by some erudite
young officer:

> And the heads of the horses were as the heads of
> lions; and out of their mouths issued fire and smoke
> and brimstone ... For their power is in their mouth,
> and in their tails; for their tails were like unto serpents
> ... and with them they do hurt. (Revelations 9:17)

The scholar would of course have been RNVR; we who
had been dragged up at Dartmouth were "state educated"
and unenlightened.

Starting our approach from inshore was good for surprise, and although there was no chance of sending one
boat round to the other side we could at least separate
from each other and perhaps cause mutual diversions. I
stopped to hold a careful briefing, and then we padded in
at slow speed on whichever engine exhausted away from
the enemy. The 14th VP Flotilla suspected nothing until
0335 but then their reaction was very fast; 234 in the center, and slightly ahead of the other two boats, was first to
be seen and a concentrated fire was opened at 600 yards
which I should call murderous except that no one was
killed or even hurt. My sight was lined up on the third
ship, speed setting five knots course south, but as soon as
the shooting started the point of aim was obscured; I loosed
off at a gunflash, but who could tell whether my hand
shook a little? I could, and it did; furthermore the German
Senior Officer in VP 1401 took the bold emergency action
of turning his group towards us, combing the tracks. So I

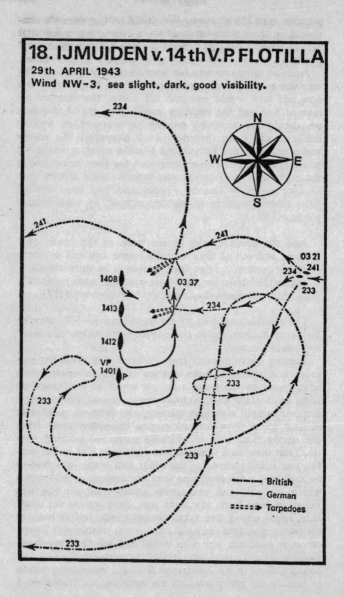

18. IJMUIDEN v. 14th V.P. FLOTILLA
29th APRIL 1943
Wind NW-3, sea slight, dark, good visibility.

missed, but Mac was directly helped by the enemy's concern with me and had a clear run in for a few more vital seconds. White told him, "If we don't hit this time . . . ," and indeed it just had to be. Mac pressed in ever closer, the repeater sight did everything expected of it and White held the boat steady until the torpedoes were well into the water.

Then 241 was seen, fiercely engaged by her own target at close range, and White finished his sentence, ". . . we've had it." She was only hit twice, once in the turret which slightly wounded Harry the Gunner but his life was saved by the bulletproof plating, and then the enemy's guns were carried below the surface. The enemy's turn had helped 241 who had had to fire from the quarter, because it meant that his beam was presented to the torpedoes when they arrived; one of them hit, and the explosion was so massive that spray fell on to 241 as she disengaged close astern.

Mac and 241 were justified; and more than that they had avenged Jamie's death by a coincidence so strange that were this story fictional it would stretch credulity too far, for they had sunk the very ship which had killed him, VP 1408. She was only a tiny tug of 107 tons, the Cycloop, but her epitaph must be that she was a plucky fighter whose gunners knew their business; she went down so quickly that only the captain and 15 men, mostly wounded, floated off, two officers and 19 men being lost.

Peter Standley was wonderful in 233. He had the farthest to go to reach the leading ship and the battle started before he was in position; blinded by tracer he felt unjustified in firing into the brown and disengaged, returning immediately for another try but with no better luck. Then he zoomed right round the enemy and came in again from the other side, but alas the 14th Flotilla was not to be caught by this sort of thing twice and was ready for him.

As Peter disengaged again he signalled to me, "Attack completed," not realizing that this conventionally implied that torpedoes had been fired. I therefore told all boats to disengage; but that was not at all what Peter meant so he turned his blind eye—"Leave off action? Now damn me if I do!"—and circled the enemy yet again to the inshore side. If only he had been with us a little longer he would have thought of telling me, "Intend attacking from inshore," and I should at once have dashed in again from seaward to distract the enemy. As it was 233 found herself too fine on her chosen target's bow and was seen and heavily engaged before Peter could do anything about it; this time she was hit five times by 20mm shells and the starboard torpedo damaged, though very luckily no one was hurt. Peter decided to break off then, and fair enough; for a first effort he earned full marks *with* a bonus for trying, because although only results count in war, battle experience should properly be regarded as a part of training.

We should have found some of the enemy's comments after this skirmish of absorbing interest. In précis form again:

By 1st Sicherungsdivision

The loss of *VP 1408* is the second in nine days to S-boats. Material and personnel losses of this kind are scarcely bearable as we have no replacements. Our patrol boats with their deep draught, slow speed, and poor maneuverability cannot compete with S-boats which reach torpedo firing range, and the fitting of radar is therefore most urgent.

By Befehlshaber der Sicherung der Nordsee

The loss of our own patrol boats in April must be considered more serious than the sinking of three enemy boats and the damaging of five or six others.* As well as the high losses of personnel, 34, they represent a sensible material loss which cannot be made up.

Our crews have behaved excellently in the most trying circumstances. Nevertheless there is a danger that morale might sink in this "trench warfare at sea" unless we can deploy fast well-armed craft which can act offensively instead of just sitting waiting to be attacked. I propose that six newly built fast boats should be equipped as MTB hunters with 37mm and 20mm guns but without torpedoes, and sent to my command with the utmost urgency.

Our policy of changing the times when the convoys pass along the Dutch coast has not paid off because casualties from air attack have been heavy.

By Marineoberkommando Nordsee (C-in-C North Sea)

Of first importance is the absolute necessity to

_____
*Not so of course.

strengthen our escort forces against air and S-boat attack, otherwise we shall have to expect greater losses. But increasing the number of escorts can only be done if other important defense measures are reduced; and our lack of defensive forces, which will not improve in the foreseeable future, can only be overcome in practical terms by re-organizing the present convoy and escort procedures. We agree with the request for S-boat pursuit craft.

The demands made on leaders and crews in April were unusually heavy and their performance deserves particular recognition.

To all this pleasing despondency should be added the fact that the Swedes did not take at all kindly to a steady trickle of their ships being sunk by mine, aircraft or MTB on the Rotterdam run; and they now felt brave enough, the general pattern of the war increasingly favoring the Allies, to refuse to allow them any further than Emden. This strained the German inland transport system considerably.*

That the sinking of a 100-ton tug should, when added to the achievements of the RAF and other MTB Flotillas, become significant in the realms of strategy by a few short and logical steps would have astonished us. Whether it would have had the same effect on our Commander-in-Chief I cannot say, but I suspect so for had he realized the importance of our activities he would surely have said so and encouraged us to greater efforts; but all we got was, "You might as well attack the trawlers . . ."

The crucial factor of morale, on which success or failure in battle absolutely depends, was at stake. I do not mean the total failure that results in mutiny or turning tail on the enemy, though such things can happen and are often nearer the surface than is fashionable to admit; and I believe that few individuals complete a prolonged tour of active duty without either cracking up or coming very close to it at some time. I am concerned now with the top end of the morale scale, that extra, almost superhuman push that gives victory over an otherwise equal foe. An MTB Captain might close to say 600 yards because he was told

_____

*S.W. Roskill, *The War at Sea*, Vol. II, p. 390.

to; or because he knew that Big Brother was watching and
did not want it said that he had failed; or because he might
earn a DSC with a bit of luck; or because, being intelligent,
honest, loyal, he would do his duty because it was his
duty—all my people were like that. But he would press
home to 500 yards and hit for sure, only when he was absolutely convinced in his own mind that what he was doing
overrode in importance all personal considerations so that
the risk to his own life became acceptable to him. Just
imagine the setback to the Germans had we sunk five or
six ships in our three trawler actions as analysis shows
would have been by no means impossible. As it was we
were given little leadership or Intelligence, and thought
we had done pretty well to bag two; and so we had in the
light of our directive, "You might as well . . ."

XII

HITS AND NEAR MISSES

"A drunken woman is an abomination." That quotation is not from the Good Book but from Tommy Kerr, delivered in dreadful tones at Wrens Defaulters to some lass who had emerged from a boat more sinned against, I suspect, than sinning. I nevertheless include it as the simple expression of a fundamental truth, and also because it struck me as funny at a time when I began to feel very much in need of something to laugh at.

Strain, when it has insinuated itself into one's system, becomes self-perpetuating and predominant. In assessing the wind strength before an operation I could not stop myself hoping that it would be too strong; we should win the war of course, but the end was nowhere in sight and I did so wish it was like a term at school when one at least knew how long one had to stick it out. Excitement in the early days had comprised part eagerness, part fear, but now we had seen it all and there was little to inspire eagerness; only one radically new experience remained—to die. Yet I was fearfully conscious that without eagerness, tactical innovation, forceful training, convincing leadership, quick and accurate decision—my *raisons d'être* as Senior Officer —would become dull, and inadequate for defeating a virile enemy or for discharging my awesome responsibilities to my own people. Whether I tried to ignore the tension or faced it squarely made little difference; it gnawed my vital energy, never excessive at the best of times, and I was tired, so tired. I wanted to talk it out with others who felt the same but that was taboo; I wanted to get drunk but knew the hangover would be unbearable; so I laughed brittlely and overloud, and fell back on the old expedient of pretending to be brave. The real answer was to trust in God and keep my powder dry, but I had not yet learned even the beginning of wisdom.

19. MINESWEEPERS (I)
14th MAY 1943

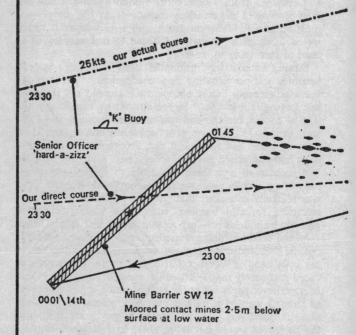

—·—·— British
———— German

25 kts our actual course

23 30

'K' Buoy

Senior Officer
'hard-a-zizz'

01 45

Our direct course
23 30

23 00

0001 \ 14th

Mine Barrier SW 12
Moored contact mines 2·5m below
surface at low water

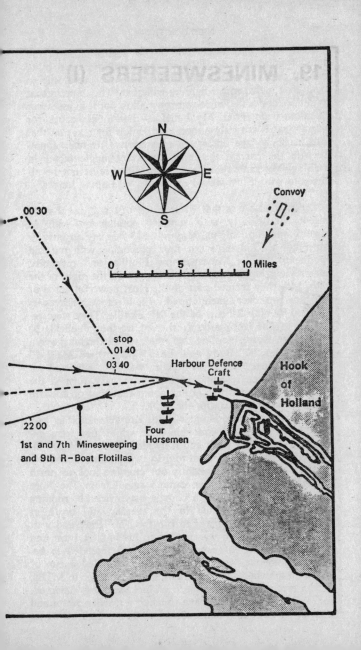

N

W   E

S

Convoy

00 30

0   5   10 Miles

stop
01 40

03 40   Harbour Defence   Hook
          Craft   of
                        Holland

22 00

1st and 7th Minesweeping
and 9th R–Boat Flotillas

Four
Horsemen

Being tired and lonely but by no means finished, my state of mind was no different from millions of fighting men all over the world. My only reason for presuming to mention it is that much fighting will always be done in that condition, and a nation at war must allow for it in assessing its military potential. My belief is that a just cause for waging war is not only a moral obligation for a nation that calls itself civilized but, given approximate strategic equality with the enemy, the most important single factor in winning. My generation *knew* that Hitler must not be allowed to win, it just wasn't on; so we kept going longer.

The silly part was that I felt much better at sea than in harbor, particularly with summer coming on with its warmth and short nights. May of 1943 was not so busy as April but we did have our final reckoning with our old opponents the 1st Minesweeping Flotilla, and redeemed our previous humiliation at their hands. On the night of the 13th/14th they formed part of the most powerful force of warships we ever encountered, 12 Fleet Minesweepers escorted by nine R-boats of the 9th Flotilla.. They were returning to The Hook after freshening up the minefields 30 miles to seaward, "fouling the area" in minelaying jargon, not far from "K" Buoy and the position where *MTB 30* had been mined. It was an activity we never expected for one moment, or I should certainly not have formed the habit of taking a cat nap at just about that spot on the trip across, so as to be fresh for the battle.

That we did not blunder into Korvettenkapitän von Grumbkow and his formidable team while they were engaged in their dirty work and fully alert was a stroke of ill-deserved luck. We had been told to sweep from Noordwijk to The Hook and consequently our crossing took us north of their minefield; but then came a signal from The Nore to say that the southbound convoy was evidently running late, having been sighted in the evening still north of Ijmuiden. My reaction was to run for The Hook and wait for it there; but Alan was not up to his highest form and put us five miles to seaward of where I intended to be. Perhaps someone jogged his elbow or up-ended a cup of cocoa on the chart, navigational hazards endemic to MTBs.

The error was another piece of luck, still less deserved, for without it we should have run into a trawler patrol and a group of Harbor Defense Craft which were all keyed up and waiting to receive the convoy; and much worse, we should have been immobile as we did so, for as we cut engines Leading Stoker Clarke hauled himself out of the engine room, only just succeeding despite his toughness, to report that an exhaust pipe had leaked and that Cuthbert and Gilbert were unconscious. I strongly suspect a degree of heroism from all three to have kept going for so long, but now there was no doubt of it; the two limp forms having been instantly fished out and laid in the fresh air, Cuthbert stirred after some minutes, vomited, clutched his head in excruciating pain and staggered below again to mend the pipe.

In a very short time we were operational; but Cuthbert and Clarke were both very weak while Gilbert remained completely *hors de combat*, for their trouble was not just lack of air but acute carbon monoxide poisoning. Our training paid off however, for Mayers was able to take charge of Gilbert's engine and our excellent Third Officer from New Zealand, Natusch, took general charge below; everything worked perfectly from then on.

We were allowed two hours' grace before von Grumbkow arrived and then we heard him on the hydrophone, first by a succession of metallic clicks as from an echosounder or acoustic minesweep, and then by loud and confused propeller noises from a large number of ships, obviously the convoy. The direction was southwest, but after a few minutes we deduced by the change of bearing that the enemy's course was east towards The Hook; but the hydrophone gave us no range and it was hard to guess the visibility, for although the weather was fine and the last quarter moon was setting in the southwest there seemed to be a slight haze. So in order to sight on the flank rather than ahead of the enemy I steered at slow speed straight down the bearing, with *244* (Ken Hartley) to port, and *241* (Mac) and *232* (O) forming the 2nd Division to starboard.

Two minutes later there they were, four large ships with smaller escorts steering east, and we were perfectly positioned on their port bow. I wondered whether to go in with all my boats in line abreast, separating as we closed as we had done the last time, but the escorts were all well placed and might rumble us too early; I decided therefore to try the diversionary scheme in depth, the idea being for Ken and me to go in first and disengage to the flanks so as to

20. MINESWEEPERS (II)

Calm, phosphorescence, poor visibility, setting moon.

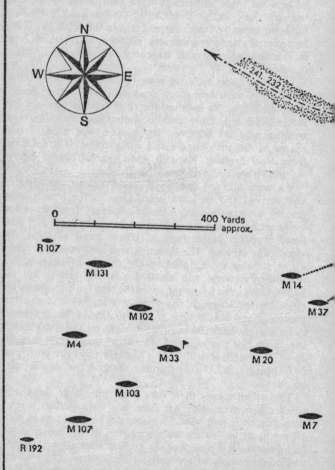

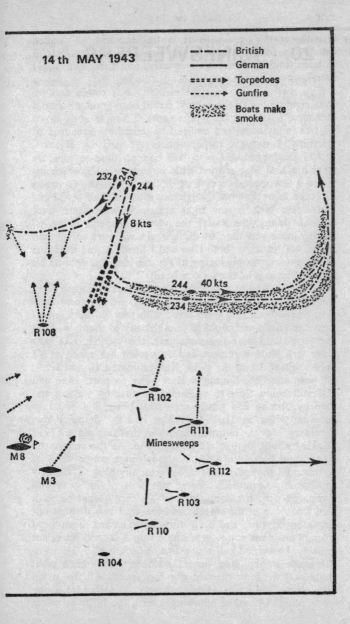

14th MAY 1943

Legend:
- ·—·—·—· British
- —————— German
- ▷▷▷▷▷▷▷ Torpedoes
- - - - - → Gunfire
- ▨▨▨▨▨ Boats make smoke

232 241 234 244

8 kts

244 40 kts

234

R 108

R 102

R 111

Minesweeps

M 8

M 3

R 112

R 103

R 110

R 104

take the enemy's fire with us, while Mac and "O" waited
behind to follow through the fire-vacuum thus left. I
stopped, told them the plan quickly, and then Ken and I
set off.

This was a quick one; the visibility was rotten and we
were right on top of the enemy; had it been good we should
of course have seen his whole force. I had to scale down
his size in my mind and realized he must be a squadron of
warships, I thought torpedo-boats escorted by E-boats.
R 108 challenged *241* who had had no time to separate
from me, and Mac replied with a random letter which in-
stilled a few seconds' worth of doubt. In fact the Germans
had seen us in time but thought we must be their own Four
Horsemen; Nelson was right again, "I wish there were
twice as many, the easier the victory, depend upon it."
Before there was time to think again we were at torpedo
range, 400 yards, so both Ken and I lined up and fired just
as the enemy was beginning to get the idea and lobbed his
first uncertain rounds over our heads.

I had told Ken to ease away from me but of course there
was no time for him to do that, nor for me to allocate targets; and although we were faced with four ships apparently in line ahead and could have taken any of them, we both
had to go and pick the same one, the second. Her bow
wave was phosphorescent and I guessed her speed at 12
knots, setting 10 on the sight; Ken estimated 10 and set 7;
off went the fish. I nudged Ken away to port, Mac and
"O" still being close to starboard, at first by waving and
then by turning *234* gently across his bows; it seemed an
occasion when, as Their Lordships had it, "despatch was
necessary," for the number of guns in that line did not bear
thinking about, though we soon had to. As the cannonade
roared and blazed into life as though at a single word of
command I thought I had never seen anything so vulgarly
flamboyant; nevertheless even that wall of fire was dim
compared with the flare from *M 8*'s fore magazine as it
blew up. Alan in the wheelhouse reported two distinct underwater crumps, and four torpedoes having been fired
from point-blank range at a single ship a second hit is not
unlikely. I awarded half a swastika to each boat.

I made smoke, Ken turned inside me through a right
angle and we soon reached our top speed. All the strain
had left me and I was a boy again; the skimming hulls, the
white plume of smoke billowing astern, the brilliant tracer

like giant matches being struck, the fierce, wild, elemental cacophony of noise, success behind us, all were glorious. Retaining a degree of prudence however I ducked behind the armor plating, popping up briefly to see what was happening and to wonder why Ken did not turn the whole way and put my smoke between himself and the enemy. Enough was enough, dash it, and if he was staying there spellbound with the beauty of it all I resolved to speak to him seriously on the matter of priorities; especially as he was close on my port bow and I could not turn away until he did.

Poor Ken's heart was in the right place but his binoculars were not. He ordered "hard-a-port," ducked, and simultaneously with his coxswain's spinning the wheel with right goodwill the strap caught in a spoke. If the man thought it strange that his captain's head had become fixed on a level with his stomach, more important was the fact that the wheel would not turn; bracing himself he hove mightily, but the only effect was to close Ken's windpipe and prevent him from bringing the light of reason to bear on this whimsical misunderstanding.

Meanwhile the two boats hurtled towards what we thought was the shore but was probably the Four Horsemen; bullets came inboard, I suspect mainly from *R 102* and *R 111*, but just as the issue seemed to have passed beyond our competence Ken, with his last gasp and near-nerveless fingers, found his knife and severed the strap. In carrying one he proved himself a true seaman, for cutting something quickly has ensured a happy outcome from many afflictions, not all of them readily predictable. The wheel spun, triple rudders wrenched us round, and Ken emerged to breathe the sweet, cool air of freedom behind the smoke; only Ordinary Seaman Pollard of *244* was slightly wounded with a splinter in his arm, and all our many hits were of small caliber causing only superficial damage. Whew!

If my mood was gay, and in my description of it I have tried to allow for the absence today of an immediate prospect of having my head cut off, the enemy's certainly was not. I find myself absurdly angry with him for allowing us to hurt him so horribly. He reported:

According to those saved from *M 8*, the torpedo entered the magazine and the fore part of the ship was

torn apart; much of the bridge was destroyed and the
fore deck blown upwards. Some of the bridge personnel were killed outright and some (O God!) were
squashed; only von Grumbkow and the helmsman
survived and they were wounded. The forward gun's
crew and those off watch below sank with the fore
part of the ship.

He had no need to let us come so close, and why in
heaven's name had there been anyone off watch when
S-boat attack was likely and there was no early warning
system of any sort?

Much steam escaped but the engines went on working,
although the ship slowed down. Adjacent ships did
not realize the extent of the damage and continued
on their course, and since all communications were
destroyed in *M 8* the wounded Senior Officer was unable to control the situation. Ten minutes after the hit
M 8 ordered *M 4* to come alongside by loud hailer,
but the damaged ship was moving in a circle and hit
her rescuer, holing her. *R 192* succeeded in closing to
take off the wounded, some of her crew going on
board and trying to free those trapped on the bridge.
M 8 was now stopped, bows west, and *M 14* passed a
tow to her stern, while *M 4* screened the two ships on
their northern side.

As was normal, MTBs and torpedo tracks were sighted
on all sides as soon as we had gone away, and the weight
of ammunition expended was impressive.

Mac was very reasonably annoyed with me afterwards
for leaving him behind; the right thing to have done as it
turned out was to press in with all four boats and get eight
torpedoes into the water during the minute or so when the
enemy was still coming to life. As it was *242* and *232* found
themselves baulked by *R 108* in the first instance, and then
it was too late with the whole enemy force erupting and
starshells allowing no concealment. After a fierce little
engagement with *R 108* the two boats escaped to the west,
and there I met them again.

Our torpedo hit having been unmistakable I reasoned
that other enemy ships would even now be standing by the
wreck or picking up survivors; moreover we knew precise-

ly where they would be. This was a nasty dilemma and pleasure vanished. Was it inhuman to torpedo a ship engaged in rescue work? Yes; but was it right? Yes, of course it was; our whole purpose in life was to sink ships and humanity could only begin when the enemy called for quarter. There was no chance whatever of that and I took the team back to the scene of the crime, though feeling more like a sneaking assassin than I care to remember. My squeamishness was however quite unnecessary; the enemy had had 15 minutes to institute an impenetrable screen around the wreck and brought his troubles on himself by failing to do so.

M 8 was clearly visible from 1,000 yards as a square lump without a bow, and we only saw one other ship which became our target. I could have taken *244* and caused a diversion on the far side but thought that would just scare the target away; I could have sent both *241* and *232* in together but two silhouettes would be easier to see than one and I expected the enemy to be very alert. I therefore sent Mac in on his own, which I admit was not entirely logical but my sixth sense told me he would not be seen, and nor was he. I apologize to him though, for he tells me he felt like David advancing on Goliath while the hosts of Israel sat back contentedly and cheered him on; worse, when he looked back we three shone like road signs in the light of the setting moon.

Poor Mac! His target was the almost continuous silhouette of *M 14* and the wreck, he allowed two knots' enemy speed at 600 yards, *M 14* saw the tracks and went full ahead, parting the tow, and the torpedoes went slap between the two ships. Quiet still persisted, however, and as Mac crept softly away to the southwest I sent *232* in to bowl, again our last hope. When she had reached 600 yards and "O," John Hawkins, his First Lieutenant and Valentine his coxswain were discussing the important matter of the enemy's speed, the Germans pulled themselves together at last and opened fire. "O" quickly decided on five knots, and it seems that his target was *M 4* who was circling the wreck from the east; he would have fired at once but had to wait until the range was down to 400 yards because Valentine had trouble steadying the boat. The shooting built up in intensity until at last "O" was satisfied and pulled his triggers.

It was a gallant effort, but the port torpedo misfired and

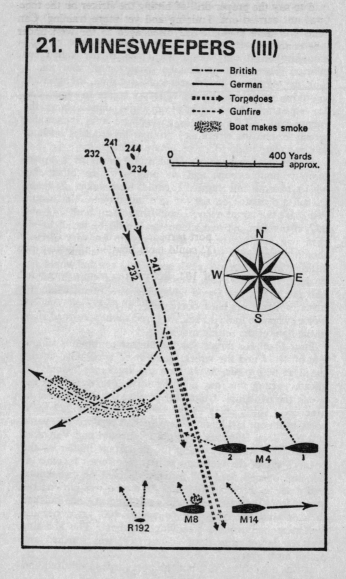

21. MINESWEEPERS (III)

—·—·— British
———— German
▪▪▪▪▶ Torpedoes
- - -▶ Gunfire
▓▓▓ Boat makes smoke

232   241   244
          234

0 | | | | | 400 Yards
                      approx.

N
W — E
S

232   241

2   M4   1

R192   M8   M14

sad to say the proper drill of hitting the striker on the tube
was not carried out. Training and yet more training! Can
one ever have enough? *232* disengaged to the west under
the concentrated fire of *M 4*, *M 8*, *M 14* and *R 192* who
claimed her as sunk, but they only hit her with small caliber
bullets and caused no damage or casualties to speak of;
indeed *232* gave rather better than she got, scoring hits on
all three minesweepers. "O" 's target was very close to the
wreck of *M 8* when he fired, and it was her that his one
torpedo hit. According to the Germans:

> . . . on the starboard side abreast the funnel and the
> result was very destructive. The rest of the bridge was
> blown off and sank, the stern sank shortly afterwards,
> and the center stuck out of the water for an hour
> floating on a cushion of air.

Putting their report with ours, the intriguing possibility
arises that had *232*'s port torpedo been fired it might well
have hit *M 4*, and "O" could have boasted of getting two
ships with one shot.

From *M 8*'s crew of 104, thirty-three were unwounded.
Eighteen were hurt including the Flotilla Leader von
Grumbkow. Fifty-three died, among them the captain,
Oberleutnant zur See Hardamm.

Focke-Wulf Fw 190

We then left for home but the enemy could not know that. The Four Horsemen engaged the leading R-boats as they approached and fire was returned; then they themselves were shot at from the dark inshore side and replied smartly, wounding four men in the Harbor Defense Group off the river mouth; and lastly the minesweepers engaged their own escort of R-boats from time to time, thinking they were us.

With the dawn came four Focke-Wulf 190 fighters, and we took up a diamond formation so as to bring as many guns to bear in any direction as possible. Simultaneously we sent an urgent summons to our own Air Force in the coded form "Help!" followed by our own callsign which happened to be "Violet"; it also happened to be the name of Saunders's wife and he wondered how she could be of assistance. We waited uncomfortably for what would be a new experience in MTBs and prepared to sell our lives dearly, reasonably confident in being well-gunned, small, and very maneuverable. But it was an almost embarrassing flop, for the airmen just stayed at about 2,000 feet, loosed off their guns in our general direction, and went home. Two Spitfires came zooming in soon afterwards, but delay was to be expected 70 miles from their base at Martlesham and we thought they had done extremely well; we waved heartily, and invited them down to the boats for a drink or two as soon as we reached harbor.

It had been a bad night for the Germans, and the morning brought no relief for then no less a Titan than the Befehlshaber der Sicherung der Nordsee himself flew urgently to Holland. Some of Admiral Lucht's comments make interesting reading:

Tactical measures were hampered by the Senior Officer being out of action right at the start—these flotillas had little experience—lack of plan made second enemy attack easier—our considerable fire-power not used to full effect—fire discipline lacking— some boats thought own starshell were aircraft flares and fired into the air though there were no aircraft— plans must be worked out and communicated beforehand—VHF communications failed—poor W/T reporting, two signals speak of mines when it must have been obvious that the damage was caused by S-boat torpedoes—intensive training is to be instituted to ensure a marked increase in efficiency—reasons for the exchanges of fire between friendly forces are to be rendered in writing.

Without exactly sympathizing, indeed I am glad that sort of thing happened on the other side of the hill too, I confess to a fellow feeling. That the enemy was very irked indeed was revealed by his press release:

The British Admiralty has spread the false report that two German ships were sunk on May 14 ... This is what actually occurred; six S-boats were spotted by the German naval coastguard and engaged. The British gunnery was inferior and their boats were hit repeatedly; two caught fire over their whole lengths and a third capsized owing to heavy damage, in clear moonlight it could be seen that she sank. Apart from some personnel losses the German boats suffered no damage and have reached their base in full numbers.

Although Lord Haw-Haw's imagination was always vivid, such a transparently blatant lie was unusual. One of Their Lordships' lackeys wrote on the docket: "As Lieutenant Dickens and his team presumably swam home, propose they be granted survivor's leave and the long distance record."

As well as MTBs and MGBs, a flotilla of four motor launches (MLs) was based on *Beehive;* the vessels' function was entirely minelaying off the enemy coast. Their senior officer was an almost circular officer called Tubby Cambridge whose popularity matched his girth, and whose well-concealed, persistent efficiency exceeded both. He and his team probably achieved more for the war effort than any number of fighting patrols, and in the latter part of May and June 1943 we too were switched temporarily to minelaying. Having 40 knots available for dodging trouble, which the MLs did not, I must say I found the occupation restful. I liked prowling in the dark, and for every enemy we saw whom I was not expected to attack, whom indeed it was my positive duty to avoid without ourselves being seen, I felt that ten years had been added to my life—or 24 hours anyway.

The great bulk of offensive minelaying was done by

the Air Force with great effectiveness which gradually
increased as aircraft were fitted with ever more accurate
navigational aids. But the enemy's shore radar could often
detect them at their business; and although that did not
invalidate the minefield because he would still have to go
to great trouble and expense sweeping it, and could never
be sure he had succeeded what with the devilish con-
trivances of the mine designers, we would much rather he
discovered it through a ship blowing up. Coastal Forces
had the ability to go practically anywhere undetected; and
now the 21st Flotilla could also fulfil the other essential of
minelaying, accuracy, so long as we had Tom Neill's 223
with us since she was fitted with a radio position-finder.

So we come to July and my last two battles. If I was a
bit weary, not perhaps so much from the fear of danger
but of the nervous energy recurrently expended in screw-
ing myself up to the highest pitch of endeavor, most mem-
bers of the Flotilla had not yet had their share of action
and were keen to earn their swastikas. A welcome addition
was General Lee who took over 224 from Peter Magnus
and brought her back from Poole in tip-top form; and a
new era was beginning at Beehive with Ian Trelawny, now
fully recovered from his Barfleur wounds, starting to build
up his 11th Flotilla with which he was to perform outstanding feats. On the night of July 17/18 Ian joined me with
his first new boat, 356, and I put him in charge of the
2nd Division with General; I rode in 223, with Ken
Hartley's 244.

That the Germans cared about our mines is well-shown
by our meeting no fewer than 11 minesweeping trawlers
under Oberleutnant zur See Witsch, clearing the Weg Rot
between The Hook and Ijmuiden. We were coming down
the other way keeping four miles from the coast, which we
could actually see because a full moon above thin cloud
shone a diffused light and the visibility was perfect. It
was therefore a bad night for MTB operations, and I
longed for the time when such loveliness could be greeted
as wholly good. Still, I had a first-class team who all knew
what they had to do and were thoroughly trained in it.

223's radar seemed to be working well and I was very
keen to use it, not for detection on such a night but to
plot the enemy's movement and determine his course and
speed for use in torpedo firing; so when we sighted him
at four to five miles I held on slowly, waiting for an echo

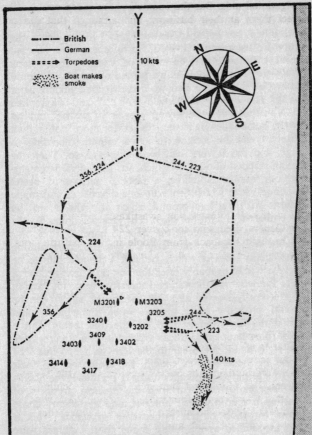

22. SCHEVENINGEN

18th JULY 1943

Full moon behind cloud, visibility excellent, sea slight.

to appear. That was a mistake, because none did until
the range was down to 2,500 yards, and the enemy being
quite clearly approaching no time was left for fancy ploys;
though it did not greatly matter in the event. I separated
the divisions, Ian going to seaward and I to landward, the
position I must admit I coveted, for no enemy ever seemed
to think it possible that he might be attacked from there.

We were seen as soon as we turned outwards, as would
not have been the case had we done so immediately after
sighting. The enemy challenged with "J" and we replied
with "L"; that, was the wrong answer of course and he
knew it, but challenging often generates more doubt than
it resolves and he took a full two minutes deciding to
engage, and did it very half-heartedly even so. Then the
shooting stopped altogether which was odd, until I remembered our new camouflage, a tasteful pattern of pastel
shades and white which broke up our silhouettes and made
us merge with the background which at night at sea, be
it remembered, is light not dark. The idea was Peter Scott's
and I warmly acknowledge our debt to him.

I went well inshore and crept down the coast aiming
for the enemy's center which, because I thought him to be
a convoy, would probably offer the best and least defended
targets. Ian went for the van and therefore came into action
first. He was re-sighted at 1,500 yards and had I been he
I should probably have turned away immediately and
assumed the diversionary role for the time being. But a
curious thing happened; tracer arrived in two streams, one
to the right hand, the other to the left, with *356* and *224*
immune in the center as though the Lord was on their
side. An alternative explanation might be that Peter Scott's
camouflage endowed them with the magical property of
appearing to multiply their number, and the enemy chose
shadows for their targets rather than substance. This is
not so far-fetched as it sounds if our ghostly shapes were
visible only out of the corner of the eye and vanished
in the center; and the fact is that Witsch reported seeing
12 to 15 of us in the first instance (that is before he had
any reason to be confused by our tactics); these split into
three groups, one to the left, one to the right, and one
which came straight at him down the middle—and was
of course not there at all.

Ian was thus able to press on with *224* close on his starboard quarter, and achieved a range of 700 yards. The fire now becoming hot and *356* having been hit forward by three 20mm shells, Ian fired at the leading ship, Witsch's big trawler *M 3201* of 460 tons, from 55 degrees on her port bow and with a speed setting of four knots. Then he disengaged to starboard, a bit too sharply for General's comfort, being hit twice again as he did so. General flung his boat to port under *356*'s stern, and being tossed high on her wake suffered an almost disastrous catastrophe; the sea suction of the port engine came clear of the water and formed an airlock; the cooling water boiled and burst its tank, scalding all three of the engine room crew, Stoker Lucy severely; the starboard engine ran a bearing in sympathy and whined to a halt. *224* was thus nakedly exposed at close range, with but one engine and that operable only from the bridge. She had an Oerlikon however, and used it and her 0.5s with magnificent determination and coolness to cover her withdrawal; she succeeded, and wounded two men in *M 3201* while doing so.

Ian's torpedo shot was perfectly accurate; if it had not been, one or the other would have hit, but as it was they passed within 10 yards of *M 3201*'s bow and stern respectively.

Using this splendid diversion I started my approach and at first the Germans thought we were dikes or breakwaters ashore, but then a fairly heavy fire was opened and I turned away. Remembering how the gunners had lost us before as soon as their own tracer obscured their vision, I kept our speed down to only ten knots, and on a sudden inspiration made a few quick puffs of smoke. Sure enough the firing stopped, and when the gunners could see again they let fly at the smoke. When all was again quiet on our side we turned back, and I told Ken to diverge on my starboard beam as we closed, and pointed out the ship he should take for his target; that and the one I chose for myself I thought were coasters in a convoy but they must have been *M 3205* and *M 3202*. It was as astonishing to us then as it must seem now that we were not sighted again until after firing at a range of about 600 yards, well inside the radar ground wave at 1,000 yards.

The explanation was Ian's magnificent diversion on the other side; he dashed up and down and in and out, the enemy reporting no fewer than three attacks during this period, each by at least three boats and some accompanied by torpedo tracks. All were beaten off, the Germans said, by consummate gunnery and fire discipline.

We fired unobserved and turned to our escape course, still at slow speed until the torpedoes had run the distance. There was no result. "Oh God!" Tom and I wailed to each other; "*never* was there such a perfect attack, they *must* have run under." The torpedoes had been set to only six feet and I doubt whether we really believed that to be the explanation; as an excuse on return to base it would certainly sound unconvincing, but it was true. If my analysis of the two sides' records is correct, one of Tom's torpedoes ran under *M 3202*, and Ken's right-hand one passed two yards astern of *M 3205*. While praising Witsch for his successful defense, 1st Sicherungsdivision also felt it necessary to point out that he had been very lucky.

Full ahead; but not soon enough to prevent tragedy being added to failure. Only one 20mm shell hit *244* but that exploded within a few inches of Ken's face and wounded him so horribly that I hope I may be excused for not giving the details; Proctor, his Coxswain, was also badly hurt but made a complete recovery. The First Lieutenant, Mitford-Burgess, sprang to the wheel and followed *223* out of trouble, keeping behind her smoke; then he went to Ken where they had dragged him and found he had written "Morph . . ." on the turret in his own blood.

As soon as I knew I sent Mitford-Burgess home at full speed, and *244* really was a good boat because she made the crossing without a check, at engine revolutions not normally permitted except in short bursts. That started a saga of devotion in which, first Ken's life was saved, and then he was given a new jaw and much of his face and throat, and with them the chance to live again. The brilliant RAF doctor at Felixstowe, Squadron Leader Knipe, to whom many in Coastal Forces have cause to be eternally grateful, succeeded in an emergency operation which at the outset promised little hope; and he then arranged for Ken to be looked after by the intensive care unit at Ely which catered for flying casualties and was probably the most efficient of its kind in the country. After that there followed three years of plastic surgery under the great McIndoe at East Grinstead; and always June was with him, at first as his Wren fiancée and as soon as possible his wife, giving him extra strength and resolution to add to his own. He will never be really fit, though courage has overcome that. One must never be too relieved at the "wounded" part of a casualty list, for although, thank God, they are alive they may need our sympathy for a very long time and it is so easy to forget to give it.

XIII

SAD ENDING

Not being able to confirm our near-misses we were bewildered and disheartened. Always before there had been some reasonable explanation for missing, but this time there was none and we had failed completely in the most favorable circumstances we had ever had; two serious casualties rubbed salt into the wound.

I had another cause for depression for I was quite severely criticized, and perhaps even sacked though of that I can only conjecture. If so it was all done in the nicest possible way by the nicest possible chap, our new Commander-in-Chief Admiral Sir Jack Tovey, and I have no complaint. Such things are part of life, and misunderstandings, particularly in war, are more the rule than the exception; conclusions are sometimes drawn from the wrong premises yet strangely they are quite often right.

It must have been before the last battle that I was either sent for by the great man or paid my official call on him, I think the latter, and I remember well the unaccustomed luxury of his beautifully furnished study in Admiralty House, and his superbly tailored and valeted uniform, ablaze with gold and medal ribbons of every color like a line of Vorpostenboote in full blast. He was charming and I felt no undue awe, for he asked me all about life in MTBs and I was nothing loth to tell him, deeming it indeed to be my duty to do so for was I not one of the older hands on the coast? And he, though hero of the *Bismarck* and many North Russian convoys, would surely wish to hear my accumulated wisdom on a matter of which presumably, in common with all RN officers, he knew nothing.

I was greatly encouraged at first by his desire to get at the enemy and sink ships, but when he spoke about such tactics as pressing home attacks through concentrated enemy gunfire, or using gunboats to force a way through a screen, I explained patronizingly that we had tried all that and the right way to do it was my way, which I expounded at length. In my naivete I quite failed to understand that the Admiral was by no means asking my opinion but urging me, on the probable assumption that an MTB was a scaled-down battleship, to get stuck into combat and stay there until victory or death. I continued to press my case with much enthusiasm and more stupidity, rather as Jamie would have done in his precollaborative days and as, I should have known well, was not calculated to endear juniors to their seniors; I felt deeply that such methods would only lose men and boats to no profit and ought to be scotched at birth. Whether the Admiral found me insubordinate and lily-livered I cannot tell, but I should not be at all surprised if he detected the strain in me and thought I was ready for a move, whatever my tactics.

What the Admiral did not tell me was *why* it was so important to sink ships; he made no mention of iron ore, and certainly none of the beneficial results to be gained from destroying a steady succession of auxiliary warships. He was a bit like me saying, "Come on chaps, we need more boost!" without knowing what boost was. If one is in the unenviable position of having to lead men from behind, one must tell them with perfect frankness the importance of the objective and the degree of risk its attainment warrants. We British are not like Japanese who apparently delighted in dying for any or no reason; but we will do it when the stake is great as our record shows.

The interview ended with something less than effusive cordiality and sure enough, or purely coincidentally as the case may be, relief was appointed for me. The C-in-C's comments on the last action showed that I had conveyed none of my points and my tactics were designated as "bad." The same old battering-ram misconceptions were put forward as new ideas, and yet I could understand so well how they came to be raised. In describing the solid wall of tracer one would have to penetrate it was almost impossible not to convey the impression of faintheartedness; but it was not mainly damage which deterred me but the fact of not being able to see the target, and that was vital when torpedoes had to be used as precision weapons.

All was well for posterity, and my ego is slightly re-stored, by Their Lordships replying to C-in-C Nore in almost the language I should have used myself, give or take the odd "it should be borne in mind that." But there was irony in the 21st Flotilla's little cloud on two counts. From April to July we had fought five actions in three of which enemy ships were sunk. The other two, the "Bottom" and this latest, were total failures and in both I had described the enemy as convoys, whereas his forces had contained nothing larger than auxiliary warships. This was a grave tactical error on my part, for it was merchant ships in convoy that the Admiral wanted sunk and he of course concluded that we had done no more than poke ineffectually at the screen and needed a thorough gingering-up. Secondly, trawlers were extremely difficult targets, for which our weapon system had never been designed, whereas merchant ships of several thousand tons were dead easy ones as our only two encounters with them had shown.

Those are excuses but they are valid ones, and far from being a dismal performance Ken Hartley's battle can truly be described as the apex of our tactics, training and fighting ability. Our misses against three small enemy targets, two torpedoes by ten yards, one at two yards and one under, denote bad luck or divine ill-will of no ordinary degree; and although I could only be very humble before learning the enemy's story, to remain so now would be falsely modest. Worse, it would be grossly unappreciative of Ken's and Proctor's sacrifices, and of the sustained enthusiasm, dedication and loyalty of that great little team which I am so very proud to have commanded.

Heigh ho! Tony Hollings arrived to relieve me, and being RN and knowing nothing about the business he was allowed a couple of weeks in which to take over. Tony was a very cheerful and pleasant soul whom I thought would have a reasonable chance of learning, but Mac, Tom, General, Peter, "O" and the rest eyed him with the same barely concealed mistrust which I too had initially been accorded. I was cynically though sympathetically amused; poor Tony would have to sort that one out for himself and it is the most important single factor of command, for it embraces every quality from personality to professional competence but is often the least considered before accepting a job.

*   *   *

The long turnover period allowed me one last battle which I approached with turbulently mixed feelings. I dearly wished it to be a really outstanding success such as our silent attack on the convoy, and even better if possible. On the other hand there was only one proper reason for fighting battles and that was to help the war along; the idea of demanding an all-out effort in order to give me a last-night personal benefit was abhorrent, and every death in such a fight would forever be a haunting, accusing, personal ghost. On a much lower plane I wanted to survive, and suddenly the prospect was tremblingly bright.

But there was yet a third reason for playing it cool; I had been ordered to go harder by my Admiral, and because I thought he was wrong to issue such a blanket instruction and my loathing of sycophancy being almost pathological, I was damned—*damned*—if I would necessarily do so. If the composition of the enemy—fat convoy, ocean raider, large warship—warranted the full treatment he would get it, and nobody need tell me. No wonder I never got very far in the Navy and quite right too, you can't have that attitude in a disciplined service. That may all sound fierce, manly, dogmatic, even Scottish; but being in reality a prey to every doubt I am glad to have the backing of Ian Trelawny—successful, enterprising, forceful, gentle *and* a great fighter.

"If it's a battleship, well you just get your head down and go in; but you don't do that sort of thing with good boats and nice boys for a couple of bloody trawlers."

Unless of course you realize that trawlers are key targets which we did not.

We sailed on July 27, 1943 with no fewer than seven boats; they were available and I considered we had reached a sufficiently high state of training for such a large number to be handled in one unit. Mac was there in *241; 244* had been taken over by Jack Saunders, a firm and trusted friend who had been in the 4th Flotilla at *Beehive* for a long time and with whom I had often operated; Ian brought *356* and his second new boat, *351* commanded by Nick Morrow, and *234*'s crew and I took out *225*, the eighth and last boat of the 21st Flotilla. She had no crew of her own under a sensible new scheme whereby a flotilla was allowed six crews and eight boats to ensure the most efficient use of men and materials. Tony Hollings came with me to learn the trade, and Coxswain Jim Saunders

23. NOORDWIJK 25th JULY 1943

Wind NE-3. No cloud, visibility moderate.
Moon rose 0140.

—·—·— 1st Division 225, 241.
—▪—▪— 2nd Division 223, 224. } British
—▪▪—▪▪— 3rd Division 356, 244, 351.
———— German
●●●➤ Torpedoes

VP 1401 P   M 3417 , M 3418
VP 1410   M 3402 – Leader
VP 1412   M 3409

0100

223
hit

223
on fire

224

0130   0345

0300

0200

0245

0230

said afterwards: "That'll have taught him what it's all about. Very nice bloke for an RN man."

It was another beautiful summer night with the moon due to rise at 0140 and the sea brilliantly and dismayingly phosphorescent. First contact, two miles to the northeast, was made by radar as we closed the coast just north of Noordwijk, and as an unobserved attack was clearly out of the question I put the usual plan into effect and split the force into three divisions with orders not to attack trawlers. Ian therefore took the 3rd Division (*356, 351* and *244*) inshore; Tom Neill (*223*) and General Lee (*224*) formed the 2nd Division and were allotted the sector to the southwest of the enemy, and Mac and I went to the northwest. We never fully discovered the composition of the enemy although we had the next three hours in which to do so; and though I can now describe it I would ask that it should be forgotten whenever viewing the situation through our eyes, otherwise it will certainly seem that we were even less inspired than we actually were.

This was again a routine minesweeping operation, by four trawlers of the 32nd Minesweeping Flotilla led by Obersteuermann Mohrbacher and escorted by three Vorpostenboote of the 14th Patrol Flotilla. We were old acquaintances, for the minesweepers had been present the week before and this would be the fifth time we had dealt a hand to the 14th; such an experienced enemy together with the bright night meant that the cards favored our opponents, but although we could only see the backs of theirs at this stage they very soon began to be played face upward on the table.

Ian steered southeast to get inshore, but ran into the minesweepers who were extremely quick on the draw so that he had to disengage to the south for a short distance. *244* lost her leader in her smoke, pressed on eastwards and was heavily engaged with serious damage to her engines. Ian stopped, saw the enemy for the first time and identified them as trawlers shooting at us to seaward; nevertheless he continued farther inshore to see what else there might be, and luckily met *244* whom he sent home when he discovered her condition.

The hallmark of this battle was that whenever we closed the enemy he saw only our phosphorescent wakes

before we saw him, and because he was very alert we rarely
did. I first met the 14th, which was stationed as a group
on the sweepers' starboard beam and who let me have it
from far outside torpedo range. I tried the slow disengaging technique which worked again, and returned, which
did not. On my third approach however I found myself
being engaged by the 14th from the port beam, while right
ahead and quite separate were the minesweepers, momentarily clearly visible as trawlers. With relief, for our situation was thoroughly unpromising, I ordered all boats to
withdraw from the action; but it was too late to forestall
tragedy.

Tom Neill in the 2nd Division was not clear which group
he went for, but the German report makes it fairly clear
that it was the minesweepers. He could not identify them
as trawlers, and indeed picked what he took for a torpedo-
boat as his target so that he was probably much closer than
he thought. Simultaneously Mohrbacher altered the course
of his unit towards Tom by a turn together, an effective
move for it both combed any torpedo tracks and brought
his guns into killing range. 223 and 224 were suddenly and
accurately illuminated by a starshell, fired by the 14th
who would have been on their port beam, and Tom's boat
was hit savagely by the minesweepers ahead while still at
her slow approach speed. Lillicrap's shipwrights could not
afterwards count the number of 20mm hits because the
holes merged into one another; the messdeck and galley
blazed up, and then a big 37mm came into the wheelhouse
and killed the First Lieutenant, Midshipman R. H. Jones.
He was so young, at nineteen, so sickeningly young.

The blast from this big shell knocked down everyone
on the bridge, and Tom and his Coxswain received minor
splinter wounds. Tom was first up and found the boat to
be still heading for the enemy, now very close indeed;
he grabbed the wheel and wrenched it to starboard, leaning on his throttles with all his might. He did not fire
torpedoes; there was no aiming point, just a network of
blinding tracer, and had he done so they would merely
have passed between the end-on enemy ships. Was this
what the C-in-C wanted us to do every time? Beehive
mothered only sixteen MTBs; how long would they have
lasted?

The engines responded, all 223's wounds having been

honorably in front, but now as she turned she caught another withering blast and Able Seaman Cyril Paddick died in his turret. He too was nineteen.

223 got away, just how it is difficult to say but perhaps she was partly hidden by the smoke from her own fire, though the enemy continued to observe it for Mohrbacher reported it with justifiable satisfaction. General Lee had followed Tom and was appalled to see the punishment being taken by *223;* but the enemy had eyes only for her and *224* was unhurt. As soon as practicable General closed to offer help, but Tom waved him away: "I'm all right, you go on."

All right? Well done, Tom; well done indeed.

So General went on, back towards the minesweepers which he had on his radar, at nine knots and all alone. The 14th Flotilla spotted him and closed on his port quarter, opening fire, but because the enemy ahead was looking the other way, perhaps at Ian Trelawny on the far side, General kept going without allowing himself to be flustered; he saw three trawlers and something much larger which he took for a merchant ship of 1,100 tons. At 400 yards by radar—notice the technical improvement—hitting started; one 20mm entered the port forward petrol tank but no fire resulted, one nicked the steering cable and parted most of the wire strands but left a filament holding, and three hit along the port tube bearer. General gave himself no excuses, a quick examination by the Seaman Torpedoman showed that the tube was probably usable, and at 350 yards from the target both torpedoes were fired and ran true. As *224* turned to starboard, still at slow speed, the minesweepers caught her with what General called, "an extremely heavy and accurate fire," and he was by no means given to exaggeration; but sandwiched between the two groups he acknowledged that it was time to increase speed and make smoke, and he brought his whole crew out unscathed. There was no merchant ship, the targets were but trawlers and small ones at that, and the torpedoes passed between *M 3402* and *M 3417.* No one could have tried harder; well done, General!

I saw *224* coming back towards me and intercepted her. General told me about the merchant ship without bringing in his gallantry and I thought, "Hell, another bloody miss!"

But the battle must now continue and I cancelled my withdrawal signal, adding, "Attack with torpedoes."

Now Ian and I probed and probed again on our respective sides, I being thwarted at every attempt by the 14th who were exceptionally mobile, a new tactic in our experience, and Ian by the moon which rose behind him, as well as both of us by the phosphorescence. The order not to attack trawlers still held, but we had to go on trying to find General's merchant ship. I saw something firing farther south and took a short leg in that direction before coming in again, but with no better result because the 14th seemed to know exactly what I was up to.

Ian was engaged so much that he became disoriented and found himself on the seaward side of the enemy at one point. There he met *223;* and it was just what Tom needed for he and his crew were in the last stages of exhaustion having just, and only just, succeeded in mastering their fire after thirty minutes of superhuman exertion with buckets of water, the extinguishers having been long expended. Furthermore a solid 20mm bullet was punched through the port tube and into the torpedo, preventing it from being fired. Tom would not have left on his own account with one torpedo remaining, but Ian told him to go, and no nonsense.

I took a longer leg to the southwest at 25 knots and then crept in again; but it was no use because the accursed 14th arrived at the same moment, having been able to steer along one side of a triangle to our two. We did however come closer to the minesweepers than usual and I thought in my wishful thinking that they really looked quite big, but then saw to my dismay that they were steering northeast with us on their quarter and hopelessly placed. I felt hopeless too and weary, lacking all inspiration; though if I had been told the shaming truth that Mohrbacher had not merely fought us off but was continuing undeterred with his minesweeping, and had now reversed course only because he had reached the limit of his task, I should have known anguish indeed.

Yet I realized how fortune could change, and how often in the history of war men had given up at the very moment the enemy was giving up too, so we must plug on. As we temporarily disengaged at 25 knots I did not worry about the gunnery after we had passed the 1,000 yard mark,

outside which experience had shown that we were usually
safe; indeed I welcomed the enemy's expenditure of ammunition, because the feeling was growing that if we went
on like this for long enough he might run out, particularly
of starshell. But now came a new experience whose significance I did not realize; large single splashes arose in
our vicinity, caused I presume by 88mm guns in the 14th,
the minesweepers having nothing bigger than 37mm. If I
thought anything it was to recall *Cotswold* days when I
could not hit an E-boat with four 4inch guns and a
sophisticated control system at a quarter the present range,
which I estimated as 4,000 yards, and I told Tony blandly
that he needn't worry about that sort of stuff.

Then a shell struck *225*. The considerable crack made
Alan stone deaf for a while, but I just kicked myself for
a slow-witted fool because a zigzag at high speed would
have made us impossible targets. It was no thanks to me
that the damage was amazingly slight; the hit was right
aft in the transom itself so no one was hurt, and although
the narrow compartment contained the steering gear that
still worked, and directly underneath, the three propellers,
shaft, hull brackets and rudders all seemed to be unim-
paired. The space was flooded of course, and splinters had
penetrated the adjacent petrol compartment; but the excellent self-sealing compound enveloped the holes in the
tanks and there was little space for water around them.
After gingerly trying all the systems it seemed that our
only handicap was a reduction of full speed to about 25
knots, owing to the weight of water tucking the stern down
and preventing it lifting to the planing position.

The time was 0330 and we had been engaged off and on
for two and a half hours; only an hour remained before
twilight so I decided to have one last stab at whatever
turned up next, including trawlers. Back we went to the
northeast for six miles so as to overtake the enemy, and
then in again; but when we saw them we were still on their
quarter as Mohrbacher had recovered his sweeps and was
steaming faster. He wrote:

> At 0340 we sighted two S-boats steering towards us
> from the port quarter. In spite of heavy protective
> fire they came within 500m and fired two torpedoes,
> each of which was avoided, at the same time as en-

gaging with gunfire. Thereupon the enemy disappeared to the southwest.

That at least sounds as though we tried, but I knew all along that our firing angle was almost hopeless. The gunnery was indeed heavy, and old Ginger Harry, *241*'s gunner, was wounded again though not seriously; but otherwise we suffered only superficial hull damage and it was deduced afterwards that *241*'s starboard warhead must have been hit by a 20mm before the torpedo was fired, so the pistol might not have worked.

Mac and I then stayed around in case we could be of any help to Ian, who had all this time been bashing his head against the same brick wall from the other side, and very nobly too for he spent more time under fire than we did. He never saw anything but trawlers, but two unexpected intruders did come his way. One was our own 4th MTB Flotilla from *Beehive* who came roaring up from the south, reflecting a terrible lapse in operational planning on somebody's part; but they did no harm—it would have been difficult for anyone to have made things worse—and Ian used them as a diversion for one of his attacks.

Then came an enemy craft—and indeed their report mentions a minesweeping unit on its way north to meet a convoy in the morning—which blundered into the battle and challenged Ian with the letter "Y." Quick as a flash he gave her back her "Y" as though he were challenging her, and the two of them then continued exchanging "Y's" like a cross-talk act. The German never vouchsafed the correct reply which would have been useful, but evidently concluded that Ian was stupid and inefficient for he started making a signal on a bright light, "Können Sie . . ." Ian felt sympathetic because the chap was obviously just as bewildered as himself, but there was no chance to enlighten him because the old enemy interrupted with a renewed burst of firing.

It was all a sad, sad fade-out. Oh, there were bright spots to be sure, chiefly provided by my grand team who did all and more than I asked of them. Ian was wonderful, Tom and General were superb; Mac says,

My chief recollection is of the unity which had grown between you and me. Several times we were flying

along at over 30 knots and you wanted to stop and
review the position. No signal passed, you simply
stopped and cut your engines, and being close on your
quarter I could see the cooling water stop coming out
of your exhausts so I did the same, and in a few
seconds we were able to talk in dead quiet except for
the faint hiss of water as we glided on. To have received such a pitch of coordination and understanding
gave me quite a thrill of pride.

The pride is mine, Mac, old friend.

The enemy did well too, and I am not so grovelling in
self-abasement as not to admit that he was a formidable foe.
Mohrbacher and his team were alert, steady and highly
trained, using their advantage of the light to the full and
never neglecting one sector while engaging in another;
there was no wilderness in their gunnery, they engaged
only visible targets and then they shot straight. The 14th
VP Flotilla too had a most successful night and must
have enjoyed themselves; whoever was leading them possessed imagination and flair for he always put them in
the right spot and foiled our every move. I wish I knew
who he was, but the 14th were men of deeds rather than
words and their reports were always terse and unsigned.
That was modest but ill-advised, for the pen is mightier
than the sword and no Iron Cross or visit to Buckingham
Palace follows from a deed that nobody knows anything
about, and this night's work only brought the 14th a
reproof for swanning off chasing MTBs and leaving the
minesweepers unguarded. In principle that was a valid
criticism, but circumstances alter cases and if 1st
Sicherungsdivision had been told how brilliantly they had
used the moon and phosphorescence in their aggressive
defense, the rap over the knuckles would surely have
become a pat on the back. Kapitänleutnant Schennen was
the Flotilla Leader and to him, in default of any other
name, and to Obersteuermann Mohrbacher I tip my cap.

The sky had lightened even as we made our last attack,
and soon the sun rose astern for the last time in those
waters and assured me that I still had my life and would
probably keep it for longer than it had been reasonable,
yesterday, to hope. But that being so it now seemed not

to matter very much and the ambience was all of sadness; the sadness of unavailing casualties, the sadness of failure, and the sadness of no longer belonging to the goodly fellowship of the 21st MTB Flotilla for I realized with a start that the break had already occurred; even though I was still at sea and in command they and I were looking ahead as all men must do, and our courses diverged.

What had it all been about? Had all the sound and fury signified—anything? What had we learned that might help us see more clearly into the future?

I had learned how it felt to command a force in battle, but although that is a privilege and challenge accorded to few I have no urge or qualification to preach on the subject which is far better left to the great captains and their historians. One point only so surprised and disappointed me that it might be worth mentioning, the messiness of battle. This has been summed up in the precept that everyone makes mistakes and the winner is he who makes the fewest, but it is often difficult in peacetime to visualize what that implies, and the absence of an intelligent enemy means that tactics tend to evolve around the capabilities and limitations of weapons, and the impact of mind upon mind is underplayed. There follows an expectation that the outcome will be clear-cut and tidy, with one side winning and the other losing depending on pure logic that might just as well and less painfully be left to a computer than tested in battle. But in real life men will change logic out of recognition, with their flair or indecision, resolution or cowardice, and their awareness of the enemy as another man who can dominate or be manipulated. Except in the hands of a master like Nelson, or in unusually favorable circumstances such as a completely unobserved attack, actual battles are usually messy and unsatisfying; yet they may well be worth fighting if their effects are felt beyond the battlefield. That having been said I readily concede that some of my efforts, particularly this last one, were messier than they need have been. The enemy's human intelligence had also upset the logic of my diversionary tactics and new ideas were needed, but these were not to be mine.

I have related how the Germans found our attacks irritating and sometimes a downright nuisance. That is no justification for our existence by itself, for the true balance

can only be struck by weighing the total effort devoted to
MTBs against the results achieved, an involved and difficult
calculation. I believe our force to have been inevitable as
is borne out, partly by its very existence when few in high
places liked or wanted it, and by Admiral Lucht, Befehlshaber der Sicherung der Nordsee, who wrote with feeling, "We must not leave the enemy free use of the area
off our coast at night."

Why not? Because the convoys had to pass and were in
danger both from direct attack and from mines laid in
their paths; because if they were safe at night they could
avoid the greater threat of air attack by day; because we,
the enemy, could not be allowed to reconnoiter the coast
for invasion purposes, or pass secret agents across it (an
activity continuously undertaken by Coastal Forces though
it did not fall to our lot); and because of the unknown—
if we could operate as we would we might do anything
and the Germans would only find out when it was too
late. Every iron ore ship sunk meant fewer tanks; but every
trawler sunk meant one less antiaircraft escort, patrol vessel or minesweeper, and a growing shortage of either meant
an increased risk to the ore carriers or imposed delay on
their sailings which was significant in itself, as well as
making it impossible to send any escorts to the Baltic
where they were desperately needed to support the vast
military campaign in Russia.

So the arguments in support of our small-scale activities
ranged far and wide, and I suggest that an aggressive Allied
presence off the occupied coast was as necessary to our
strategy as its neutralization was to the Germans'; and
since only small craft could operate in those mined and
shallow waters, and join with the Air Force in completing
the diurnal cycle of pressure, MTBs had to be invented.
That however was not enough to make them fully effective
which I frankly admit they were not, and I believe the
underlying cause to have been the ingrained dislike of
flashy little boats by the RN Establishment. There were
thus scarcely any boats to begin with, and then only bad
ones until four years after the outbreak of war; but worse
even than that, many RN officers appointed to Coastal
Forces in the early days lacked inspiration, one or two
being downright bad, and it was left to a forceful few,
RN and RNVR both, to get the business moving at all.

In my day I found operational unconcern and material neglect, together with faintly concealed disdain for our chances of doing anything worthwhile; and I have little doubt that the publicity we attracted when we accomplished anything at all was resented and made matters worse. Yet though limited in scope we only could do the job and the Navy's aim should have been to ensure that we did. That seemed difficult but was not. I grant that young men in fast craft with the ability to dash all over the ocean take a deal of harnessing; and on top of that a more than nodding acquaintance with all the military virtues was demanded of the captain of a warship however small, for he was on his own and must decide for himself in complex and tense situations. He could not be briefed before setting off like a bomber pilot for his tactics would depend on many factors which, I assert, were no less involved than those confronting a squadron of battleships. But youth could do it right, no question of that, and at least as well as many battleship captains who were not invariably remarkable for initiative and enterprise. But in common with them and all other leaders in war they should have been made to feel an essential part of a great purpose, and themselves led by men with all those high qualities which we in the services were taught to expect and emulate from our youth up but did not necessarily find.

So, the Navy called Coastal Forces into existence reluctantly and expected little from them, concluded when it got them that small craft were no use anyway, and reconsigned the whole disagreeable paraphernalia to oblivion as soon after the war as was decently possible—for the second time. Now that may be right in the changed conditions of the 1970s and I am no nostalgic partisan. Certainly I love small fast fighting craft. Who would not after my experience? But then I also love sailing ships for their beauty and the thrill of an aircraft carrier's flight deck in full operation, both being achieved by skills long in evolution in milieus of great hazard. But I believe, although it brings a lump to my throat, that the heavy carrier must follow the sailing ship into history, and that the small craft must go too if it is not vital to our defense. Our deepest love must be for whatever we believe to be fundamental, in my case the pursuit of civilization in freedom, and lesser loves as for example the companionships and weapons of war needed to preserve the greater must bow before it. Nevertheless fast, missile-armed craft of far higher relative potential than the last-war MTB proliferate in most navies but ours, particularly the Russian; they were used with very great effect in the India-Pakistan war of 1971 and the Israeli-Arab wars of 1967 and 1973.

I should be content were I to detect any awareness of importance of narrow waters in our defense planning; for although the world and its weapons have changed beyond recognition in the last thirty years, geography has not. Narrow seas remain and enemies will continue to glare at each other across them, each needing desperately to use them for their own purposes, whether to transit, traverse or secure the offshore oilfields, while denying them to the other. Because they differ essentially from continents, the preserve of armies, and oceans, while possessing a degree of affinity with both, he who wishes to dispute their control will find he needs different weapons and methods than those with which he has provided himself for the other two theaters; and if the enemy only has them, too bad! Such specialization in narrow waters during the last two wars was most marked; practically no air or naval forces designed for other tasks could be used in these effectively without substantial modification and retraining, while most could not be used at all for they were far too vulnerable and expensive. Arms like Coastal Forces had to be created especially for the role and there were many others, including those hitherto undreamed of monstrosities, the forts guarding the Thames Estuary, which adapted themselves so readily as pop radio stations in the piping times of peace.

The combination of aircraft, surface craft, submarines, shore-based missiles, electronic measures and countermeasures, mines, satellites and other developments which would be effective in a narrow-waters conflict today should be the subject of deep study which I fear is being neglected. Since I shall be accused, should anyone read these words and take them seriously, of excessive zeal over a matter of little consequence, I would add this: no one can say that the safety of our merchant shipping is a minor concern for all know it to be our life's blood; yet we have a still more alarming blind spot about that and have entered both

World Wars with scarcely any forces designed to protect
it. Twice we were almost defeated in consequence, yet with
that terrifying memory so recently behind us we have put
ourselves in exactly the same position today. That makes
two rust holes in our armor; another is naval aviation, for
although in my view the heavy carrier is dead the fixed-
wing aircraft at sea is not and there are other means
of getting it there, yet we seem to have written it off. But
of course today we have in effect written off any idea of
defending ourselves at all, against a potential enemy of
such immense strength that Germany of 1939 is like a
midget beside him, and who also disposes of a subversive
fifth column that is fearsome in its universal extent and influence. So what use is it to cry for mere changes in
priorities? We really do not deserve to survive; and I truly
doubt whether we shall unless something happens to
terrify us and our allies into awareness of our stark peril
in time to buck up.

As these thoughts occupy me I am back in *MTB 225*,
lumbering along with her stern tucked down ungracefully
on that fine summer morning, and with Saunders and the
lads desultorily occupied in baling out the seeing trickles
from various bullet holes with tin hats. We sailed the empty
sea where none dared venture but we, the small craft of
both sides; the same waters which today carry nearly all
the trade of northern Europe with the outside world. When
we reached our home channels a convoy passed, then a
unit of minesweepers plying its trade, and a few fishing
smacks and Thames sailing barges completed the picture
of maritime Britain going sturdily about its business. I
started to whistle "Sheep may safely graze" as I often did,
not that it was particularly appropriate to our offensive
task though the Navy as a whole could take satisfaction in
its achievement; but this morning the breath would somehow not come, for I was in a limbo, wondering what I was
and where I was going, with dissatisfaction predominating.

As we phut-phutted into Felixstowe Dock, looking as
smart as Alan and Saunders could contrive with our ungainly attitude, I could tell that all was quiet ashore despite
the noise of our own exhausts; and sure enough, after
"Ring off—finished with main engines" and the last
throaty, expectorant cough had slurped on to the much

polluted dock wall, none of the watchers raised so much as a whisper. Ready and willing to accord us a triumphant coda, but finding the tune to be a Requiem played *andante doloroso*, all was anticlimax. The tide was low and the high, greasy ladder needed an inordinate amount of strength to climb; at the top I just managed a wan smile and heavy sigh for Tommy Kerr who returned silent sympathy, before clambering heavily down the next ladder into *233* to condole with Tom Neill and his men. Black charring, splintered wood, tortured metal, blood and an acrid, haunting smell that was the quintessence of hopelessness. Tom was almost more depressed than I, blaming himself, but that at least I could correct by showering praise on them all with the greatest sincerity.

It was best that I go quickly, and leave the Flotilla in fresh hands to recover from what was after all only a setback—in the light of history quite a minor one since there were no merchant ships—and press forward to new achievements; which it did. Tony Hollings had a most unlucky accident very soon, and then Tommy Kerr did the right thing and had Mac promoted to Senior Officer although he was still only twenty-one. Despite his youth he had the stuff of leadership and inspired complete loyalty and endeavor; when *241* was shot from under him he took over *234*, which it pleased me to hear, and remained in the job until the very end of the war when he accepted the E-boats' surrender. Now he is Deputy City Engineer of Wellington, New Zealand, which is indebted to him for many inventions in the field of civil engineering. Arthur "General" Lee also went the distance and stuck by Mac in friendship and loyalty though he was the elder, becoming his Best Man in the first days of peace. Now he runs the Ministry's Fish Laboratory at Lowestoft and is engaged in such exciting pioneering projects as turbot farming.

Ian Trelawny took our little dock at Felixstowe which had been built for sailing barges and turned it into Britain's first and foremost container port, and did it in such complete harmony with his employees that the place is an object lesson in leadership to Industry and the Navy alike. Ken Hartley beat his great handicap, as I have said, and is now a successful salesman. Tom Neill makes jam in Glasgow as his family has always done, and very good it is. Henry Franklin sells oil, drinks beer and exudes perpetual youth. Alan Jensen runs a department for the Central Electricity Generating Board and makes model steam engines, precisely accurate down to the last self-made screw. Val Ohlenschlager owns a charming hotel in Cornwall and has assumed the girth appropriate to a good publican. Basil Gerrard is a County Court Judge, and I have made a note to avoid appearing before him lest I should treat him like a newly joined Spare Officer to my disadvantage. David Felce is a successful and imaginative architect; and Peter Standley is back among the deeds and files ensuring civilized good order in Wymondham.

At the top of the industrial tree is John Perkins of CIBA, and here again harmonious staff relations are a feature of his success. Ted Smyth is a senior executive in Courtaulds, and Peter Magnus too is way up in the clouds. Seemingly as rich as any of my humble acquaintanceship is Jim Saunders, who with his brother took their £80 war gratuities and bought a very old lorry; when I next met him in the 1960s he drove into Chatham Dockyard in his new Bentley to write a cheque for £25,000 for surplus stores. He too is a leader, and with his success he remains completely unspoiled, looking at life with alert wonder, going straight to the heart of a matter without inhibition or self-consciousness, and being a tonic to flagging spirits. Tommy Kerr is happily still with us, his punkish, perceptive, often astringent but always human wisdom undimmed.

To all these; to those others whom I have mentioned in the narrative, and to many more whom I have not for fear of confusing the reader with too many names, notably Ken Harris and Dave Moore; to those who died, above all to those who died, I offer my gratitude for their loyalty and support. That is of course conventional at the end of a book of this kind, but I mean it with a sincerity so deep that it is part of my very self. To me those were the days, never to be repeated, and it was the Officers and Men whom I had the honor to command who made them so.

I wish it could all have happened without our having to kill more than 120 Germans and Swedes; but it could not. The enemy fought honorably as I hope he thought we did, and I trust and believe that nothing happened then to prejudice our friendship and collaboration now.

I fell everybody in and made them a speech, which flopped. They gave me a cheer which was not at all a bad effort in the circumstances but we were all rather embarrassed. There were many handshakes and shy good wishes, which were truly sincere but sounded banal for we were young and expressed our lives in deeds rather than carefully chosen words. Then I bolted; to the broad, sun-lit uplands of the future? Not a bit of it, for the dark tun-nel of the war stretched interminably ahead.

"Switch out that bloody light!"

Appendix I

British Ships and Craft

The Vosper 1941 Class

Motor Torpedo-boat, etc.

Dimensions

Length overall, including rudders	72ft 6in.
Beam	19ft 3in.
Draft at rest	5ft 6in. to 6ft
Displacement at rest	
new and dry:	47 tons
with added weapons and equipment and soakage of timber:	55 tons plus

Hull

Double diagonal mahogany, hard chine, planning hull.

Engines

Three Packard V-12, supercharged, 1,250h.p. each. The wing engines drove direct through thrust blocks to the propellers; the center shaft which drove forward was turned under the engine by a V-Drive.

Maximum speed 38–40 knots. 2,500 gallons of 100-octane gas gave a radius of action on operations of about 140 miles, cruising at 25 knots.

Two Ford V-8 auxiliary engines could be clutched to the wing shafts for silent running at about 6½ knots. Good drill was needed to change from auxiliaries to mains quickly in emergency.

In 1943 the main engines were silenced with Dumbflows (see p. 123) and one auxiliary engine was removed.

Steering

Originally hydraulic which gave fingertip control but was far too vulnerable in action to the smallest puncture. This was replaced by a direct wire system with power assistance at the rudders; it was heavier to operate it but most coxswains preferred it as the "feel" of the boat was transmitted back to the wheel. The original two rudders gave too wide a turning circle and a third was added, one directly abaft each propeller.

Torpedoes

Two above-water 21inch tubes angled outwards 7½° from the bow. On entering the water the torpedoes turned forward 6½°, giving a spread of 2° or about 120ft at 1,000 yards. Firing by small explosive charge in a combustion chamber at the rear of the tube.

In 1942 we were fitted with the Mark V Torpedo, 35 knots and 500lb. warhead. This was an old type which had never achieved full service with the fleet but we had to use it owing to general shortage. It was unreliable to say the least, having been known to do everything but loop the loop, through it never failed us in action. In 1943 we were given the Mark VIII Submarine Torpedo, 45 knots and 750lb. warhead, which was admirable in all respects; safety range 100 yards, contact-only pistol.

Torpedo control was achieved by aiming the boat, the Captain firing by remote control (see pp. 51–53). Optimum boat speed on firing was 12 knots; above or below that speed the torpedoes would dive progressively deeper before achieving their set depths which was a handicap in shallow water.

Guns

Two 0.5inch Vickers machine guns, high angle/low angle, 700 rounds per minute; armor-piercing, incendiary and tracer ammunition. Twin power-operated mounting fed with hydraulic pressure by a pump on the center main engine; joystick control.

0.303inch Vickers gas-operated machine guns could be mounted on the torpedo tubes.

In 1943 as a result of private enterprise a single hand-worked 20mm Oerlikon, 450 r.p.m., was fitted on the fore deck. High explosive, armor-piercing solid and tracer ammunition.

Since we used guns mainly to deter the enemy gunners and to cause diversions, a high proportion of tracer was included in the loading.

Mines

Four could be carried instead of torpedoes. They were "A" Type ground magnetic/acoustic, 9ft 6in. long by 18in. diameter, released from chocks abaft the torpedo tubes.

Depth Charges

Two.

Smoke

Chlorosulphonic acid (C.S.A.) in a container right aft, the vapor being expelled by compressed air. Being cold the cloud hugged the surface and was very effective. In order to expedite generation of smoke in moments of stress I had the air-line led to a cock by my hand on *234*'s bridge.

Communications

One medium frequency W/T set which was supposed to have a voice capability but did not. When boats were separated we used short groups of one or two figures or letters from the Coastal Forces Signal Pamphlet by morse code, e.g.:

Enemy's course is . . .
Create a diversion from seaward
Attack from inshore of enemy
Attack with torpedoes
Attack completed . . . hits, *or* unsuccessful
Am in danger of sinking
Return to base
My engines have broken down

When in company we used the dimmest of dim blue-shaded lamps, which demanded constant training for efficiency. Only I had a signalman and in the other boats the signalling was done mainly by officers; a ten-minute daily practice session was rewarding though not popular.

Recognition

The challenge was a single letter flashed by morse code, the reply another. To identify herself, often necessary with considerable urgency, a boat could flash the reply letter, fire a two-star firework, or switch on her colored recognition lights on the mast. The letters and the colors of the stars and lights were changed at stated times.

Radar

Type 286 with fixed aerials pointing ahead and on each bow. A good idea but premature for MTBs in my time for we never had any worthwhile information from it, despite valiant efforts by the base staffs, notably Sub-Lieutenants Breadner and Bennett at *Beehive*.

Crew

The basic crew in 1942 was:

Captain—Lieutenant or Sub-Lieutenant
First Lieutenant—Lieutenant, Sub-Lieutenant or Midshipman
Coxswain—Petty Officer or Leading Seaman
Petty Officer Motor Mechanic
Leading Stoker
Able Seaman, Seaman Torpedoman
Able Seaman, Seaman Gunner
Telegraphist
Stoker
Ordinary Seaman, Trained Man

This number grew as new weapons and equipment came into service. A number of Spare Officers were borne at every base and it became normal for one to be carried in each boat, making three officers; one in command, one navigator and one for general supervision.

Further Details are contained in *Warship Profile No. 7* by David Cobb (Profile Publications Ltd).

Motor Gunboats (MGB)

MGBs *18, 21*   British Power Boat, Scott-Paine design
    31 tons, 70 × 20 × 4ft, 40 knots
    Guns: 1—20mm Oerlikon aft
    21 had two sided, twin 0.5inch turrets abreast the

bridge, *18* had one twin turret on the centerline abaft the bridge.

Depth charges

MGBs *82, 84, 86, 91* Scott-Paine design, built by Electric Boat Co., USA (Elco)

33 tons, 70 × 20 × 4ft, 44 knots

Guns: 1—20mm Oerlikon
      4—0.5inch machine guns in twin turrets abreast bridge

Depth charges

Motor Launches (ML)

Fairmile "A" Minelayers

60 tons, 110 × 17½ × 6½ ft, 25 knots

Guns: 1—3pdr
      3—20mm Oerlikon

Mines: 6 ground or 9 moored

Fairmile "B" Patrol/Escort

65 tons, 112 × 18¼ × 4¾ ft, 20 knots

Guns: 1—3pdr
      2—machine guns
      20mm added later

Asdic and depth charges

HMS *Somali*   Tribal Class Destroyer

1,870 tons, 377 × 36½ × 9ft, 32 knots

Guns: 8—4.7inch HA/LA (max. elev. 40°)
      4-barrelled 2pdr pom-pom
      8—0.5inch machine guns

Torpedoes: 4

HMS *Cotswold*   Hunt Class Escort Destroyer

907 tons, 280 × 29 × 8ft, 25 knots

Guns: 4—4inch HA/LA
      1—4-barrelled 2pdr pom-pom
      1—single-barrelled 2pdr pom-pom bow-chaser (anti E-boat)

Appendix II

Operational Statistics

Torpedoes:	Fired	55	
	Hit	11	or 12
Enemy Ships:	Sunk	6	
	Severely damaged	3	
Boats Lost:		2	
Casualties:	Own—killed	5	
	wounded	22	
	Enemy—killed or missing	122	
	wounded	51	

(Enemy totals are likely to be higher as not all actions were fully reported.)

Appendix III

Enemy Ships and Craft

Torpedo-boats (Torpedoboote)

   T 23   1,294 tons, 315 × 31 × 9ft, 33 knots
      Guns: 4—105mm, 4—37mm, 9—20mm
      Torpedoes: 6
   Kondor   924 tons 278 × 27½ × 9ft, 32 knots
      Guns: 3—105mm, 4—20mm
      Torpedoes: 6

Fleet Minesweepers (Minensuchboote)

   M 3 to M 131   717 tons, 216½ × 27¼ × 7ft, 18 knots
      Guns: 2—105mm, 2—37mm, 6—20mm
      Mines: 30

Fleet Escort (Flottenbegleiter)

   F 4   700 tons, 222½ ft, 28 knots
      Guns: 2—105mm and smaller

Motor Torpedo-boats (Schnellboote–E-boats)

   There were several types; typical was the *S 30* Class
built in 1940/41:
   82 tons, 108 × 16 × 6ft, 36 knots
   Torpedoes: 2—21inch
   Guns: 2—20mm

Motor Launches (Räumboote—R-boats)

   R 102 to R 192   125 tons, 124 × 19 × 4¾ ft, 20 knots
      Guns: 1—37mm, 3—20mm

Patrol Craft, Vorpostenboote (VP), and
Auxiliary Minesweepers

   (M)
   These requisitioned vessels were mostly fishing craft of

various types and sizes, with correspondingly different armaments; the minesweepers had fewer guns than the VPs as might be expected. The 88mm was the starshell gun; by no means all craft had one though we normally, but not invariably, found at least one in a patrol or minesweeping force. Typical craft:

> VP 1234   176 tons, ex-Dutch Motor Drifter *Koningen Emma*
>> Guns: 2—20mm, 1—15mm, machine guns
>
> VP 1415   186 tons, ex-trawler *Irene*
>> Guns: 1—37mm, 2—20mm, 1—13.2mm, machine guns
>
> VP 1413   256 tons, ex-trawler *Adelante*
>> Guns: 1—88mm, 2—20mm, 1—13.2mm, machine guns
>
> M 3800   585 tons, ex-steam pilot vessel *Stoomloodsvaartuig-16*
>> Guns: 1—75mm, 1—40mm, 4—20mm, 2—13.2mm, machine guns

The first two figures in a boat's number denoted the Flotilla.

Bibliography

Cobb, David, *Warship Profile No. 7* "HM MTB/Vosper 70 ft." Windsor: Profile Publications, 1972.

Cooper, Bryan, *The Battle of the Torpedo Boats*. London: Macdonald, 1970.

Cooper, Bryan, *The Buccaneers*. London: Macdonald, 1970.

Hichens, Robert, *We Fought Them in Gunboats*. London: Michael Joseph, 1944.

Hunt, Cecil (ed.), *More Last Words*. London: Sampson Low, Marston, 1946.

Roskill, S.W., *The War at Sea*. London: H.M.S.O.

Scott, Peter, *The Battle of the Narrow Seas*. London: Country Life, 1945.

INDEX

NOTE: *Decorations, where known, have been included though they may have been earned after the
events in the book.*

ABOUT THE AUTHOR

Born in 1917, the son of Admiral Sir Gerald Dickens and the great-grandson of Charles Dickens, Peter Dickens joined the navy at thirteen and at the outbreak of war in 1939 had just been promoted to lieutenant. Service in the destroyer *Somali* in the Norwegian campaign, in a little ship at Dunkirk and as first lieutenant of the destroyer *Cotswold* on east coast escort duties, preceded his work as Senior Officer of 21st MTB Flotilla which the present book describes. Command of HMS *Blencathra* at the end of the war, including the D-day operations, and a spell as a house officer at Dartmouth were followed in peace by command of three destroyers.

While on the staff he was concerned with the escape of HMS *Amethyst* from communist hands in the Yangtse, and later married his admiral's stepdaughter. They have two daughters and one son (beginning his naval career) and live in Sussex.